Reading Architectural History

CW00734454

Architectural history is more than just the study of buildings. Architecture of the past and present remains an essential emblem of a distinctive social system and set of cultural values and as a result it has been the subject of study of a variety of disciplines. But what is architectural history and how should we *read* it?

Reading Architectural History examines the historiographic and socio/cultural implications of the mapping of architectural history with particular reference to eighteenth- and nineteenth-century Britain. Discursive essays consider a range of writings from biographical and social histories to visual surveys and guidebooks to examine the narrative structures of histories of architecture and their impact on our perception and understanding of the architecture of the past. Alongside this, each chapter cites canonical histories juxtaposed with a range of social and cultural theorists, to reveal that these writings are richer than we have perhaps recognised and that architectural production in this period can be interrogated in the same way as that from the more recent past – and can be *read* in a variety of ways.

The essays and texts combine to form an essential discussion of methods and critical approaches to architectural history, and more generally provide examples of the kind of evidence used in the formation of architectural histories, while also offering a thematic introduction to architecture in Britain and its social and cultural meaning.

Dana Arnold is Professor of Architectural History and Director of the Centre for Studies in Architecture and Urbanism at the University of Southampton.

Reading Architectural History

Dana Arnold

London and New York

First published 2002
by Routledge
11 New Fetter Lane, London EC4P 4EE

Simultaneously published in the USA and Canada
by Routledge
29 West 35th Street, New York, NY 10001

Routledge is an imprint of the Taylor & Francis Group

© 2002 Dana Arnold

Typeset in Galliard by M Rules
Printed and bound in Great Britain by
TJ International Ltd, Padstow, Cornwall

All rights reserved. No part of this book may be reprinted or reproduced
or utilised in any form or by any electronic, mechanical, or other means,
now known or hereafter invented, including photocopying and recording,
or in any information storage or retrieval system, without permission in
writing from the publishers.

British Library Cataloguing in Publication Data
A catalogue record for this book is available from the British Library

Library of Congress Cataloging in Publication Data
A catalog record for this book has been requested

ISBN 0–415–25049–8 (hbk)
ISBN 0–415–25050–1 (pbk)

For my mother Jose
who has always encouraged me
to think for myself

Contents

Figures

Acknowledgements

The process of constructing a discourse around the discipline of architectural history has been complex and rewarding. The purpose of this book is to place the architectural history of Britain *c.* 1600–1840 centre stage to reveal its pivotal role for any exploration of the social and cultural map of both the past and the present. This aim is founded on the belief that if we treat architecture as a text with a range of readings we can learn ever-expanding amounts about a given point in time, and about ourselves.

The writing of this book has been a huge undertaking. Looking back it seems more daunting than when I began and there are many to thank for their help and encouragement. My colleagues in the Department of Archaeology at the University of Southampton have been unfailingly supportive and helpful of this project. I am also particularly grateful to Professor Andrew Ballantyne and Professor Adrian Rifkin who talked through some of my ideas with me and commented on the draft of my text. Any omissions and oversights are my own.

Collaborative work and interdisciplinarity are important aspects of present-day academic research. To this end I have included a selection of texts to provide a variety readings of the architecture and its histories of the period under review together with writings on social and cultural theory. The collation of these texts and the securing of copyright permission has been a major undertaking in its own right and I would like to thank Mark Westgarth for his invaluable assistance and for the preparation of the index.

And, yet again, Ken Haynes has shown exemplary patience throughout the writing of this book, and that *is* a fact!

Dana Arnold
London, January 2002

Extract acknowledgements

What is history? E H Carr: Extracts from *What is History?*, London, Macmillan, 1961, pp. 7–30. Copyright the Estate of Edward Hallet Carr, 1961. Used by permission of Macmillan Ltd.

The fictions of factual representation Hayden White: Extract from Angus Fletcher (ed.) *The Literature of Fact*, New York, Columbia University Press, 1976. Copyright 1976 Columbia University Press. Reprinted with permission of the publisher.

Biographical Dictionary Sir Howard Colvin: Extracts from *A Biographical Dictionary of British Architects 1600–1840*, 3rd edn, New Haven, CT and London, Yale University Press, 1995, pp. 17, 18, 29–45, 51–54. Copyright 1995 Yale University Press. Reprinted with permission.

What is an author? Michel Foucault: Translated from the French by Josué V. Harari, in *Textual Strategies: Perspectives in Post-structuralist Criticism*, edited by J. Harari, London, Methuen and Co. Ltd, 1979, pp. 141–160. Copyright 1979 Cornell University Press. Used by permission of the publisher, Cornell University Press.

Architecture in Britain, 1530–1830 John Summerson: Extracts from *Architecture in Britain, 1530–1830*, New Haven, CT and London, Yale University Press, 1993, pp. 317–320, 322, 324–5, 372–374, 376–378, 380–384, 386–389, 391–393. Copyright 1953, 1955, 1958, 1963, 1969, 1970, 1977, 1983, 1991, 1993 Yale University Press. Reprinted with permission.

Art history and class struggle Nicos Hadjinicolaou: Extracts from *Art History and Class Struggle*, trans. Louise Asmal, London, Pluto, 1978, pp. 9–12, 95, 100–104. Copyright Librarie François Maspero, 1973. English translation copyright Pluto Press, 1978. Used by permission of Pluto Press.

Life in the English country house Mark Girouard: Extracts from *Life in the English Country House: A social and architectural history*, New Haven, CT and London, Yale University Press, 1978, pp. 126, 128, 135–136, 138–139, 140–154, 156, 158, 160–162, 184, 189–190, 191, 193–194, 199–200, 203–206, 208. Copyright 1978 by Yale University Press. Used by permission of Yale University Press.

In search of cultural history E H Gombrich: Extract from E.H. Gombrich, 'In Search of Cultural History', the Philip Maurice Deneke Lecture delivered at Lady Margaret Hall, Oxford, 19 November 1967; reprinted in *Ideas and Idols: Essays on Values in History and in Art*, Oxford, 1979; reprinted, London, 1994, pp. 42–59. Copyright 1969 Oxford University Press. Used by permission of Oxford University Press.

The buildings of England Sir Nikolaus Pevsner: Extracts from *The Buildings of England*, volumes covering the Cities of London and Westminster (1957, pp. 15–17), Wiltshire (1963, pp. 573, 580–583), Hampshire (1967, pp. 536–537), and Buckinghamshire (1960, pp. 239–241), all published in Harmondsworth by Penguin. Copyright (London) the estate of Sir Nikolaus Pevsner, 1957, 1962, 1973, 1984, 1985; (Wiltshire) Sir Nikolaus Pevsner, 1963 and Sir Nikolaus Pevsner and Bridget Cherry, 1975; (Hampshire) Sir Nikolaus Pevsner and David Lloyd, 1967; (Buckinghamshire) Sir Nikolaus Pevsner 1960 and Andrew Martin, Geoffrey K. Brandwood, Roger Evans, Michael Farley, Andrew Pike, John Chenevix Trench, Elizabeth Williamson and the estate of Sir Nikolaus Pevsner, 1994.

The Blue Guide Roland Barthes: Extract from R. Barthes, *Mythologies*, London, Jonathan Cape, 1972, pp. 74–77. Used by permission of The Random House Group Ltd

Sexism and the star system in architecture Denise Scott Brown: 'Room at the Top? Sexism and the star system in architecture', from Ellen Perry Berekeley (ed.) *Architecture: A place for women*, London and Washington, DC, Smithsonian Institution Press, 1989, pp. 237–246. Copyright 1989 The Smithsonian Institution. Used by permission of the publishers.

Planning and representation in the early modern country house Alice T Friedman: Extracts from 'Architecture, Authority and the Female Gaze: Planning and representation in the early modern country house', *Assemblage*, 18 (August 1992), pp. 41–61. Copyright 1992 The Massachusetts Institute of Technology.

Introduction

This book is the result of over twenty years of reading architectural history. As an historian of eighteenth- and early nineteenth-century British architecture I have enjoyed and benefited from the map of the subject set out by such canonical writers as Sir John Summerson, Sir Nikolaus Pevsner and Mark Girouard, to name but a few. This book is then partly about my engagement with their writings and partly about their influence on the discipline. But it is also about how I constructed my own map of the subject to allow me to cross the same terrain with a different set of co-ordinates and destinations. My aim is not to replace the pioneers of the discipline of architectural history nor destructively to criticise their writings. Rather, it is to engage with their ideas, approaches, and their role in the historiography of architectural history and the effect this has on the subject today. Moreover, in juxtaposing canonical texts with the thinking of a range of social and cultural theorists my aim is to reveal that these writings are richer than we have perhaps recognised, and that they are in themselves an archive worthy of academic enquiry.

The chapters in this volume concentrate on fundamental texts in the study of architectural history pre-nineteenth-century Britain[1] with special reference to the long eighteenth century.[2] In each of the sections, discursive essays preface the texts under discussion and highlight the key themes or methods they address in the construction of architectural histories. Alongside this, philosophical or theoretical writings which consider the abstract issues under review in each chapter texts are presented as a kind of exegesis on the chosen texts. More generally, these writings provide a dialogue around the central themes of the volume. Indeed, all the texts cited are intended to interact and intersect beyond their specific groupings to present a transdisciplinary discourse around the discipline of architectural history. The chapters cover a broad range of writings, including canonical histories, contemporary commentaries, guidebooks and visual surveys. And the resonance between the verbal and the visual, the historical and the theoretical is a core theme in the volume.

The texts cited serve not only as an essential reader for methods and approaches to architectural history, and more generally as examples of the kinds of evidence used in the construction of histories, but also as a thematic introduction to architecture in Britain and its social and cultural meaning. In this way I hope to show that architectural production in this period can be interrogated in the same way as that from the more recent past. This is particularly relevant as the architecture of the long eighteenth century is often seen through the lens of the historical thinking of the period in which it was produced. From the later nineteenth century onwards architecture was conceived and written about in a more historicising and self-conscious way, which either provided or facilitated the formulation of a theoretically based historical analysis. In our period, however, at the moment when history was emerging as a quasi-scientific, historical discipline, the duty of the historian was, according to key thinkers such as Ranke, writing in the 1830s, 'simply to show how it really was'. This has resonance through three generations of historians and has in many ways continued to the present day in the strong empirical tradition in architectural history whereby 'hard' facts, 'established' at the expense of interpretation, are allowed 'to speak for themselves'. I do not deny that architecture has a language. Rather, I would question whether this language has only one meaning. If facts are part of the grammatical apparatus necessary for the act of speaking, who decides and deciphers the syntax or can this be innate in the facts themselves?

In attempting to answer this I have turned round this historical lens to look out rather than in. Instead of focusing simply on the facts and attempting to let them speak for themselves, I want to see the vast temporal and intellectual context in which they exist, and also see how we comprehend them. To do this we must consider architecture – its facts and its histories – as texts which can be read in a variety of ways – and the theoretical writings can provide the apparatus for doing this. *Reading Architectural History* can then reveal the subject in all its richness and complexities as a fluid discourse around the built environment in its social and cultural contexts. But the main problem is how to get round the canon of British architectural history in order to leave it coherent yet interrogated, unpacked yet intact.

How, for instance, does an historian of eighteenth- and nineteenth-century architecture negotiate the work of Sir John Summerson? His giant, monolithic figure dominates the history of the country house and the urban environments of the period, especially London. Should I attempt to challenge what has proved to be a fundamental touchstone of the discipline? Or should I, as others have, try to write the replacement for *Architecture in Britain 1530–1830* or *Georgian London* by offering a slightly new spin on the same set of observed, teleological processes? Without a substantial philosophical or theoretical core these attempts can appear flimsy, derivative and, to some extent, petty. There is a substantial body of writing that has shifted the sights to thematic considerations – for instance M H Port's excellent study of Imperial London[3] – or drawn attention away from architects by concentrating on building process, as seen in the innovative work in this area by Malcolm Airs.[4] These fascinating and very valuable micro-histories add necessary detail and a specificity of approach whilst at the same time expanding our knowledge of architecture in Britain.

Here my aim is rather different. I want to construct a meta-discourse around the discipline of architectural history. In many ways this follows the Foucauldian idea of a kind of universal system that is 'an attempt to establish between elements that may have been split over the course of time, a set of relationships that juxtapose them, set them in opposition or link them together, so as to create a sort of shape.'[5] I differ in my use of theory from those who have theory as their focus of study – whether it be the theoretical writings *per se* or the historiography of theory. I am interested in the historiography of histories of architecture – their meanings and consequences – and it is to this end that I use theory as an interlocutor or lens through which to *read* this part of my archive. But the discourses in this book also stress the provisional nature of readings – or histories – which will inevitably shift and change over time. In this way the architecture and the histories of Britain remain a constant focus but the viewpoint and perception are in flux. Consequently, the questions of the viewer become important, as I want also to explore the nature of architectural history: What are we studying? Is it the built form, the histories or the broader social and cultural meaning and through this what then becomes of the subject/object relationship. In other words, what do our constructions of histories of architecture tell us about ourselves?

I think we have the component parts – the archive, the facts, the theoretical paradigms – it is a question of putting them together and then pulling them apart.

Notes

1 Here I use Britain to refer to the British Isles although the emphasis in the histories I discuss is on England. This Anglocentric view in terms of its formulation and influence on architectural history is an important theme in this volume.

2 By this I refer to architecture from the late seventeenth to the early nineteenth century.

3 M H Port, *Imperial London: Civil government building in London 1850–1915*, New Haven and London, Yale University Press, 1995.

4 See M Airs, *The Tudor and Jacobean Country House: A building history*, New York and Stroud, Sutton, 1995.

5 M Foucault, 'Of other spaces' trans. J Miskowice, *Diacritics,* Spring 1986, pp. 22–27.

1
Reading the past
What is architectural history?

Architectural History is more than just the study of buildings. Architecture of the past and the present remains an essential emblem of a distinctive social system and set of cultural values, and as a result it has been the subject of study of a variety of disciplines. But what is architectural history and how should we *read* it? This book examines both the role of architecture in the construction of its histories and, equally, the way in which histories of architecture are written – in other words how the forces of history impact on our perception and understanding of the architecture of the past. But first what is meant by architecture? And what is history?

History

Let's begin by unpacking the term 'history'. History is about the past. Yet it exists only in the present – the moment of its creation as history provides us with a narrative constructed after the events with which it is concerned. The narrative must then relate to the moment of its creation as much as its historical subject. History presents an historian with the task of producing a dialogue between the past and the present. But as these temporal co-ordinates cannot be fixed, history becomes a continuous interaction between the historian and the past. As such, history can be seen as a process of evaluation whereby the past is always coloured by the intellectual fashions and philosophical concerns of the present. This shifting perspective on the past is matched by the fluid status of the past itself. In this way structuralist and post-structuralist[1] discourse has fundamentally altered our view and understanding of knowledge and history. The preoccupation with the nature of history and historical truth is scrutinized in terms of its linguistic and textual possibilities. Similarly, such thoughts and questions as 'What is history?' were voiced by historians in the 1960s as part of a discourse around the discipline. Historians were beginning to question what they were doing and the philosophical implications of their construction of the discipline. In this way we see that the concern with what history is is not merely the preoccupation of social and cultural theorists intent on dismantling traditional canons of thought, it is a fundamental core of the historiography of history.

One of the principal concerns when considering of the nature of history is the question of subjectivity. Now that human knowledge is no longer viewed as being a stable and immutable – a kind of humanistic or enlightenment vision of the subject knowing both the world and itself – we define subjectivity as a state of flux and change. History, as a part of human knowledge, cannot then be seen as a solid ever-expanding discourse developing along generally accepted trajectories. We have dissembled these certainties in order to question established principles of knowledge upon which historical thought is based.

The recognition of the role and importance of subjectivity in the construction of histories does, by implication, negate the possibility for objectivity in the writing of history. But there will always be historical narrative and, consequently, a narrative voice, be it hidden in the syntactical structure of the writing by, for instance, the absence of first person or the use of simple past tense. But this is a sleight of hand which gives the reader a sense of immediate contact with the past without the presence of an interlocutor. This apparently 'unmediated' contact gives history a kind of privileged status of objective knowledge.

Narrative and its role in history is the concern of Roland Barthes' influential essay on *Historical Discourse*

> What really happens is that the author discards the human persona but replaces it by an 'objective' one; the authorial subject is as evident as ever, but it has become an objective subject . . . At the level of discourse objectivity, or the absence of any clues to the narrator, turns out to be particular form of fiction, where the historian tries to give the impression that the referent is speaking for itself.[2]

Here we see how the theoretical preoccupations with language and textuality enable us to examine the kinds of narrative constructions used in the telling of histories and the consequences these different modes of narrative have on the subject. Historical reality is then a 'referential illusion', in which we try to grasp the reality (the referent of language) that we believe lies beyond the barrier of the linguistic construction of its narratives. In this way history becomes a Myth or an ideology as it purports to be reality. Indeed, storytelling is often seen as one of the most important functions of writing histories and fundamental to the nature of the discipline. A story requires a beginning, middle and end, based on a series of events that take place over a period of time. Lawrence Stone sums up this understanding of narrative:

> Narrative is taken to mean the organization of material in a chronologically sequential order and the focussing of the content into a single coherent story, albeit with sub-plots. The two essential ways in which narrative history differs from structural history is that its arrangement is descriptive rather than analytical and that its central focus is on man not circumstances. It therefore deals with the peculiar and the specific, rather than the collective and statistical. Narrative is a mode of historical writing, but it is a mode which also affects and is affected by content and method.[3]

Coherence is then an essential part of narrative in order for it to work as a story and for it to work in Barthes' terms as a myth or reality. This coherence or linearity is a selective process that requires the exclusion of material and the imposition of a unity on a disparate set of historical events or circumstances. This consequence of the desire for narrative relates to the empirical tradition; it is one way of ordering facts – 'letting them speak for themselves' – and has a built-in notion of progress. Two orders of narrative used frequently in architectural history are the narrative of style and the narrative of the author (architect). The narrative of style allows the ordering of architectural production, whether anonymous or not, through aesthetic categories. Here the heterogeneity, discordance and lack of synchronization between different strands of architectural production can be unified into what Laura Mulvey has called 'parabolic patterns of narrative',[4] with elements/movements coming into ascendancy and then declining. This provides a dominant narrative thrust in history within which the ideas of progress movement and development are expressed through a narrative of opposition and polarisation. This is evident in stylistic histories where teleological patterns of stylistic

Figure 1.1 The Banqueting House, Whitehall, London by Inigo Jones, *c.* 1622 (photo, author).

dominance and recession are imposed. In this way English Palladianism, typified by Inigo Jones (Figure 1.1), is followed by English Baroque, typified by Sir John Vanbrugh (Figure 1.2) is followed by English Palladianism, typified by Lord Burlington (Figure 1.3). Vanbrugh rejected the style of Jones in the same way that Burlington rejected the style of Vanbrugh. But what of the substance of these narratives – the factual information?

The choice of narrative is an important way of making the facts *speak*. But this was rarely recognised by nineteenth-century historians, many of whom were oblivious to the nature and consequences of the narrative choices available to them. They believed, instead, that at some point all facts would be known and thus to provide an archival *truth*. There are traces of this today where narrative choices, centred for instance on biography, style or social history, stem from the belief that an empirical reiteration of the facts presents reality. The adoption of 'scientific' techniques of narration from the early nineteenth century onwards, where the historian dissociated himself (usually) from literature in favour of science, reinforces the primacy of factual accuracy and empirical information and the myth of truthful reality.

Wilhelm von Humboldt's essay entitled *The Historian's Task*, written in 1821, leaves us in no doubt as to the prevalent view:

> The historian's task is to present what actually happened. The more purely and completely he [note 'he'] achieves this, the more perfectly has he solved this problem. A simple presentation is at the same time the primary indispensable condition of his work and the highest achievement he will be able to attain. Regarded in this way, he seems to be merely receptive and productive, not active and creative.

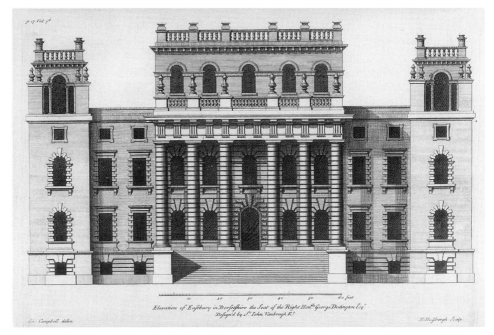

Figure 1.2 Eastbury, Dorset by Sir John Vanbrugh, illustrated in *Vitruvius Britannicus*, Volume III, plate 17, 1725 (private collection).

Facts are the substance of this 'objective' historical narrative. But what are they? And what is the relationship of the historian to the facts? Is it the duty of the historian, as Ranke amongst others suggests, to let the facts speak for themselves? But the facts history purports to describe are in the past – no longer accessible to direct inspection or empirical observation. They are untestable and have no yardstick of known reality to which they can be compared.

Again, this was a concern of historians before the post-structuralist discourses began to permeate historical thinking. W H Walsh in his *Introduction to the Philosophy of History* considered the question of truth and fact in history, which he saw as relating to the more general theory of knowledge.

> We are apt to suppose that the facts in any branch of meaning must be in some way open to direct inspection, and that the statements of experts in each branch can be tested by their conformity with them . . .
>
> The most striking thing about history is that the facts it purports to describe are past facts; and past facts are no longer accessible to direct inspection. We cannot, in a word, test the accuracy of historical statements by simply seeing whether they correspond to a reality which is independently known. How then can we test them? . . .
>
> . . . we do so by referring to historical evidence. Although the past is not accessible to direct inspection it has left ample traces of itself in the present, in the shape of documents, buildings, coins, institutions, procedures and so forth.[5]

Every assertion must be based, therefore, on some kind of evidence. If there is no evidence history, according to Walsh, becomes an inspired guess or a fiction. But the original sources

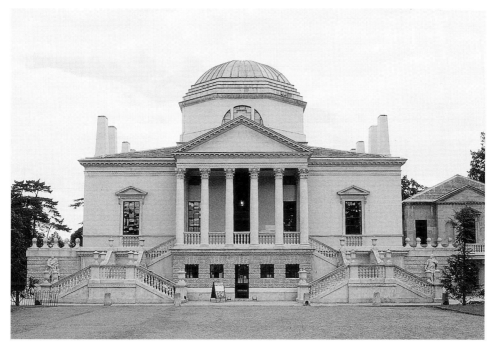

Figure 1.3 Chiswick House, London by Lord Burlington, *c.* 1725 (photo, author).

need scrutiny and the historian has to decide whether or not to believe them; they are not the 'ultimate datum to which we can refer to test historical judgements'. Walsh places historical thinking firmly in the present so that the historical truth arrived at by the historian is a product of the present and not the past.

The past does leave traces of itself in the present in the form of archives, whether they be documents, institutions or indeed buildings. This archive of knowledge about the past, no matter how incomplete, allows the historian to present an argument or reconstruction based on this body of 'evidence' or facts. But the 'facts of history can never come to us in a pure state', as the historian E H Carr observed: 'they are always refracted through the mind of the recorder'.[6] So we not only have an imperfect and uncorroborated archive, but we also have the subjectivity of the historian. Indeed, Carr advises that 'It follows that when we take up a work of history, our first concern should be not with the facts which it contains but with the historian who wrote it.'[7]

Architectural historians and their histories of architecture are the substance of this enquiry. The dialogue between the historian and his/her facts is an essential element Michel de Certeau calls it 'the particularity of place where discourse is produced'. He argues that this

> . . . [puts] the subject-producer of knowledge into question . . . One can, of course, either maintain that the personal status of the author is a matter of indifference (in relation to the objectivity of his or her work) or that he or she alone authorizes or invalidates the discourse (according to whether he or she is 'of it' or not). But this debate requires what has been concealed by an epistemology, namely, the impact of subject-to-subject

relationships (men and women, blacks and whites, etc.) on the use of apparently 'neu-tral' techniques and in the organization of discourses that are, perhaps, equally scientific. For example, from the differentiation of the sexes, must one conclude that a woman produces a different historiography from that of a man? Of course, I do not answer this question, but I do assert that this interrogation puts the place of the subject in question and requires a treatment of it unlike the epistemology that constructed the 'truth' of the work on the foundation of the speaker's irrelevance.[8]

De Certeau is particularly concerned with histories and the historiography of 'other', but this sensitivity to the subject-to-subject relationship outlined here has resonance with the con-cerns of this study. And de Certeau sees these categories of historical discourse as magnifying more general concerns about the narratives and subjects of history outlined in this chapter. At this point I would add a third party to this perceived dialogue between historian and nar-rative – the reader. What do we bring to and what do we want from these discourses? And what is our 'experience' of the past?

The past is encountered and mapped through the discovery and ordering of facts which are not static, fixed – or indeed certain. Foucault amongst many other thinkers asserts that there is no essential order, meaning or framework as knowledge is forever changing and is itself sub-ject to periodisation or fashion, as is the discipline of history itself. These epistemes, as Foucault referred to them, were both a means of exploring and understanding the historical discourses of the past and a way of discovering and interpreting the production of the present.

> If interpretation were the slow exposure of the meaning hidden in an origin, then only metaphysics could interpret the development of humanity. But if interpretation is the violent or surreptitious appropriation of a system of rules, which in itself has no essen-tial meaning, in order to impose a direction, to bend it to a new will, to force its participation in a different game, and to subject it to secondary rules, then the devel-opment of humanity is a series of interpretations. The role of genealogy is to record its history: the history of morals, ideals, and metaphysical concepts, the history of the con-cept of liberty or of acetic life; as they stand for the emergence of different interpretations, they must be made to appear as events on the stage of historical process.[9]

History can then imply chronology and sequence, perhaps even a sense of development and progress. Linearity is not necessarily problematic – it is only one route through knowl-edge – but if we accept that architecture and urban environments are complex entities with interwoven meanings, this straightening out of the different strands or chains of facts/events can both clarify and obscure our readings of these phenomena.

Architecture

'Architecture' may at first appear to be a more fixed and finite term. It has a three-dimensional, tangible, useable form. But questions remain about what can be considered architecture and what cannot, and by this I mean that we usually understand architecture to incorporate aesthetic as well as functional consideration into its structure. Anything that does not fall into this category can be described as 'just a building'. This may seem too simple. Can architecture be determined solely by the use of refined architectural style – high or polite architecture instead of vernacular? This view reduces architecture to an aesthetic – a cosmetic transformation or intervention of which the cultural and historical meaning remains in the realms of the visual. But style has been an essential tool in the construction of the narratives of architectural history. If we then consider the function of a building, is the answer really as simple as Sir Nikolaus Pevsner's view that 'a bicycle shed is a building: Lincoln Cathedral is a piece of architecture'?[10] In one way we return to the importance of the aesthetic, whilst at the same time imposing hierarchies of utility. Moreover, can we deny that technical and structural innovations play a crucial part in the design process – both in terms of infrastructure and formal possibilities. At what point does this become 'architecture'? The complexities revealed by these questions amplify when buildings are considered in their urban context. Most would agree that buildings comprise a substantial part of a city. But do these buildings have to be 'architecture'? And if we accept buildings as constituent parts of an incoherent whole, it becomes infeasible to categorise these key features of metropolitan structures and identities in any fixed way. Instead of fixed definitions, fluid sets of relationships between buildings and the urban infrastructure demonstrate the complex interweaving of the fabricated environment to reveal at once its heterotopic and heterochronic significance.

Architecture differs from a work of art, which can be displayed in different settings and the subject-matter, form and meaning will remain unchanged. The physicality of any built structure can be altered over time as additions and alterations are made. Moreover, a building or work of architecture can change its function as it meets the different demands of its occupants, although its exterior appearance may be unaltered. And its meaning may change depending on the nature of the context. This reveals some of the problems of interpreting historic architecture from a modern-day perspective as the physical changes and different cultural contexts transform the object. So at what point do we consider architecture and how do we reconstruct this period in time? This underlines the importance of treating architecture not as a limited body of design which reflected certain social values. Instead, architecture is an essential instrument of the development and dissemination of these ideas, and this continues throughout the life of the building. By reading architecture as a text we can identify ideological debates and issues that emerge in an interdisciplinary study through which we can understand the relationships between cultural practices and artifacts at various points in time. Indeed, this approach reinforces the point that to consider a building in isolation as a total history in itself, and concentrate solely on form or appearance, is to denude it of much of its meaning. This demonstrates that the sum of the parts of 'architecture' is greater than the physical whole, that is to say the architectural form of the building itself.

If we accept architecture as a cultural artefact then we must also see its histories as a text open to a variety of readings. The process of locating 'the text' within its appropriate contexts is not merely to provide an historiography, it is to begin the process of interpretation. It is here that critical theory facilitates this kind of interrogation of histories of the built environment and architecture.

> We know now that a text consists not of a line of words, releasing a single 'theological' meaning (the 'message' of the Author-God), but of a multi-dimensional space in which are married and contested several writings, none of which is original: the text is a fabric of quotations, resulting from a thousand sources of culture.[11]

The focus is then on the interface between theory and archive and how this is manifest in the history of the historiography of architectural history. In this way critical theory, in its broadest constituency, becomes an interlocutor between me – the author narrator – and the historiographies and the 'factual' archive.

Architecture and history

The relationship between architecture and history is a predominant theme of this book. In many ways they are separate, discrete worlds which collide only to fracture each other into a variety of different meanings and possibilities. First there are the different archives of architecture. We can begin with the building, this physical, tangible archive that comes to us through time. Is this the hard evidence? We also have historic architecture – buildings of historic interest that exist in the present, thereby closing the gap between past and present – but they are loaded with social and cultural meaning and interpretation. Alongside this we have the information around the building. This is a more diverse and scattered archive. Both archives can lead the historian in different directions, and this reveals the tensions and interactions of architectural history and its interconnectedness with so many other disciplines. Architecture can be explained in so many ways – more than any other 'art form'. A building, what we might call here the primary archive, is commissioned, designed, used, re-used, conserved or demolished. It is the subject of what we might here call the secondary archive as it appears in design briefs, drawings, journals, diaries, household accounts, travel and guidebooks, architectural surveys, and we must not forget architectural histories. The building can become, through a synthesis of its primary and secondary archives, an archive in itself for enquiries from other disciplines – social history, cultural geography and so forth. Buildings can then be historicised or become the objects of history.

Architectural history

The development of the study of architecture and the kinds of histories that have been written about it is the subject of David Watkin's survey *The Rise of Architectural History*.[12] This study stands as a rather isolated account of the emergence of a discipline which remains unreflexive and unself-questioning, especially when compared to its close cousin art history. My purpose here is not to go over the ground covered by Watkin nor to challenge or reconfigure the path he lays out of the evolution of the subject. I am interested instead in looking closely at a specific moment in the development of architectural history in Britain and considering the impact this has had on the writing of architectural history and the way in which it is *read*.

The Second World War precipitated a quite considerable change in national attitudes towards historic architecture and traditional townscapes. The threat of what could be lost as well as the memory of what had already been lost sharpened interest and awareness on the part of both government and populace. In 1943 the Ministry of Town and Country Planning was instructed to draw up an inventory of buildings of national historic importance. This became the now infamous, if not controversial, listing process. It is perhaps hard for us to imagine how or why in the face of such adversity this seemed relevant. But if we accept that architecture can be a built embodiment or representation of sets of social and cultural values, the importance of the past – of historic architecture – at that moment can be seen as a signifier of the values that were at stake. Also during the war, in order to have at least a photographic/drawn record of the nation's historic architecture, the National Buildings Record (later the National Monuments Record) was set up and the Royal Commission on Historical Monuments had its remit expanded so that it was permitted to survey structures dating from after 1714.

In the immediate post-war period government and public attention was focused on historic architecture of both country and city. At the same time many large country houses fell into public ownership or were handed over to the National Trust as their owners could no longer afford to keep them on. This had the twofold effect of making more of these houses available to the visiting public and, perhaps more importantly here, their archives became freely available to scholars and the interested public in county record offices across the country. There was a range of academics and writers ready to work in these newly accessible archives in order to map out the architectural history of Britain, especially its country houses, and to make this history available to the public in order to explain the significance of the historical architecture now deemed worthy of national veneration and preservation.

The range of writing around architecture at this time reflected both the social and intellectual diversity of the historians of architecture in post-war Britain. There were those, such as Reginald Blomfield, Christopher Hussey, James Lees Milne and Sacheverall Sitwell, who continued the élitist *Country Life* tradition of architectural connoisseurship (Figure 1.4). But there was also a new generation of British academics from less grand backgrounds. Most notable here is perhaps Sir John Summerson who, although a confirmed modernist, recognised the importance of Georgian architecture to the urban fabric (Figures 1.5 and 1.6). His seminal study, *Georgian London*, first published in 1945, was partly a response to the loss to bomb damage and demolition of much of London's eighteenth-century architecture and partly a way of introducing and mapping the urban development of the city at this time for the general public. Through the connections he made between the abstract qualities of Georgian design and the principles of the Modern movement Summerson provided a bridge between historic past and forward-looking modern present. This kind of English empirical tradition in architectural history continued in Summerson's *Architecture in Britain 1530–1830*, first published in 1953, which offered for the first time a clear, illustrated route through the development of architecture in this period. The stylistic preoccupations of this book are the subject of a chapter in this study, as is the work of another empirical scholar: Sir Howard Colvin. Colvin's *Biographical Dictionary of British Architects 1600–1840* first appeared in 1954, when the flurry of academic activity concerning British architectural history was in full swing. It provided a route map for archival sources for the study of architecture, as well as being, and remaining, the most comprehensive gazetteer of architectural activity, albeit by named architects only, in the period. Colvin was not alone at this time in mapping out British cultural production. Rupert Gunnis produced his *Dictionary of British Sculptors* at the time, which also drew heavily on newly accessible country house collections There was almost a sense of urgency to discover, order and publish facts – empirical information about a past set of values and architecture that had so nearly been lost.

The influx of scholars to Britain in the mid-twentieth century, many of whom had fled persecution in Nazi-occupied Europe, meant British architecture was scrutinised for the first time in any depth by a set of intellectual and philosophical conventions that had not rested easily in existing British academic traditions. British architecture had not received much attention from European scholars. It provided neither examples of formal brilliance that would stand up to continental examples nor any significant influence on design in Europe – the traffic of ideas had for the most part been one way. In 1945 Sir Nikolaus Pevsner began his expansive survey of buildings, both urban and rural, of interest and importance to the nation in his *Buildings of England* series, the impact of which is considered later in this book. This series was followed by Pevsner's bigger and more wide-ranging *The Pelican History of Art* series of which Summerson's volume on *Architecture in Britain 1530–1830* was one of the first to be commissioned alongside the volume by Ellis Waterhouse on *Painting in Britain 1530–1790*.

Figure 1.4 Foots Cray Place, Kent. Upper-class traditions of architectural connoisseurship endured into the twentieth century. Engraving by William
Woollet (detail) 1760 (private collection).

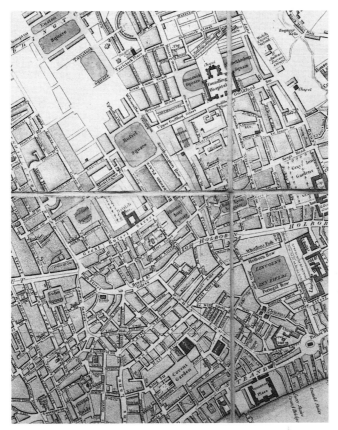

Figure 1.5 Detail of map showing Bloomsbury and Soho. Summerson was one of the first architectural historians to study London as a city. *A Pocket Guide to London*, 1812 (Yale Center for British Art, Paul Mellon Collection).

The map of British architectural history may well have been drawn up quickly – in less than a decade. This hasty appearance was in part the result of the flurry of activity as rich, new archives became available for public scrutiny. But it also coincides with the state's promotion of a 'New Elizabethan Era' in the early 1950s as part of the invention of heritage as a tool to focus national loyalty and pride in the post-war era.[13] But this archival material and the established readings of it remain of lasting importance to architectural history in Britain in terms both of the empirical information and the way this is presented, with various aspects privileged over others in the narrative interpretations.

Reading

The textuality of architectural history has many intricate layers. Fundamental to our readings are the complexities of language and syntax – the author's choice of words and the reader's understanding of them.[14] Hayden White was one of the first writers who brought the theoretical ideas of literary theory to the study of history. Here the central point is that language and linguistic protocols fundamentally shape the writing of history and by inference our understanding of the narratives of history. The historian's choice of narrative

Figure 1.6 Soho Square. The ordinariness of London's domestic architecture and planning featured in architectural histories of the city. Anonymous nineteenth-century engraving (private collection).

structures and the theoretical concepts in the analysis or explanation of events are important framing devices. More important is the linguistic paradigm by which historians 'prefigure their field of study'. This, White asserts, is the metahistorical element in all historical writing

> Histories combine a certain amount of 'data', theoretical concepts for explaining these data, and a narrative structure for their presentation . . . in addition, I maintain, they contain a deep structural content which is generally poetic, and specifically linguistic in nature, and which serves as the precritically accepted paradigm of what distinctively 'historical' explanation should be. This paradigm functions as the 'metahistorical' element in all historical works that are more comprehensive in scope then the monograph or archival report.[15]

In other words, the historian must perceive the field before investigation can begin, and in doing so creates his/her object of analysis and the nature of the conceptual strategies to be used to explain it. Thus, historians employ their narratives in particular ways and these modes of narrative give some form of explanation. An example would be the choice of beginning and end of the narrative. The sources of history are continuous; it is the historian who inserts the breaks.

   This book draws together the various ways of writing about architectural history and each chapter aims to show how this study complements them and can serve as a way of revisiting important texts. This is with a view to not only as using these texts as important sources of information but also to interrogating them in terms of their role in the construction of the canon of architectural history. As a result, we see what their preoccupations tell us of the ways in which histories have been written. Alongside this I have included texts which express some of the fundamental ideas that have informed thinking on modern and contemporary architecture and criticism. The juxtaposition of these is there to show how one can serve as a kind of exegesis of the other. The empirical survey can be revisited and re-read in the light of the theoretical paradigm, just as the theoretical paradigm can be vivified and explored through the specifics of the empirical survey. Of particular interest here is the canonical use of biography, style and social history, together with such concepts as gender, and architectural experience through guidebooks and visual analyses. This thematic exploration and *ergo* fragmentation of the canon of the historical narratives of architecture means that the discipline cannot now assert itself as having the epistemological status attributed to positivist or teleological systems of knowledge. Each fragment or theme represents and relates to current systems of thought where there can be a variety of perspectives or approaches to a subject which do not claim to be total histories in themselves. Inevitably, this challenges the long-held notion of objectivity in architectural history. But is as E H Carr asks us 'to consider the historian . . .' we will see that architectural history has been the construct of white European male subjects. Moreover, certain elements of the architectural histories of Britain of the eighteenth and nineteenth centuries can be seen as tools to promote and reinforce the hegemony of certain social and cultural élites, and so reveal much about the social dynamics of the production and consumption of the myths of architecture.

I do not intend these lines of enquiry to constitute a destructive act on the discipline of architectural history. Rather, my aim in scrutinising the canonical texts is to give a range of voices to the monolithic narrative they have constructed. In doing so the facts, such as they are, can be released from the restraints of positivist, teleological interpretative systems and be seen as fluid entities with a multiplicity of meanings and interpretations. *Reading Architectural History* becomes then at once a process of recognition and of analysis of the subject in all its complexities.

Notes

1 In this book I use the terms 'post-structuralist' and 'post-modern' interchangeably.

2 R Barthes, 'Le discours de l'histoire' trans. as 'Historical Discourse' in M Lane (ed.) *Structuralism: A reader*, London, Jonathan Cape, 1970, pp. 149–154.

3 L Stone, 'The Revival of Narrative: Reflections on a new old history' in *The Past and Present Revisited*, London, Routledge and Kegan Paul, 1987 p. 74.

4 L Mulvey, 'Changes: Thoughts on myth, narrative and historical experience', *History Workshop Journal*, 23, Spring 1987 pp. 3–19.

5 W H Walsh, *An Introduction to the Philosophy of History*, London, Hutchinson University Library, 1958 pp. 19–20 esp.

6 E H Carr, *What is History?* Harmondsworth, Penguin, 1961 p. 22.

7 E H Carr *What is History?* Harmondsworth, Penguin, 1961 p. 22.

8 M de Certeau, 'History: Science and fiction', in *Heterologies: Discourse on the Other*, trans. Brian Massimi, Minneapolis, University of Minnesota Press, 1986 pp. 217–218.

9 M Foucault, 'Nietzsche, Genealogy, History', in *Language, Counter-memory, Practice: Selected essays and interviews*, trans. and ed. Donald F. Bouchard and Sherry Simon, Ithaca, NY Cornell University Press, 1977, pp. 151–152.

10 N Pevsner, *An Outline of European Architecture*, Harmondsworth, Penguin, 1960.

11 R Barthes, 'The Death of the Author' in *Image–Music–Text*, trans. Stephen Heath, 1977, pp. 52–53.

12 D Watkin, *The Rise of Architectural History*, London, Architectural Press, 1980.

13 On this point, with specific reference to the country house see *P Mandler, The Fall and Rise of the Stately Home*, New Haven, CT and London, Yale University Press, 1997.

14 For a discussion of the linguistic complexities behind verbalising of discussion of modern architecture see A Forty, *Words and Buildings*, London, Thames and Hudson, 2000.

15 H White, *Metahistory: The historical imagination in nineteenth-century Europe*, Baltimore, MD, Johns Hopkins University Press, 1973 p. ix.

What is history?

E H Carr

The historian and his facts

> I often think it odd
> That it should be so dull,
> For a great deal of it
> must be invention.
> Catherine Morland on History
>   (*Northanger Abbey*, ch. xiv)

What is history? Lest anyone think the question meaningless or superfluous, I will take as my text two passages relating respectively to the first and second incarnations of the *Cambridge Modern History*. Here is Acton in his report of October 1896 to the Syndics of the Cambridge University Press on the work which he had undertaken to edit:

> It is a unique opportunity of recording, in the way most useful to the greatest number, the fullness of the knowledge which the nineteenth century is about to bequeath. . . . By the judicious division of labour we should be able to do it, and to bring home to every man the last document, and the ripest conclusions of international research.
>
> Ultimate history we cannot have in this generation; but we can dispose of conventional history, and show the point we have reached on the road from one to the other, now that all information is within reach, and every problem has become capable of solution.[1]

And almost exactly sixty years later Professor Sir George Clark, in his general introduction to the second *Cambridge Modern History*, commented on this belief of Acton and his collaborators that it would one day be possible to produce 'ultimate history', and went on:

> Historians of a later generation do not look forward to any such prospect. They expect their work to be superseded again and again. They consider that knowledge of the past has come down through one or more human minds, has been 'processed' by them, and therefore cannot consist of elemental and impersonal atoms which nothing can alter. . . . The exploration seems to be endless, and some impatient scholars take refuge in scepticism, or at least in the doctrine that, since all historical judgements involve persons and points of view, one is as good as another and there is no 'objective' historical truth.[2]

Where the pundits contradict each other so flagrantly, the field is open to inquiry. I hope that I am sufficiently up-to-date to recognize that anything written in the 1890s must be nonsense. But I am not yet advanced enough to be committed to the view that anything written in the 1950s necessarily makes sense. Indeed, it may already have occurred to you that this inquiry is liable to stray into something even broader than the nature of history. The clash between Acton and Sir George Clark is a reflection of the change in our total outlook on society over the interval between these two pronouncements. Acton speaks out of the positive belief, the clear-eyed self-confidence, of the later Victorian age; Sir George Clark echoes the bewilderment and distracted scepticism of the beat generation. When we attempt to answer the question 'What is history?' our answer, consciously or unconsciously, reflects our own position in time, and forms part of our answer to the broader question what view we take of the society in which we live. I have no fear that my subject may, on closer inspection, seem trivial. I am afraid only that I may seem presumptuous to have broached a question so vast and so important.

The nineteenth century was a great age for facts. 'What I want', said Mr Gradgrind in *Hard Times*, 'is Facts. . . . Facts alone are wanted in life.' Nineteenth-century historians on the whole agreed with him. When Ranke in the 1830s, in legitimate protest against moralizing history, remarked that the task of the historian was 'simply to show how it really was (*wie es eigentlich gewesen*)', this not very profound aphorism had an astonishing success. Three generations of German, British, and even French historians marched into battle intoning the magic words '*Wie es eigentlich gewesen*' like an incantation – designed, like most incantations, to save them from the tiresome obligation to think for themselves. The Positivists, anxious to stake out their claim for history as a science, contributed the weight of their influence to this cult of facts. First ascertain the facts, said the Positivists, then draw your conclusions from them. In Great Britain, this view of history fitted in perfectly with the empiricist tradition which was the dominant strain in British philosophy from Locke to Bertrand Russell. The empirical theory of knowledge pre-supposes a complete separation between subject and object. Facts, like sense-impressions, impinge on the observer from outside and are independent of his consciousness. The process of reception is passive: having received the data, he then acts on them. The Oxford Shorter English Dictionary, a useful but tendentious work of the empirical school, clearly marks the separateness of the two processes by defining a fact as 'a datum of experience as distinct from conclusions'. This is what may be called the commonsense view of history. History consists of a corpus of ascertained facts. The facts are available to the historian in documents, inscriptions and so on, like fish on the fishmonger's slab. The historian collects them, takes them home, and cooks and serves them in whatever style appeals to him. Acton, whose culinary tastes were austere, wanted them served plain. In his letter of instructions to contributors to the first *Cambridge Modern History* he announced the requirement 'that our Waterloo must be one that satisfies French and English, German and Dutch alike; that nobody can tell, without examining the list of authors, where the Bishop of Oxford laid down the pen, and whether Fairbairn or Gasquet, Liebermann or Harrison took it up'.[3] Even Sir George Clark, critical as he was of Acton's attitude, himself contrasted the 'hard core of facts' in history with the 'surrounding pulp of disputable interpretation'[4] – forgetting perhaps that the pulpy part of the fruit is more rewarding than the hard core. First get your facts straight, then plunge at your peril into the shifting sands of interpretation – that is the ultimate wisdom of the empirical, commonsense school of history. It recalls the favourite dictum of the great liberal journalist C. P. Scott: 'Facts are sacred, opinion is free.'

Now this clearly will not do. I shall not embark on a philosophical discussion of the nature of our knowledge of the past. Let us assume for present purposes that the fact that Caesar crossed the Rubicon and the fact there is a table in the middle of the room are facts of the same or of a comparable order, that both these facts enter our consciousness in the same or in a comparable manner, and that both have the same objective character in relation to the person who knows them. But, even on this bold and not very plausible assumption, our argument at once runs into the difficulty that not all facts about the past are historical facts, or are treated as such by the historian. What is the criterion which distinguishes the facts of history from other facts about the past?

What is a historical fact? This is a crucial question into which we must look a little more closely. According to the commonsense view, there are certain basic facts which are the same for all historians and which form, so to speak, the backbone of history – the fact, for example, that the Battle of Hastings was fought in 1066. But this view calls for two observations. In the first place, it is not with facts like these that the historian is primarily concerned. It is no doubt important to know that the great battle was fought in 1066 and not in 1065 or 1067, and that it was fought at Hastings and not at Eastbourne or Brighton. The historian must not get these things wrong. But when points of this kind are raised, I am reminded of Housman's remark that 'accuracy is a duty, not a virtue'.[5] To praise a historian for his accuracy is like praising an architect for using well-seasoned timber or properly mixed concrete in his building. It is a necessary condition of his work, but not his essential function. It is precisely for matters of this kind that the historian is entitled to rely on what have been called the 'auxiliary sciences' of history – archaeology, epigraphy, numismatics, chronology, and so forth. The historian is not required to have the special skills which enable the expert to determine the origin and period of a fragment of pottery or marble, to decipher an obscure inscription, or to make the elaborate astronomical calculations necessary to establish a precise date. These so-called basic facts, which are the same for all historians, commonly belong to the category of the raw materials of the historian rather than of history itself. The second observation is that the necessity to establish these basic facts rests not on any quality in the facts themselves, but on an *a priori* decision of the historian. In spite of C. P. Scott's motto, every journalist knows today that the most effective way to influence opinion is by the selection and arrangement of the appropriate facts. It used to be said that facts speak for themselves. This is, of course, untrue. The facts speak only when the historian calls on them: it is he who decides to which facts to give the floor, and in what order or context. It was, I think, one of Pirandello's characters who said that a fact is like a sack – it won't stand up till you've put something in it. The only reason why we are interested to know that the battle was fought at Hastings in 1066 is that historians regard it as a major historical event. It is the historian who has decided for his own reasons that Caesar's crossing of that petty stream, the Rubicon, is a fact of history, whereas the crossing of the Rubicon by millions of other people before or since interests nobody at all. The fact that you arrived in this building half an hour ago on foot, or on a bicycle, or in a car, is just as much a fact about the past as the fact that Caesar crossed the Rubicon. But it will probably be ignored by historians. Professor Talcott Parsons once called science 'a selective system of cognitive orientations to reality'.[6] It might perhaps have been put more simply. But history is, among other things, that. The historian is necessarily selective. The belief in a hard core of historical facts existing objectively and independently of the interpretation of the historian is a preposterous fallacy, but one which it is very hard to eradicate.

But let us turn to the different, but equally grave, plight of the modern historian. The ancient or medieval historian may be grateful for the vast winnowing process which, over the years, has put at his disposal a manageable corpus of historical facts. As Lytton Strachey said, in his mischievous way, 'ignorance is the first requisite of the historian, ignorance which simplifies and clarifies, which selects and omits.'[7] When I am tempted, as I sometimes am, to envy the extreme competence of colleagues engaged in writing ancient or medieval history,

I find consolation in the reflexion that they are so competent mainly because they are so ignorant of their subject. The modern historian enjoys none of the advantages of this built-in ignorance. He must cultivate this necessary ignorance for himself – the more so the nearer he comes to his own times. He has the dual task of discovering the few significant facts and turning them into facts of history, and of discarding the many insignificant facts as unhistorical. But this is the very converse of the nineteenth-century heresy that history consists of the compilation of a maximum number of irrefutable and objective facts. Anyone who succumbs to this heresy will either have to give up history as a bad job, and take to stamp-collecting or some other form of antiquarianism, or end in a madhouse. It is this heresy which during the past hundred years has had such devastating effects on the modern historian, producing in Germany, in Great Britain, and in the United States, a vast and grow-ing mass of dry-as-dust factual histories, of minutely specialized monographs of would-be historians knowing more and more about less and less, sunk without trace in an ocean of facts. It was, I suspect, this heresy – rather than the alleged conflict between liberal and Catholic loyalties – which frustrated Acton as a historian. In an early essay he said of his teacher Döllinger: 'He would not write with imperfect materials, and to him the materials were always imperfect.'[8] Acton was surely here pronouncing an anticipatory verdict on him-self, on that strange phenomenon of a historian whom many would regard as the most distinguished occupant the Regius Chair of Modern History in this university has ever had – but who wrote no history. And Acton wrote his own epitaph, in the introductory note to the first volume of the *Cambridge Modern History* published just after his death, when he lamented that the requirements pressing on the historian 'threaten to turn him from a man of letters into the compiler of an encyclopedia'.[9] Something had gone wrong. What had gone wrong was the belief in this untiring and unending accumulation of hard facts as the foun-dation of history, the believe that facts speak for themselves and that we cannot have too many facts, a belief at that time so unquestioning that few historians then thought it neces-sary – and some still think it unnecessary today – to ask themselves the question 'What is history?'

The nineteenth-century fetishism of facts was completed and justified by a fetishism of documents. The documents were the Ark of the Covenant in the temple of facts. The rev-erent historian approached them with bowed head and spoke of them in awed tones. If you find it in the documents, it is so. But what, when we get down to it, do these documents – the decrees, the treaties, the rent-rolls, the blue books, the official correspondence, the pri-vate letters and diaries – tell us? No document can tell us more than what the author of the document thought – what he thought had happened, what he thought ought to happen or would happen, or perhaps only what he wanted others to think he thought, or even only what he himself thought he thought. None of this means anything until the historian has got to work on it and deciphered it. The facts, whether found in documents or not, have still to be processed by the historian before he can make any use of them: the use he makes of them is, if I may put it that way, the processing process.

Of course, facts and documents are essential to the historian. But do not make a fetish of them. They do not by themselves constitute history; they provide in themselves no ready-made answer to this tiresome question 'What is history?'

At this point I should like to say a few words on the question why nineteenth-century his-torians were generally indifferent to the philosophy of history. The term was invented by Voltaire, and has since been used in different senses; but I shall take it to mean, if I use it at all, our answer to the question, 'What is history?' The nineteenth century was, for the intel-lectuals of western Europe, a comfortable period exuding confidence and optimism. The facts were on the whole satisfactory; and the inclination to ask and answer awkward questions about them was correspondingly weak. Ranke piously believed that divine providence would take care of the meaning of history, if he took care of the facts; and Burckhardt, with a more modern touch of cynicism, observed that 'we are not initiated into the purposes of the eternal wisdom'. Professor Butterfield as late as 1931 noted with apparent satisfaction that 'historians have reflected little upon the nature of things, and even the nature of their own subject'.[10] But my predecessor in these lectures, Dr A. L. Rowse, more justly critical, wrote of Sir Winston Churchill's *World Crisis* – his book about the First World War – that, while it matched Trotsky's *History of the Russian Revolution* in personality, vividness, and vitality, it was inferior in one respect: it had 'no philosophy of history behind it'.[11] British historians refused to be drawn, not because they believed that history had no meaning, but because they believed that its meaning was implicit and self-evident. The liberal nineteenth-century view of history had a close affinity with the economic doctrine of laissez-faire – also the product of a serene and self-confident outlook on the world. Let everyone get on with his particular job, and the hidden hand would take care of the universal harmony. The facts of history were themselves a demonstration of the supreme fact of a beneficent and apparently infinite progress towards higher things. This was the age of innocence, and historians walked in the Garden of Eden, without a scrap of philosophy to cover them, naked and unashamed before the god of history. Since then, we have known Sin and experienced a Fall; and those historians who today pretend to dispense with a philosophy of history are merely trying, vainly and self-consciously, like members of a nudist colony, to recreate the Garden of Eden in their garden suburb. Today the awkward question can no longer be evaded.

During the past fifty years a good deal of serious work has been done on the question 'What is history?' It was from Germany, the country which was to do so much to upset the comfortable reign of nineteenth-century liberalism, that the first challenge came in the 1880s and 1890s to the doctrine of the primacy and autonomy of facts in history. The philosopher who made the challenge are now little more than names. Dilthey is the only one of them who has recently received some belated recognition in Great Britain. Before the turn of the century, prosperity and confidence were still too great in this country for any attention to be paid to heretics who attacked the cult of facts. But early in the new century, the torch passed to Italy, where Croce began to propound a philosophy of history which obviously owed much to German masters. All history is 'contemporary history', declared Croce,[12] meaning that history consists essentially in seeing the past through the eyes of the present and in the light of its problems, and that the main work of the historian is not to record, but to evaluate; for, if he does not evaluate, how can he know what is worth recording? In 1910 the American historian, Carl Becker, argued in deliberately provocative language that 'the facts of history do not exist for any historian till he creates them'.[13] These challenges were for the moment little noticed. It was only after 1920 that Croce began to have a considerable vogue in France and Great Britain. This was not perhaps because Croce was a subtler thinker or a better stylist than his German predecessors, but because, after the First World War, the facts seemed to smile on us less propitiously than in the years before 1914, and we were therefore more accessible to a philosophy which sought to diminish their prestige. Croce was an important influence on the Oxford philosopher and historian Collingwood, the only British thinker in the present century who has made a serious contribution to the philosophy of history. He did not live to write the systematic treatise he had planned; but his published and unpublished papers on the subject were collected after his death in a volume entitled *The Idea of History*, which appeared in 1945.

The views of Collingwood can be summarized as follows. The philosophy of history is concerned neither with 'the past by itself' nor with 'the historian's thought about it by itself', but with 'the two things in their mutual relations'. (This dictum reflects the two current meanings of the word 'history' – the inquiry conducted by the historian and the series of past events into which he inquires.) 'The past which a historian studies is not a dead past, but a past which in some sense is still living in the present.' But a past act is dead, i.e. meaningless to the historian, unless he can understand the thought that lay behind it. Hence 'all history is the history of thought', and 'history is the re-enactment in the historian's mind of the thought whose history he is studying'. The reconstitution of the past in the historian's mind is dependent on empirical evidence. But it is not in itself an empirical process, and cannot consist in a mere recital of facts. On the contrary, the process of reconstitution governs the selection and interpretation of the facts: this, indeed, is what makes them historical facts. 'History', says Professor Oakeshott, who on this point stands near to Collingwood, 'is the historian's experience. It is 'made' by nobody save the historian: to write history is the only way of making it.'[14]

This searching critique, though it may call for some serious reservations, brings to light certain neglected truths.

In the first place, the facts of history never come to us 'pure', since they do not and cannot exist in a pure form: they are always refracted through the mind of the recorder. It follows that when we take up a work of history, our first concern should be not with the facts which it contains but with the historian who wrote it.

For if, as Collingwood says, the historian must re-enact in thought what has gone on in the mind of his dramatis personae, so the reader in his turn must re-enact what goes on in the mind of the historian. Study the historian before you begin to study the facts. This is, after all, not very abstruse. It is what is already done by the intelligent undergraduate who, when recommended to read a work by that great scholar Jones of St Jude's, goes round to a friend at St Jude's to as what sort of chap Jones is, and what bees he has in his bonnet. When you read a work of history, always listen out for the buzzing. If you can detect none, either you are tone deaf or your historian is a dull dog. The facts are really not at all like fish on the fishmonger's slab. They are like fish swimming about in a vast and sometimes inaccessible ocean; and what the historian catches will depend, partly on chance, but mainly on what part of the ocean he chooses to fish in and what tackle he chooses to use – these two factors being, of course, determined by the kind of fish he wants to catch. By and large, the historian will get the kind of facts he wants. History means interpretation. Indeed, if, standing Sir George Clark on his head, I were to call history 'a hard core of interpretation surrounded by a pulp of disputable facts', my statement would, no doubt, be one-sided and misleading, but no more so, I venture to think, than the original dictum.

The second point is the more familiar one of the historian's need of imaginative understanding for the minds of the people with whom he is dealing, for the thought behind their acts: I say 'imaginative understanding', not 'sympathy', lest sympathy should be supposed to imply agreement. The nineteenth century was weak in medieval history, because it was too much repelled by the superstitious beliefs of the Middle Ages, and by the barbarities which they inspired, to have any imaginative understanding of medieval people. Or take Burckhardt's censorious remark about the Thirty Years War: 'It is scandalous for a creed, no matter whether it is Catholic or Protestant, to place its salvation above the integrity of the nation.'[15] It was extremely difficult for a nineteenth-century liberal historian, brought up to believe that it is right and praiseworthy to kill in defence of one's country, but wicked and wrong-headed to kill in defence of one's religion, to enter into the state of mind of those who fought the Thirty Years War. This difficulty is particularly acute in the field in which I am now working. Much of what has been written in English-speaking countries in the last ten years about the Soviet Union, and in the Soviet Union about the English-speaking countries, has been vitiated by this inability to achieve even the most elementary measure of imaginative understanding of what goes on in the mind of the other party, so that the words and actions of the other are always made to appear malign, senseless, or hypocritical. History cannot be written unless the historian can achieve some kind of contact with the mind of those about whom he is writing.

The third point is that we can view the past, and achieve our understanding of the past, only through the eyes of the present. The historian is of his own age, and is bound to it by the conditions of human existence. The very words which he uses – words like democracy, empire, war, revolution – have current connotations from which he cannot divorce them. Ancient historians have taken to using words like *polis* and *plebs* in the original, just in order to show that they have not fallen into this trap. This does not help them. They, too, live in the present, and cannot cheat themselves into the past by using unfamiliar or obsolete words, any more than they would become better Greek or Roman historians if they delivered their lectures in a *chlamys* or a *toga*. The names by which successive French historians have described the Parisian crowds which played so prominent a role in the French revolution – *les sans-culottes, le peuple, la canaille, les bras-nus* – are all, for those who know the rules of the game, manifestos of a political affiliation and of a particular interpretation. Yet the historian is obliged to choose: *the use of language forbids him to be neutral* [emphasis added]. Nor is it a matter of words alone. Over the past hundred years the changed balance of power in Europe has reversed the attitude of British historians to Frederick the Great. The changed balance of power within the Christian churches between Catholicism and Protestantism has profoundly altered their attitude to such figures as Loyola, Luther, and Cromwell. It requires only a superficial knowledge of the work of French historians of the last forty years on the French revolution to recognize how deeply it has been affected by the Russian revolution of 1917. The historian belongs not to the past but to the present. Professor Trevor-Roper tells us that the historian 'ought to love the past'.[16] This is a dubious injunction. To love the past may easily be an expression of the nostalgic romanticism of old men and old societies, a symptom of loss of faith and interest in the present or future.[17] Cliché for cliché, I should prefer the one about freeing oneself from 'the dead hand of the past'. The function of the historian is neither to love the past nor to emancipate himself from the past, but to master and understand it as the key to the understanding of the present.

If, however, these are some of the insights of what I may call the Collingwood view of history, it is time to consider some of the dangers. The emphasis on the role of the historian in the making of history tends, if pressed to its logical conclusion, to rule out any objective history at all: history is what the historian makes. Collingwood seems indeed, at one moment, in an unpublished note quoted by his editor, to have reached this conclusion:

> St Augustine looked at history from the point of view of the early Christian; Tillamont, from that of a seventeenth-century Frenchman; Gibbon, from that of an eighteenth-century Englishman; Mommsen from that of a nineteenth-century German. There is no point in asking which was the right point of view. Each was the only one possible for the man who adopted it.[18]

This amounts to total scepticism, like Froude's remark that history is 'a child's box of letters with which we can spell any word we please'.[19] Collingwood, in his reaction against 'scissors-and-paste history', against the view of history as a mere compilation of facts, comes perilously near to treating history as something spun out of the human brain, and leads back to the conclusion referred to by Sir George Clark in the passage which I quoted earlier, that 'there is no "objective" historical truth'. In place of the theory that history has no meaning, we are offered here the theory of an infinity of meanings, none any more right than any other – which comes to much the same thing. The second theory is surely as untenable as the first. It does not follow that, because a mountain appears to take on different shapes from different angles of vision, it has objectively either no shape at all or an infinity of shapes. It does not follow that, because interpretation plays a necessary part in establishing the facts of history, and because no existing interpretation is wholly objective, one interpretation is as good as another, and the facts of history are in principle not amenable to objective interpretation. I shall have to consider at a later stage what exactly is meant by objectivity in history.

But a still greater danger lurks in the Collingwood hypothesis. If the historian necessarily looks at his period of history through the eyes of his own time, and studies the problems of the past as a key to those of the present, will he not fall into a purely pragmatic view of the facts, and maintain that the criterion of a right interpretation is its suitability to some present purpose? On this hypothesis, the facts of history are nothing, interpretation is everything. Nietzsche had already enunciated the principle: 'The falseness of an opinion is not for us any objection to it. . . . The question is how far it is life-furthering, life-preserving, species-preserving, perhaps species-creating.'[20] The American pragmatists moved, less explicitly and less wholeheartedly, along the same line. Knowledge is knowledge for some purpose. The validity of the knowledge depends on the validity of the purpose. But, even where no such theory has been professed, the practice has often been no less disquieting. In my own field of study I have seen too many examples of extravagant interpretation riding roughshod over facts not to be impressed with the reality of this danger. It is not surprising that perusal of some of the more extreme products of Soviet and anti-Soviet schools of historiography should sometimes breed a certain nostalgia for that illusory nineteenth-century haven of purely factual history.

How then, in the middle of the twentieth century, are we to define the obligation of the historian to his facts? I trust that I have spent a sufficient number of hours in recent years chasing and perusing documents, and stuffing my historical narrative with properly footnoted facts, to escape the imputation of treating facts and documents too cavalierly. The duty of the historian to respect his facts is not exhausted by the obligation to see that his facts are accurate. He must seek to bring into the picture all known or knowable facts relevant, in one sense of another, to the theme on which he is engaged and to the interpretation proposed. The commonest assumption appears to be that the historian divides his work into two sharply distinguishable phases or periods. First, he spends a long preliminary period reading his sources and filling his notebooks with facts: then, when this is over, he puts away his sources, takes out his notebooks and writes his book from beginning to end. This is to me an unconvincing and unplausible picture. For myself, as soon as I have got going on a few of what I take to be the capital sources, the itch becomes too strong and I begin to write – not necessarily at the beginning, but somewhere, anywhere. Thereafter, reading and writing go on simultaneously. The writing is added to, subtracted from, re-shaped, cancelled, as I go on reading. The reading is guided and directed and made fruitful by the writing: the more I write, the more I know what I am looking for, the better I understand the significance and relevance of what I find. Some historians probably do all this preliminary writing in their head without using pen, paper, or typewriter, just as some people play chess in their heads without recourse to board and chessmen: this is a talent which I envy, but cannot emulate. But I am convinced that, for any historian worth the name, the two processes of what economists call 'input' and 'output' go on simultaneously and are, in practice, parts of a single process. If you try to separate them, or to give one priority over the other, you fall into one of two heresies. Either you write scissors-and-paste history without meaning or significance; or you write propaganda or historical fiction, and merely use facts of the past to embroider a kind of writing which has nothing to do with history.

Our examination of the relation of the historian to the facts of history finds us, therefore, in an apparently precarious situation, navigating delicately between the Scylla of an untenable theory of history as an objective compilation of facts, of the unqualified primacy of fact over interpretation, and the Charybdis of an equally untenable theory of history as the subjective product of the mind of the historian who establishes the facts of history and masters them through the process of interpretation, between a view of history having the centre of gravity in the past and a view having the centre of gravity in the present. But our situation is less precarious than it seems. We shall encounter the same dichotomy of fact and interpretation again in these lectures in other guises – the particular and the general, the empirical and the theoretical, the objective and the subjective. The predicament of the historian is a reflexion of the nature of man. Man, except perhaps in earliest infancy and in extreme old age, is not totally involved in his environment and unconditionally subject to it. On the other hand, he is never totally independent of it and its unconditional master. The relation of man to his environment is the relation of the historian to his theme. The historian is neither the humble slave nor the tyrannical master of his facts. The relation between the historian and his facts is one of equality, of give-and-take. As any working historian knows, if he stops to reflect what he is doing as he thinks and writes, the historian is engaged on a continuous process of moulding his facts to his interpretation and his interpretation to his facts. It is impossible to assign primacy to one over the other.

The historian starts with a provisional selection of facts, and a provisional interpretation in the light of which that selection has been made – by others as well as by himself. As he works, both the interpretation and the selection and ordering of facts undergo subtle and perhaps partly unconscious changes, through the reciprocal action of one or the other. And this reciprocal action also involves reciprocity between present and past, since the historian is part of the present and the facts belong to the past. The historian and the facts of history are necessary to one another. The historian without his facts is rootless and futile; the facts without their historian are dead and meaningless. My first answer therefore to the question 'What is history?' is that it is a continuous process of interaction between the historian and his facts, an unending dialogue between the present and the past.

Notes

1 *The Cambridge Modern History: Its Origin, Authorship and Production* (1907), pp. 10–12.

2 *The New Cambridge Modern History*, i (1957), pp. xxiv–xxv.

3 Acton, *Lectures on Modern History* (1906), p. 318.

4 Quoted in the *Listener*, 19 June 1952, p. 992.

5 *M. Manilii Astronomicon: Liber Primus* (2nd ed., 1937), p. 87.

6 T. Parsons and E. Shils, *Towards a General Theory of Action* (3rd ed., 1954), p. 167.

7 Lytton Strachey, Preface to *Eminent Victorians*.

8 Quoted in G. P. Gooch, *History and Historians in the Nineteenth Century*, p. 385; later Acton said of Döllinger that 'it was given him to form his philosophy of history on the largest induction ever available to man' (*History of Freedom and Other Essays*, 1907, p. 435).

9 *Cambridge Modern History*, i (1902), p. 4.

10 H. Butterfield, *The Whig Interpretation of History* (1931), p. 67.

11 A. L. Rowse, *The End of an Epoch* (1947), pp. 282–3.

12 The context of this celebrated aphorism is as follows: 'The practical requirements which underlie every historical judgement give to all history the character of "contemporary history", because, however remote in time events thus recounted may seem to be, the history in reality refers to present needs and present situations wherein those events vibrate' (B. Croce, *History as the Story of Liberty*, Engl. transl. 1941, p. 19).

13 *Atlantic Monthly*, October 1910, p. 528.

14 M. Oakeshott, *Experience and Its Modes* (1933), p. 99.

15 J. Burckhardt, *Judgements on History and Historians* (1959), p. 179.

16 Introduction to J. Burckhardt, *Judgements on History and Historians* (1959), p. 17.

17 Compare Nietzsche's view of history: 'To old age belongs the old man's business of looking back and casting up his accounts, of seeking consolation in the memories of the past, in historical culture' (*Thoughts Out of Season*, Engl. transl., 1909, ii, pp. 65–6).

18 R. Collingwood, *The Idea of History* (1946), p. xii.

19 A. Froude, *Short Studies on Great Subjects*, i (1894), p. 21.

20 *Beyond Good and Evil*, ch. i.

The fictions of factual representation

Hayden White

In order to anticipate some of the objections with which historians often meet the argument that follows, I wish to grant at the outset that *historical events* differ from *fictional events* in the ways that it has been conventional to characterize their differences since Aristotle. Historians are concerned with events which can be assigned to specific time-space locations, events which are (or were) in principle observable or perceivable, whereas imaginative writers – poets, novelists, playwrights – are concerned with both these kinds of events and imagined, hypothetical, or invented ones. The nature of the kinds of events with which historians and imaginative writers are concerned is not the issue. What should interest us in the discussion of 'the literature of fact' or, as I have chosen to call it, 'the fictions of factual representation' is the extent to which the discourse of the historian and that of the writer of imaginative fictions overlap, resemble, or correspond with each other. Although historians and writers of fiction may be interested in different kinds of events, both the forms of their respective discourses and their aims in writing are often the same. In addition, in my view, the techniques or strategies that they use in the composition of their discourses can be shown to be substantially the same, however different they may appear on a purely surface, or dictional, level of their texts.

Readers of histories and novels can hardly fail to be struck by their similarities. There are many histories that could pass for novels, and many novels that could pass for histories, considered in purely formal (or, I should say, formalist) terms. Viewed simply as verbal artifacts histories and novels are indistinguishable from one another. We cannot easily distinguish between them on formal grounds unless we approach them with specific preconceptions about the kinds of truths that each is supposed to deal in. But the aim of the writer of a novel must be the same as that of the writer of a history. Both wish to provide a verbal image of 'reality.' The novelist may present his notion of this reality indirectly, that is to say, by figurative techniques, rather than directly, which is to say, by registering a series of propositions which are supposed to correspond point by point to some extra-textual domain of occurrence or happening, as the historian claims to do. But the image of reality which the novelist thus constructs is meant to correspond in its general outline to some domain of human experience which is no less 'real' than that referred to by the historian. It is not, then, a matter of a conflict between two kinds of truth (which the Western prejudice for empiricism as the sole access to reality has foisted upon us), a conflict between the truth of correspondence if it is to pass as a plausible account of 'the way things *really* were.' For the empiricist prejudice is attended by a conviction that 'reality' is not only perceivable but is also coherent in its structure. A mere list of confirmable singular existential statements does not add up to an account of reality if there is not some coherence, logical or aesthetic, connecting them one to another. So too every fiction must pass a test of correspondence (it must be 'adequate' as an image of something beyond itself) if it is to lay claim to representing an insight into or illumination of the human experience of the world. Whether the events represented in a discourse are construed as atomic parts of a molar whole or as possible occurrences within a perceivable totality, the discourse taken in *its* totality is an image of some reality, bears a relationship of correspondence to that *of which* it is an image. It is in these twin senses that all written discourse is cognitive in its aims and mimetic in its means. And this is true even of the most ludic and seemingly expressivist discourse, of poetry no less than of prose, and even of those forms of poetry which seem to wish to illuminate only 'writing' itself. In this respect, history is no less a form of fiction than the novel is a form of historical representation.

This characterization of historiography as a form of fiction making is not likely to be received sympathetically by either historians or literary critics who, if they agree on little else, conventionally agree that history and fiction deal with distinct orders of experience and therefore represent distinct, if not opposed, forms of discourse. For this reason it will be well to say a few words about how this notion of the *opposition* of history to fiction arose and why it has remained unchallenged in Western thought for so long.

Prior to the French Revolution, historiography was conventionally regarded as a literary art. More specifically, it was regarded as a branch of rhetoric and its 'fictive' nature generally recognized. Although eighteenth-century theorists distinguished rather rigidly (and not always with adequate philosophical justification) between 'fact' and 'fancy,' they did not on the whole view historiography as a representation of the facts unalloyed by elements of fancy. While granting the general desirability of historical accounts that dealt in real, rather than imagined events, theorists from Bayle to Voltaire and De Mably recognized the inevitability of a recourse to fictive techniques in the *representation* of real events in the historical discourse. The eighteenth century abounds in works which distinguish between the 'study' of history on the one side and the 'writing' of history on the other. The 'writing' was a literary, specifically rhetorical exercise, and the product of this exercise was to be assessed as much on literary as on scientific principles.

Here the crucial opposition was between 'truth' and 'error,' rather than between 'fact' and 'fancy,' with it being understood that many kinds of truth, even in history, could only be presented to the reader by means of fictional techniques of representation. These techniques were conceived to consist of rhetorical devices, tropes, figures and schemata of words and thoughts, which, as described by the classical and Renaissance rhetoricians, were identical with the techniques of poetry in general. 'Truth' was not equated with 'fact,' but with a combination of fact and the conceptual matrix within which it was appropriately located in the discourse. The imagination no less than the reason had to be engaged in any adequate representation of the truth: and this meant that the techniques of fiction-making were as necessary to the composition of a historical discourse as erudition might be.

In the early nineteenth century, however, it became conventional, at least among historians, to identify truth with fact and to regard fiction as the opposite of truth, hence as a hindrance to the understanding of reality rather than as a way of apprehending it. History came to be set over against fiction, and especially the novel, as the representation of the 'actual' to the representation of the 'possible' or only imaginable.' And thus was born the dream of a historical discourse that would consist of nothing but factually accurate statements about a realm of events which were (or had been) observable in principle, the arrangement of which in the order of their original occurrence would permit them to figure forth their true meaning or significance. Typically, the nineteenth-century historian's aim was to expunge every hint of the fictive, or merely imaginable, from his discourse, to eschew the techniques of the poet and orator, and to forego what were regarded as the intuitive procedures of the maker of fictions in his apprehension of reality.

In order to understand this development in historical thinking, it must be recognized that historiography took shape as a distinct scholarly discipline in the West in the nineteenth century against a background of a profound hostility to all forms of myth. Both the political Right and the political Left blamed mythic thinking for the excesses and failures of the Revolution. False readings of history, misconceptions of the nature of the historical process, unrealistic expectations about the ways that historical societies could be transformed – all these had led to the outbreak of the Revolution in the first place, the strange course that Revolutionary developments followed, and the effects of Revolutionary activities over the long run. It became imperative to rise above any impulse to interpret the historical record in the light of party prejudices, utopian expectations, or sentimental attachments to traditional institutions. In order to find one's way among the conflicting claims of the parties which took shape during and after the Revolution, it was necessary to locate some standpoint of social perception that was truly 'objective,' truly 'realistic.' If social processes and structures seemed 'demonic' in their capacity to resist direction, to take turns unforeseen, and to overturn the highest plans, frustrating the most heartfelt desires, then the study of history had to be de-mythified. But in the thought of the age, de-mythification of any domain of inquiry tended to be equated with the de-fictionalization of that domain as well.

The distinction between myth and fiction which is a commonplace in the thought of our own century was hardly grasped at all by many of the foremost ideologues of the early nineteenth century. Thus it came about that history, the realistic science par excellence, was set over against fiction as the study of the real versus the study of the merely imaginable. Although Ranke had in mind that form of the novel which we have since come to call 'Romantic' when he castigated it as mere fancy, he manifested a prejudice shared by many of his contemporaries when he defined history as the study of the real and the novel as the representation of the imaginary. Only a few theorists, among whom J. G. Droysen was the most prominent, saw that it was impossible to write history without having recourse to the techniques of the orator and the poet. Most of the 'scientific' historians of the age did not see that for every identifiable kind of novel, historians produced an equivalent kind of historical discourse. Romantic historiography produced its genius in Michelet. Realistic historiography its paradigm in Ranke himself. Symbolist historiography produced Burckhardt (who had more in common with Flaubert and Baudelaire than with Ranke), and Modernist historiography its prototype in Spengler. It was no accident that the Realistic novel and Rankean historicism entered their respective crises at roughly the same time.

There were, in short, as many 'styles' of historical representation as there are discernible literary styles in the nineteenth century. This was not perceived by the historians of the nineteenth century because they were captives of the illusion that one could write history without employing any fictional techniques whatsoever. They continued to honor the conception of the opposition of history to fiction throughout the entire period, even while producing forms of historical discourse so different from one another that their grounding in aesthetic preconceptions of the nature of the historical process alone could explain those differences. Historians continued to believe that different interpretations of the same set of events were functions of ideological distortions or of inadequate factual data. They continued to believe that if one only eschewed ideology and remained true to the facts, history would produce a knowledge as certain as anything offered by the physical sciences and as objective as a mathematical exercise.

Most nineteenth-century historians did not realize that, when it is a matter of trying to deal with past facts, the crucial consideration for him who would represent them faithfully are the notions he brings to his representation of the ways parts relate to the whole which they comprise. They did not realize that the facts do not speak for themselves, but that the historian speaks for them, speaks on their behalf, and fashions the fragments of the past into a whole whose integrity is – in its *re*presentation – a purely discursive one. Novelists might be dealing only with imaginary events whereas historians are dealing with real ones, but the process of fusing events, whether imaginary or real, into a comprehensible totality capable of serving as the *object* of a representation, is a poetic process. Here the historian must utilize precisely the same tropological strategies, the same modalities of representing relationships in words, that the poet or novelist uses. In the unprocessed historical record and in the chronicle of events which the historian extracts from the record, the facts exist only as a congeries of contiguously related fragments. These fragments have to be put together to make a whole of a particular, not a general, kind. And they are put together in the same ways that novelists use to put together figments of their imaginations, to display an ordered world, a cosmos, where only disorder or chaos might appear.

So much for manifestos. On what grounds can such a reactionary position be justified? On what grounds can the assertion that historical discourse shares more than it divides with novelistic discourse be sustained? The first ground is to be found in recent developments in literary theory – especially in the insistence by modern Structuralist and text critics on the necessity of dissolving the distinction between prose and poetry in order to identify their shared attributes as forms of linguistic behavior that are as much constitutive of their objects of representation as they are reflective of external reality, on the one side, and projective of internal emotional states, on the other. It appears that Stalin was right when he opined that language belonged neither to the Superstructure nor the Base of cultural praxis, but was, in some unspecified way, *prior to both*. We don't know the origin of language and never shall, but it is certain today that language is more adequately characterized as being neither a free creation of human consciousness nor merely a product of environmental forces acting on the psyche, but rather the *instrument of mediation* between consciousness and the world that consciousness inhabits.

This will not be news to literary theorists, but it has not yet reached the historians buried in the archives hoping, by what they call a 'sifting of the facts' or 'the manipulation of the data,' to *find* the form of the reality that will serve as the object of representation in the account that they will write when 'all the facts are known' and they have finally 'got the story straight.'

So, too, contemporary critical theory permits us to believe more confidently than ever before that 'poetizing' is not an activity that hovers over, transcends, or otherwise remains alienated from life or reality, but represents a mode of praxis which serves as the immediate base of all cultural activity (this an insight of Vico, Hegel, and Nietzsche, no less than of Freud and Lévi-Strauss), even of science itself. We are no longer compelled, therefore, to believe – as historians in the post-Romantic period had to believe – that fiction is the antithesis of fact (in the way that superstition or magic is the antithesis of science) or that we can relate facts to one another without the aid of some enabling and generically fictional matrix. This too would be news to many historians were they not so fetishistically enamored of the notion of 'facts' and so congenitally hostile to 'theory' in any form that the presence in a historical work of a formal theory used to explicate the relationship between facts and concepts is enough to earn them the charge of having defected to the despised 'sociology' or of having lapsed into the nefarious 'philosophy of history.'

Every discipline, I suppose, is, as Nietzsche saw most clearly, constituted by what it *forbids* its practitioners to do. Every discipline is made up of a set of restrictions on thought and imagination, and none is more hedged about with taboos than professional historiography – so much so that the so-called 'historical method' consists of little more than the injunction to 'get the story straight' (without any notion of what the relation of 'story' to 'fact' might be) and to avoid both conceptual over-determination and imaginative excess (i.e., 'enthusiasm') at any price.

Yet the price paid is a considerable one. It has resulted in the repression of the *conceptual apparatus* (without which atomic facts cannot be aggregated into complex macro-structures and constituted as objects of discursive representation in a historical narrative) and the remission of the *poetic moment* in historical writing to the interior of the discourse (where it functions as an unacknowledged – and therefore uncriticizable – *content* of the historical narrative).

Those historians who draw a firm line between history and philosophy of history fail to recognize that every historical discourse contains within it a full blown – if only implicit – philosophy of history. And this is as true of what is conventionally called 'narrative' (or diachronic) historiography as it is of 'conceptual' (or synchronic) historical representation. The principal difference between history and philosophy of history is that the latter brings the conceptual apparatus by which the facts are ordered in the discourse to the surface of the text, while 'history proper' (as it is called) buries it in the interior of the narrative, where it serves as a hidden or implicit shaping device, in precisely the same way that Professor Frye conceives his *archetypes* to do in narrative fictions. History does not therefore stand over against myth as its cognitive antithesis, but represents merely another, and more extreme form of that 'displacement' which Professor Frye has analyzed in his *Anatomy*. Every history has its myth; and if there are different fictional modes based on different identifiable mythical archetypes, so too there are different historiographical modes – different way of hypotactically ordering the 'facts' contained in the chronicle of events occurring in a specific time-space location, such that events in the same set are capable of functioning differently in order to figure forth different *meanings*, moral, cognitive, or aesthetic, within different fictional matrices.

In fact, I would argue that these mythic modes are more easily identifiable in historiographical than they are in 'literary' texts. For historians usually work with much less *linguistic* (and therefore less *poetic*) self-consciousness than writers of fiction do. They tend to treat language as a transparent vehicle of representation that brings no cognitive baggage of its own into the discourse. Great works of fiction will usually – if Roman Jakobson is right – not only be *about* their putative subject-matter, but also *about* language itself and the problematical relation between language, consciousness, and reality – including the writer's own language. Most historians' concern with language extends only to the effort to speak plainly, to avoid florid figures of speech, to assure that the persona of the author appears nowhere identifiable in the text, and to make clear what technical terms mean, when they dare to use any.

This is not, of course, the case with the great philosophers of history – from Augustine, Machiavelli, and Vico to Hegel, Marx, Nietzsche, Croce, and Spengler. The problematical status of language (including their own linguistic protocols) constitutes a crucial element in their own *apparatus criticus*. And it is not the case with the great classic writers of historiography – from Thucydides and Tacitus to Michelet, Carlyle, Ranke, Droysen, Tocqueville, and Burckhardt. These historians at least had a rhetorical selfconsciousness that permitted them to recognize that any set of facts was variously, and equally legitimately, describable, that there is no such thing as a single correct original description of anything, on the basis of which an interpretation of that thing can *subsequently* be brought to bear. They recognized, in short, that all original descriptions of any field of phenomena are *already* interpretations of its structure, and that the linguistic mode in which the original description (or taxonomy) of the field is cast will implicitly rule out certain modes of representation and modes of explanation regarding the field's structure and tacitly sanction others. In other words, the favored mode of original description of a field of historical phenomena (and this includes the field of literary texts) already contains implicitly within it a limited range of modes of emplotment and modes of argument by which to disclose the meaning of the field in a discursive prose representation. If, that is, the description is anything more than a random registering of impressions. The plot-structure of a historical narrative (*how* things turned out as they did) and the formal argument or explanation of *why* 'things happened or turned out as they did' are *pre*figured by the original description (of the 'facts' to be explained) in a given dominant modality of language use: metaphor, metonymy, synecdoche, or irony.

Now, I want to make clear that I am myself using these terms as metaphors for the different ways we construe fields or sets of phenomena in order to 'work them up' into *possible objects of narrative representation* and *discursive analysis.* Anyone who originally encodes the world in the mode of metaphor, will be included to decode it – that is, narratively 'explicate' and discursively analyze it – as a congeries of individualities. To those for whom there is no real resemblance in the world, decodation must take the form of a disclosure, either of the simple *contiguity* of things (the mode of metonymy) or of the *contrast* that lies hidden within every apparent resemblance or unity (the mode of irony). In the first case, the narrative representation of the field, construed as a diachronic process, will favor as a privileged mode of emplotment the archetype of Romance and a mode of explanation that identifies knowledge with the appreciation and delineation of the particularity and individuality if things. In the second case, an original description of the field in the mode of metonymy will favor a tragic plot-structure as a privileged mode of emplotment and mechanistic causal connection as the favored mode of explanation, to account for changes topographically outlined in the emplotment. So too an ironic original description of the field will generate a tendency to favor emplotment in the mode of satire and pragmatic or contextual explanation of the structures thus illuminated. Finally, to round out the list, fields originally described in the synecdochic mode will tend to generate comic emplotments and organicist explanations of why these fields change as they do.[1]

Note, for example, that both those great narrative hulks produced by such classic historians as Michelet, Tocqueville, Burckhardt, and Ranke, on the one side, and the elegant synopses produced by philosophers of history such as Herder, Marx, Nietzsche, and Hegel, on the other, become more easily relatable, one to the other, if we see them as both victims and exploiters of the linguistic mode in which they originally describe a field of historical events *before* they apply their characteristic modalities of narrative representation and explanation, that is, their 'interpretations' of the field's 'meaning.' In addition, each of the linguistic modes, modes of emplotment, and modes of explanation has affinities with a specific ideological position: anarchist, radical, liberal, and conservative respectively. The issue of ideology points to the fact that there is no value-neutral mode of emplotment, explanation, or even description of any field of events, whether imaginary or real, and suggests that the very use of language itself implies or entails a specific posture before the world which is ethical, ideological, or more generally political: not only all interpretation, but also all language is politically contaminated.

Now, in my view, any historian who simply described a set of facts in, let us say, metonymic terms and then went on to emplot its processes in the mode of tragedy and proceeded to explain those processes mechanistically, and finally drew explicit ideological implications from it – as most vulgar Marxists and materialistic determinists do – would not only not be very interesting but could legitimately be labelled a *doctrinaire* thinker who had 'bent the facts' to fit a preconceived theory. The peculiar dialectic of historical discourse – and of other forms of discursive prose as well, perhaps even the novel – comes from the effort of the author to mediate between alternative modes of emplotment and explanation, which means, finally, *mediating between alternative modes of language use* or *tropological* strategies for originally describing a given field of phenomena and constituting it as a possible object of representation.

It is this sensitivity to alternative linguistic protocols, case in the modes of metaphor, metonymy, synecdoche, and irony, that distinguishes the great historians and philosophers of history from their less interesting counterparts among the technicians of these two crafts. This is what makes Tocqueville so much more interesting (and a source of so many different later thinkers) than either his contemporary, the doctrinaire Guizot, or most of his modern liberal or conservative followers, whose knowledge is greater than his and whose retrospective vision is more extensive but whose dialectical capacity is so much more weakly developed. Tocqueville writes about the French Revolution, but he writes even more meaningfully about the difficulty of ever attaining to a definitive *objective characterization* of the complex web of facts that comprise the Revolution as a graspable totality or structured whole. The contradiction, the *aporia*, at the heart of Tocqueville's discourse is born of his awareness that alternative, mutually exclusive, originally descriptions of what the Revolution *is* are possible. He recognizes that *both* metonymical and synecdochic linguistic protocols can be used, equally legitimately, to describe the field of facts that comprise the 'Revolution' and to constitute it as a *possible object of historical discourse*. He moves feverishly between the two modes of original description, testing both, trying to assign them to different mental sets or cultural types (what he means by a 'democratic' consciousness is a metonymic transcription of phenomena; 'aristocratic' consciousness is synecdochic). He himself is satisfied with neither mode, although he recognizes that each gives access to a specific aspect of reality and represents a possible way of apprehending it. His aim, ultimately, is to contrive a language capable of mediating between the two modes of consciousness which these linguistic modes represent. This aim of mediation, in turn, drives him progressively toward the ironic recognition that any given linguistic protocol will obscure as much as it reveals about the reality it seeks to capture in an order of words. This *aporia* or sense of contradiction residing at the heart of language itself is present in *all* of the classic historians. It is this linguistic self-consciousness which distinguishes them from their mundane counterparts and followers, who think that language can serve as a perfectly transparent medium of representation and who think that if one can only find the right language for describing events, the meaning of the events will *display itself* to consciousness.

This movement between alternative linguistic modes conceived as alternative descriptive protocols is, I would argue, a distinguishing feature of all the great classics of the 'literature of fact.' Consider, for example, Darwin's *Origin of Species*,[2] a work which must rank as a classic in any list of the great monuments of this kind of literature. This work which, more than any other, desires to remain within the ambit of plain fact, is just as much about the problem of classification as it is about its ostensible subject matter, the data of natural history. This means that it deals with two problems: how are events to be described as possible elements of an argument; and what kind of argument do they add up to once they are so described?

Darwin claims to be concerned with a single, crucial question: 'Why are not all organic things linked together in inextricable chaos?' (p. 453). But he wishes to answer this question in particular terms. He does not wish to suggest, as many of his contemporaries held, that all systems of classification are arbitrary, that is, mere products of the minds of the classifiers; he insists that there is a *real* order in nature. On the other hand, he does not wish to regard this order as a product of some spiritual or teleological power. The order which he seeks in the data, then, must be manifest in the facts themselves but not manifested in such a way as to display the operations of any transcendental power. In order to establish this notion of nature's plan, he purports, first, simply to entertain 'objectively' all of the 'facts' of natural history provided by field naturalists, domestic breeders, and students of the geological record – in much the same way that the historian entertains the data provided by the archives. But this entertainment of the record is no simple reception of the facts; it is an entertainment of the facts with a view toward the discrediting of all previous taxonomic systems in which they have previously been encoded.

Like Kant before him, Darwin insists that the source of all error is semblance. Analogy, he says again and again, is always a 'deceitful guide' (see pp. 61, 66, 473). As against analogy, or as I would say merely metaphorical characterizations of the facts, Darwin wishes to make a case for the existence of real 'affinities' genealogically construed. The establishment of these affinities will permit him to postulate the linkage of all living things to all others by the 'laws' or 'principles' of genealogical descent, variation, and natural selection. These laws and principles are the formal elements in his mechanistic explanation of why creatures are arranged in families in a time series. But this explanation could not be offered as long as the data remained encoded in the linguistic modes of either metaphor or synecdoche, the modes of qualitative connection. As long as creatures are classified in terms of either semblance or essential unity, the realm of organic things must remain either a chaos of arbitrarily affirmed connectedness or a hierarchy of higher and lower forms. Science as Darwin understood it, however, cannot deal in the categories of the 'higher' and 'lower' any more than it can deal in the categories of the 'normal' and 'monstrous.' Everything must be entertained as what it manifestly *seems to be*. Nothing can be regarded as 'surprising,' any more than anything can be regarded as 'miraculous.'

There are many kinds of facts invoked in *The Origin of Species:* Darwin speaks of 'astonishing' facts (p. 301), 'remarkable' facts (p. 384), 'leading' facts (pp. 444, 447), 'unimportant' facts (p. 58), 'well-established' facts, even 'strange' facts (p. 105); but there are no 'surprising' facts. Everything, for Darwin no less than for Nietzsche, is just what it appears to be – but what things appear to be are data inscribed under the aspect of *mere contiguity in space* (all the facts gathered by naturalists all over the world) *and time* (the records of domestic breeders and the geological record). As the elements of a problem (or rather, of a puzzle, for Darwin is confident that there is a solution to his problem), the facts of natural history are conceived to exist in that mode of relationship which is presupposed in the operation of the linguistic trope of metonymy, which is the favored trope of all *modern* scientific discourse (this is one of the crucial distinctions between modern and pre-modern sciences). The substitution of the name of a part of a thing for the name of the whole is prelinguistically sanctioned by the importance which the scientific consciousness grants to mere contiguity. Considerations of *semblance* are tacitly retired in the employment of this trope, and so are considerations of *difference* and *contrast*. This is what gives to metonymic consciousness what Kenneth Burke calls its 'reductive' aspect. Things exist in contiguous relationships that are only spatially and temporally definable. This metonymizing of the world, this preliminary encoding of the facts in terms of merely contiguous relationships, is necessary to the removal of metaphor and teleology from phenomena which every *modern* science seeks to effect. And Darwin spends the greater part of his book on the justification of this encodation, or original description, of reality, in order to discharge the errors and confusion which a *merely* metaphorical profile of it has produced.

But this is only a preliminary operation. Darwin then proceeds to restructure the facts – but *only along one axis* of the time-space grid on which he has originally deployed them. Instead of stressing the mere contiguity of the phenomena, he shifts gears, or rather tropological modes, and begins to concentrate on differences – but two kinds of differences: *variations within species*, on the one side, and *contrasts between the species*, on the other. 'Systematists,' he writes, '. . . have only to decide . . . whether any form be sufficiently *constant* and *distinct* from other forms, to be capable of definition; and if definable, whether the differences be sufficiently important to deserve a specific name.' But the distinction between a species and a variety is only a matter of degree.

> Hereafter we shall be compelled to acknowledge that the only distinction between species and well-marked varieties is, that the latter are known, or believed, to be connected at the present day by intermediate gradation, whereas *species* were formerly thus connected. Hence, without rejecting the consideration of the *present existence* of intermediate gradations between any two forms, we shall be led to weigh more carefully and to *value higher* the *actual amount of difference between them*. It is quite possible that forms now generally acknowledged to be merely varieties *may hereafter* be thought worthy of *specific names*; and in this case *scientific and common language will come into accordance*. In short, we shall have to treat species in the same manner as those naturalists treat genera, who admit that genera are merely artificial combinations made for convenience. This may not be a cheering prospect; but we shall at least be free from the vain search for the undiscovered and undiscoverable *essence* of the term species. (pp. 474–75; italics added)

And yet Darwin has smuggled in his own conception of the 'essence' of the term species. And he has done it by falling back on the geological record which, following Lyell, he calls 'a history of the world imperfectly kept, . . . written in a changing dialect' and of which 'we possess the last volume alone' (p. 331). Using this record, he postulates the descent of all species and varieties from some four or five prototypes governed by what he calls the 'rule' of 'gradual transition' (pp. 180ff.) or 'the great principle of gradation' (p. 251). *Difference* has been dissolved in the *mystery of transition*, such that *continuity-in-variation* is seen as the 'rule' and radical discontinuity or variation as an 'anomaly' (p. 33). But this 'mystery' of transition (see his highly tentative, confused, and truncated discussion of the possible 'modes of transition' – pp. 179–82, 310) is nothing but the facts laid out on a time line, rather than spatially disposed, and treated as a 'series' which is permitted to '*impress . . .* the *mind* with the *idea of an actual passage*' (p. 66). All organic beings are then (gratuitously on the basis of both the facts and the theories available to Darwin) treated (metaphorically on the literal level of the text but synecdochically on the allegorical level) as belonging to families linked by genealogical descent (through the operation of variation and natural selection) from the postulated four or five prototypes. It is only his distaste for 'analogy,' he tells us, that keeps him going 'one step further, namely, to the belief that all plants and animals are descended from some one prototype' (p. 473). But he has approached as close to a doctrine of organic unity as his respect for the 'facts,' in their original encodation in the mode of contiguity, will permit him to go. He has *transformed* 'the facts' from a structure of merely contiguously related particulars into a sublimated synecdoche. And this in order to put a new and more comforting (as well as, in his view, a more interesting and comprehensible) vision of nature in place of that of his vitalistic opponents.

The image which he finally offers – of an unbroken succession of generations – may have had a disquieting effect on his readers, inasmuch as it dissolved the distinction between both the 'higher' and 'lower' in nature (and by implication, therefore, in society) and the 'normal' and the 'monstrous' in life (and therefore in culture). But in Darwin's view, the new image of organic nature as an essential continuity of beings gave assurance that no 'cataclysm' had ever 'desolated the world' and permitted him to look forward to a 'secure future and progress toward perfection' (p. 477). For 'cataclysm' we can of course read 'revolution' and for 'secure future,' 'social status quo.' But all of this is presented, not as image, but as plain fact. Darwin is ironic only with respect to those systems of classification that would ground 'reality' in fictions of which he does not approve. Darwin distinguishes between tropological codes that are 'responsible' to data and those that are not. But the criterion of responsibility to the data is not extrinsic to the operation by which the 'facts' are ordered in his initial description of them; this criterion is intrinsic to that operation.

As thus envisaged, even the *Origin of Species*, that *summa* of 'the literature of fact' of the nineteenth century, must be read as a kind of allegory – a history of nature meant to be understood literally but appealing ultimately to an image of coherency and orderliness which it constructs by linguistic 'turns' alone. And if this is true of the *Origin*, how much more true must it be of any history of human societies? In point of fact, historians have not agreed upon a terminological system for the description of events which they wish to treat as facts and embed in their discourses as self-revealing data. Most historiographical disputes – among scholars of roughly equal erudition and intelligence – turn precisely on the matter of which among several linguistic protocols is to be used to *describe* the events under contention, not what explanatory system is to be applied to the events in order to reveal their meaning. Historians remain under the same illusion that had seized Darwin, the illusion that a value-neutral description of the facts, prior to their interpretation or analysis, was possible. It was not the doctrine of natural selection advanced by Darwin that commended him to other students of natural history as the Copernicus of natural history. That doctrine had been known and elaborated long before Darwin advanced it in the *Origin*. What had been required was a redescription of the facts to be explained in a language which would sanction the application to them of the doctrine as the most adequate way of explaining them.

And so too for historians seeking to 'explain' the 'facts' of the French Revolution, the decline and fall of the Roman Empire, the effects of slavery on American society, or the meaning of the Russian Revolution. What is at issue here is not: What are the facts? but rather: How are the facts to be described in order to sanction one mode of explaining them rather than another? Some historians will insist that history cannot become a science until it finds the technical terminology adequate to the correct characterization of its objects of study, in the way that physics did in the calculus and chemistry did in the periodic tables. Such is the recommendation of Marxists, Positivists, Cliometricians, and so on. Others will continue to insist that the integrity of historiography depends on its use of ordinary language, its avoidance of jargon. These latter suppose that ordinary language is a safeguard against ideological deformations of the 'facts.' What they fail to recognize is that ordinary language itself has its own forms of terminological determinism, represented by the figures of speech without which discourse itself is impossible.

Notes

1 I have tried to exemplify at length each of these webs of relationship in given historians in my book *Metahistory: The Historical Imagination in Nineteenth-Century Europe* (Baltimore & London: The Johns Hopkins Univ. Pres. 1973).

2 References in the text to Darwin's *Origin of Species* are to the Dolphin Edition (New York: Doubleday, n.d.).

2
The authority of the author
Biography and the reconstruction of the
canon

The influence of literary theory on its related disciplines has prompted much debate about the notion of 'authorship'. Yet the attraction of exploring architecture, or more specifically a building, through the life of its architect (author) remains a significant force in the construction of its histories. This is particularly the case when the architect has been identified as a major figure in the evolution of the architectural history. Conversely, buildings without architects are pushed to the sidelines of history. But biography as an historical method, particularly in recent times, is looked down on by many historians, since the wish to imbue historical narrative with the notion of causation gives the actions of individuals a fairly low priority. Here again we find E H Carr is a frequently cited source on this point. Carr asserts that biography is akin to what he calls 'the bad King John theory of history', that is, 'the view that what matters in history is the character and behaviour of individuals' which is in his view archaic since 'the desire to postulate individual genius as the creative force in history is characteristic of the primitive stages of historical consciousness.'[1]

But biography is an essential part of human memory. We think about ourselves in terms of what we have done – our identity is constructed around our past. Are history and biography linked or just two parallel strands? Biographers and historians make choices about how to frame their subject, they draw together fragments to present a possible glimpse of the unattainable whole. An historian might have a thesis or method which drives his/her enquiry whereas a biographer has, perhaps, a particular view of an individual they wish to present. Neither presents the truth, only an interpretation.

This is not a new problem predicated on the writings of Carr or such theorists as Michel Foucault who raised the issue in *What is an Author*, which addresses the question of author function, or Roland Barthes in the *Death of the Author*, which is concerned with how we *read* authorship. Indeed, the question can be traced back to antiquity as Plutarch differentiated between personality and historical events. In discussing the writing of biographical rather than historical accounts of individuals he defended the absence of lists of his subjects' achievements on the grounds that 'the truth is that the most brilliant exploits often tell us nothing of the virtues or the vices of the men who performed them, while on the other hand a chance remark or a joke may then reveal far more of a man's character then the mere feat of winning battles'.

Histories based on biographies can present a one-dimensional image of the architects involved, often inflating what was a portion of their existence, interests or social and cultural significance, making architecture appear to be their driving force when in reality it may have been merely one of several interests. For instance, Lord Burlington's interests included opera – his role in its development in this country is arguably as influential as the part he played in the architectural arena[2] (Figure 2.1). Recently there have been attempts to present

Figure 2.1 'Masquerade and Operas "Taste" or Burlington Gate'. A cartoon which lampoons
Burlington's involvement in the arts. Engraving by William Hogarth, 1723 (private
collection).

more rounded biographical studies of architects. See for instance Gillian Darley's work on Sir
John Soane[3] or Adrian Tinniswood's biography of Sir Christopher Wren.[4] And these provide
valuable fleshings-out of these figures along with an introduction into the social and cultural
milieux in which they operated. Yet these studies do not offer a significant rereading of the
architecture *per se* of these two men.

The biographical approach to writing architectural history is limited in chronological
terms by the life of the architect, how the building corresponds to his or her architectural
practice and whether it comes at the beginning, middle or end of the career in question. In
this way architecture is mapped against the personal development of the designer, which
implies some kind of progress. As Barthes points out

> The *author* [Barthes' emphasis] still reigns in manuals of literary history, in biographies
> of writers, magazine interviews, and in the very consciousness of litterateurs eager to
> unite by means of private journals, their person and their work; the image of literature
> to be found in contemporary culture is tyrannically centred on the author, his person,
> his history, his tastes, his passions; criticism still largely consists in saying that Baudelaire's
> oeuvre is the failure of the man Baudelaire, Van Gogh is his madness, Tchaikovsky's his
> vice: as if, through the more or less transparent allegory of fiction, it was always, ulti-
> mately the voice of one and the same person, the *author* [Barthes' emphasis], which was
> transmitting his 'confidences'.[5]

I have already noted that the preoccupation with the author in literary criticism substantially predate the points being made in this chapter. And there have been vigorous objections to and replacement of post-structuralist models of analysis that question the value of authorship. For instance, post-structuralism has been criticised by feminist historians for being a way in which western white males deal with the growing body of opinion that they can no longer control the production of knowledge and, therefore, no longer define the 'truth'. By saying there is no truth to be discovered the goalposts are shifted but still on men's terms. I do not deny these arguments and address them more specifically in a later chapter on gender. Yet, if we think about what Barthes is saying it does refocus our view of how architectural history is written and the consequences of the narrative structure used. And it must be acknowledged that most histories from our period are written by men and are about men, so I am content in this context to use, if you will forgive the phrase, a masculine yardstick.

Debates about the nature and importance of authorship do not imply that the architect has no importance, but to discuss a building solely in relation to its designer is only one way of looking at it. This might sound an obvious point. Yet the biographical canon of architectural history rests on such a notion. Named-author buildings are privileged over those whose parentage remains unknown or in question. Assignment of an architect changes the perceived status or value of the building, although in physical terms nothing has changed. In the preface to his *Biographical Dictionary of British Architects 1600–1840* Sir Howard Colvin makes the following remarks:

> . . . [the new edition] has called for many amendments, for the incorporation of much new information about individual architects and their works, and sometimes for a reassessment of their place in British architectural history . . .
> And there are many individual buildings of importance whose architects have yet to be identified. If the designers of, say, Lees Court, Kent, the Castle Ashby Screen, Tredegar House, Barnsley Park or Shobdon Church could be established, some of the biographies in this Dictionary might read very differently . . .
> . . . attributions [based only on stylistic criteria] have been included only when they have seemed to me to be so compelling as to amount to almost certainty . . . To clear away the undergrowth of irresponsible attribution that impeded British architectural scholarship earlier in this century [twentieth century] was one of the main objectives . . . (without of course denying that stylistic attribution has its place in architectural research).[6]

This offers a tidy way of bundling together the disparate strands of the evolution of architecture in Britain into a neat, coherent and progressive history. Colvin's *Dictionary* is now in its third edition and remains a benchmark or reference-point in the discipline of architectural history. The architect is the principal character involved in the design and gives the design its characteristics. Buildings in the post-medieval period are usually seen as more important if they have a named author, and if that author is recognised as part of the established canon of architectural history the building's status is commensurate with that of its architect. In this way certain buildings become the principal work of their architects. For instance, Lord Burlington's Chiswick House (*c.,* 1725) (see Figure 1.3) is seen as a fundamental example of English Palladianism and the apogee of Burlington's own architectural achievement. Similarly, Sir Robert Smirke's British Museum (1823 onwards) is seen as the architect's 'masterwork' and prime example of Greek Revivalism. But there is a divergence within the biographical approach to architectural history that has consequences for the way in which the building is presented. This also raises questions about how the identity of the architect is constructed and presented in histories, to which we will return. Robert Adam is a good example of the relationship between biography and the analysis of buildings, not least because his design work is often referred to as 'Adam Style' or Adamesque. Indeed, he is one of the few architects to have a style named after him which implies that architecture can be explained solely through the architect, that is, what he said and did – if there is any record of this. This way of looking at buildings can present further difficulties. Often a period of work or renovation or a new project was worked on by more than one architect. If we stay with Robert Adam and consider Kedleston, the Derbyshire seat of Lord Scarsdale, the difficulties become apparent.[7] Robert Adam was not the first architect to be involved with the project. Shortly after his return from Italy in 1758 he replaced Matthew Brettingham and James Paine, who had produced the initial designs and begun work on the central block and quadrants.[8] Adam was involved with the project *c.* 1760–1770 and was responsible for the south front, saloon, interior decoration and features in the grounds, including the bridge and the fishing house. But George Richardson, a member of Adam's architectural office, produced several important designs, including some for the ceilings of the principal rooms.[9] Is Kedleston then an Adam building? And by locating it within the framework of Adam's biography are other interpretations and meanings of Kedleston obscured? Houses were often worked on and developed over considerable periods of time. Again Adam's work at Osterley 1763–1780 for Robert Child, comprising the portico and interior remodelling, is only one of a series of architectural interventions in the house which dates back to the sixteenth century[10] (Figures 2.2, 2.3 and 2.4).

Figure 2.2 Osterley House, Middlesex remodelled by Robert Adam 1761 onwards, detail of portico (photo, author).

Figure 2.3 Osterley House, Middlesex remodelled by Robert Adam 1761 onwards, detail of 'Adamesque' plaster work in entrance hall (photo, author).

Figure 2.4 Osterley House, Middlesex remodelled by Robert Adam 1761 onwards, detail of 'Adamesque' ceiling decoration (photo, author).

The problem is magnified if we look at buildings over a greater period of time than the architect's own life-span. Returning to the British Museum (Figure 2.5), are we to deny that the central domed reading room added to Smirke's original structure by his nephew Sidney in 1854–7 is an integral part of the building, and what of the recent enclosing of the great court by Sir Norman Foster? Moreover, the reopening of this area to the public, albeit glazed over, returns to Robert Smirke's' original idea for the courtyard space. The important thing here is that to explain the building in terms of the biography of the architect or indeed a sequence of architects is to denude architecture of much of its meaning. Surely, here, the biography of the building is an equally useful approach as the biography of an architect or in this case the several architects involved with the building at various points in time? This presents the independent life of the building as an organic and ever-changing entity. Indeed, the life of things is an accepted way of interrogating objects in the study of material culture[11] and this facilitates the exploration of how the meaning and interpretation of objects can shift over time. And some buildings certainly have more fame than their patron or architect – anyone around in the 1960s will have heard of Cliveden. On the subject of architecture and scandal, looking across the Atlantic, Watergate remains a potent noun, often helping to formulate names for subsequent political peccadilloes, and staying in Washington the syllogisms regarding the Oval Office still have resonance and bring new meaning to the term '*architecture parlante*'.

Figure 2.5 The British Museum, London, main entrance (detail of portico) by Sir Robert Smirke, 1823 (photo, autho).

In architectural history then the focus on the biography either of an architect or sometimes a patron separates 'architecture' from the function of the building, the theory of the processes of architecture and the broader social and cultural significance. To this end architecture is presented in a kind of historical cul-de-sac divorced from any contemporary or theoretical meaning it may have. The construction of histories of the architecture of the late sixteenth through to the nineteenth century around biographies of patrons also places a distinct perimeter around the level of meaning given to the building. There is no doubt that the patron was an essential factor – s/he initiated the project, imposed personal preferences and, not least, paid for it. In this way the role of the patron also obliquely raises the question of who was responsible for the design?

We can see, for instance, how the focus on Lord Burlington as the 'leading' architect of his day has influenced the discussion about the design of Holkham, home of Thomas Coke, First Earl Leicester (Figure 2.6). The interaction of Coke, Burlington and William Kent, to all of whom the design has been attributed, alongside Matthew Brettingham the elder, remains unresolved. According to Matthew Brettingham junior 'The general ideas . . . were first struck out by the Earls of Burlington and Leicester, assisted by Mr William Kent'.[12] But subsequent studies by Leonard Schmidt and Catherine Hiskey have placed differing emphases on the roles of these individuals in the design of Holkham.[13] These assertions are based on the discovery of new archive material which can challenge established attributions, although the building itself remains unchanged.

The preoccupation with named architects is linked to the previously held view of the artist as genius/author in the discipline of art history. This view was challenged in 1970s and is now accepted as one of many diverse ways of examining the artistic production of societies.[14] But the idea of architect as genius endures and is partly due to architectural historians' ongoing obsession with identifying the designer of a building, which is seen to be linked to the idea

Figure 2.6 Holkam Hall, Norfolk, variously attributed to a number of architects (photo, author).

of value in architecture. In his appraisal of the importance of the architect Colvin links the emergence of the profession with genius:

> . . . it was the more sophisticated taste of the Stuart court that first allowed a man of genius to exercise the full functions of an architect in the modern sense. That man was Inigo Jones, and it was he who first imposed Italian discipline on English architecture . . .[15]

The bias towards classical architecture in architectural histories can be subjected to a range of readings. Here the rationality of this style as manifest in the work of named architects is seen as indicative of the intellectual processes involved in design and the need for an education for both producer (architect) and user (patron and viewer) for design to operate successfully, so giving architecture greater value.

The preoccupation with identifying architects is also part of the process of recognising and defending the professional status of the architect. Here a chronological survey of the establishment of the professional, named architect over the amateur or anonymous craftsmen, is an independent historical enquiry, but it has been grafted onto the architectural production of given societies. At moments when individual 'architects' or groups of like-minded individuals can be identified, significant changes in approach to design are looked for and stylistic homogeneity sought as a means of establishing professional design practice with an authorial, biographical stamp. Spiro Kostoff in his study of the architectural profession *The Architect: Chapters in the History of the Profession*, presents a version of this enduring view of the architect as genius, creator, author.

> Architecture cannot be the world's oldest profession – tradition has decided that issue long ago – but its antiquity is not in doubt. The presence of architects is documented as far back as the third millennium before Christ. Graphic conventions of architectural practice appear even earlier . . . Indeed even without documentation it can be fairly postulated that architects were abroad from the moment when there was the desire for a sophisticated built environment. For buildings of substantial scale or a certain degree of complexity must be conceived by someone before construction of them can begin.
>
> This is what architects are, conceivers of buildings. What they do is to design, that is, supply concrete images for a new structure so that it can be put up. The primary task of the architect, then as now, is to communicate what proposed buildings should be and look like. The architect does not initiate buildings, nor necessarily take part in the physical act of construction. The architect's role is that of mediator between the client or patron, that is, the person who decides to build, and the work force with its overseers, which we might collectively refer to as the builder.
>
> These are not of course rigidly distinct identities. When architects undertake to build their own houses they become additionally clients, and non-professional clients sometimes dispense with the services of an architect and simply produce their own designs. Even more frequently, builders put up standardised buildings for a general market without the benefit of the architect's skill. Finally the great majority of buildings, so called vernacular architecture, is the result of individual efforts – people who decide to build, settle for the common look of the community, and produce buildings in this accepted local way.

In this book we are not concerned with anonymous architecture of this kind, nor with the rare cases where architects act as their own clients and the reverse. We are dealing with the profession of architecture, the specialised skill that is called upon to give shape to the environmental needs of others. How did architects get to be architects in any given period of history? How were they educated and trained? How did they and their clients and communicate with them? To what extent did they supervise the execution of their designs? What did society think of them (as against what they thought of themselves. which is another matter)? What honours and renumeration could they command?[16]

This view of the importance of the profession and through this the genius of individual practitioners is fundamental to architectural history in Britain. Indeed, Sir Howard Colvin's agenda could not be more obvious in this regard. In the introductory remarks to the *Dictionary* Colvin sets out the relationship between biography and professionalism:

It is appropriate to begin a biographical dictionary of professional men by giving some account of the history of their profession. Indeed, the history of British architecture is bound up with its own practice, and the careers of those architects and master workmen who figure in this dictionary would scarcely be intelligible without some idea of the conditions under which they designed and built . . . The second [part of this essay] attempts to trace the rise of the architectural profession in Britain, a process that falls within – indeed very nearly coincides with – the chronological limits of this book. For in 1600 there were no architects in the sense in which we understand the term today. By 1840 there was an established architectural profession, based on a regular system of pupillage . . . This new profession had come into being through the labours and aspirations of those whose names appear in this volume, and a summary of its history may not inappropriately serve to introduce their careers.[17]

The cult of the personality – the named author genius – has then been fundamental to the construction of histories of western architecture from post medieval times to the present. But this excludes much of the built environment and restricts our understanding of architecture. Recently there have been more holistic considerations of the architectural profession and the idea of the architect. Mary Woods, in her recent illuminating study of the education of architects in the United States, addresses this in her discussion of 'Roarkism':

I never finished *The Fountainhead*, Ayn Rand's novel about art, freedom, and architecture . . . I found Howard Roark, Rand's architect-protagonist, neither sympathetic nor charismatic. I remember his monologues . . . as long-winded and pompous. What I found memorable were the settings and supporting characters . . . The mise-en-scène was always more vivid and intriguing than Roark, his designs or Rand's philosophy.

This study foregrounds the mise-en-scène of the architectural profession. It is a challenge to what one architectural historian called 'Roarkism', our discipline's traditional focus on the architect as a solitary creator to the exclusion of other narrators or narratives. . . .

My concern is with multiple participants, overlapping responsibilities, and the settings for design and building [rather than architecture] as art or problem solving. 'Roarks' . . . do have a part in this account . . . But I view them from unorthodox perspectives. Here they are not omniscient creators but collaborators, partners . . . Their narratives are interwoven with those of modest, provincial, renegade and failed architects. The first women and people of color to enter the profession contribute accounts.[18]

This to me sums up our fascination with authorial genius when we consider architecture and the influence this notion has had on its histories.

I want now to step back to late sixteenth-century England – a point in historical time not covered by Colvin's *Dictionary* or Kostoff's professionalising agenda – at a moment when the 'architect was emerging' as a recognised practitioner in the building process, as seen in building accounts and commentaries. Here the persona of Robert Smythson provides a case study of the relationship between the evidence and the will of the historian to provide a particular sequence of biographical narrative and architectural historical analysis. The archive available is the same but the outcomes or biographical historical narratives are quite different. This begins to reveal how, at an early stage in the formation of the canon of architectural history of the British Isles, the ability to identify and name an architect was important in placing limits or pause marks on the chronology of history. Architecture can be seen as 'emerging' from the 'Dark Ages' of relative anonymity to the lightness of the named designer. This helps bolster the argument for a more conscious approach to architectural form. In this way the notion of genius is explored through an individual or author.

Will the real Robert Smythson please stand up?

Robert Smythson *c.* 1535–1614 was active at a time when the profession of architect was not clearly defined and the emergence of the architect from a previous identity as craftsman was very much in its early stages. Smythson is discussed in Malcolm Airs' book, on building practice *The Tudor and Jacobean House: a building history*,[19] which concentrates on the production of architecture, and he is the subject of a monograph by Mark Girouard *Robert Smythson and the Elizabethan Country House*.[20] His involvement in the design of several great houses has also been discussed by Summerson in *Architecture in Britain 1530–1830*[21] and Pevsner in his *Buildings of England* series.[22] Smythson is a problematic and enigmatic figure. Existing at the moment when architecture in Britain is identified as responding to the developments in Renaissance Europe, Smythson's work provides extant examples of this, and partly because of the increased use of paper in architectural design some of his drawings remain, which make speculation about authorial intent and influences more attractive.[23] In this way he has captured the imagination of historians far more than, for instance, one of his predecessors John Shute who, although describing himself as an architect in 1540, has left little behind in terms of built architecture.[24]

The differing views of Smythson by key historians of the Elizabethan period show both the concern with the mapping of the emergence of the architect and how different emphasis on biography colours historical narrative. I want here to focus on masculine constructions of the 'architect' or author, even though Alice Friedman has made some fascinating feminist rereadings of the work (or not) of Smythson especially with reference to Hardwick Hall and Wollaton (Figures 2.7 and 2.8). Friedman's works concentrates more on the buildings and I will return to it in the chapter on gender.[25] First, let's read on with the 'boys'. Malcolm Airs describes Smythson as a 'working mason and professional surveyor of building operations' whilst Mark Girourard sees him as 'one of the great geniuses of English architecture'. These different views influence their narratives around Smythson as we see in Malcolm Airs' assessment:

Figure 2.7 Hardwick Hall, Derbyshire.

Figure 2.8 Wollaton Hall, Nottinghamshire.

Figure 2.9 Longleat, Wiltshire.

Another craftsman, who had spent much of his early career working as a mason at Longleat (Figure 2.9), also became in later life a professional surveyor of building operations. Robert Smythson worked for Thynne [the owner of Longleat] for twelve years starting in 1568. He was employed as one of the two principal masons, and there was no indications in the very full documentation for the building that he took any part in the administration other than supervising the other masons in his own gang. He was, however, a workman of considerable experience and reputation . . .

On the death of Thynne in 1580, Smythson moved to the Midlands to work for Sir Francis Willoughby, where, as his tombstone records, he was employed as 'Architector and Survayor unto yee most worthy house of Wollaton'.

The amount of mason's work actually carried out by Smythson was minimal. His principal job was to direct the building operation, and to prepare the designs in consultation with Willoughby. The status of his work is marked by the appellation of 'Mr' accorded him in the building accounts. Smythson remained at Wollaton for the rest of his life, and after the house had been completed he seems to have been employed by the Willoughby family in a general administrative capacity connected with their coal mining enterprises. During the same period, he continued to prepare architectural designs for other patrons, and to supervise some of the building operations of the Cavendish family. An entry in the Hardwick Hall accounts of 1597 refers to him as 'Mr Smythson, the Surveyour' although the actual building works were supervised by John Balechouse, a painter of Dutch origin.[26]

Mark Girouard offers a very different appraisal

During three generations and over seventy years Robert Smythson, his son John and his grandson Huntingdon built some of the most magnificent, romantic or ingenious houses in England . . . It is only in recent years that Robert Smythson, by far the most important of the three, has begun to receive his due as a figure of the first rank in the history of English architecture.[27]

Girouard continues

> In all this Smythson was taking part in, perhaps even leading, the general movement of English architecture, which everywhere was exploiting the shifting, the variegated, the complex and the picturesque, up till the inevitable reaction and the uncompromising blocks of Inigo Jones and Pratt . . . Robert Smithson is in a different class [to his son and grandson] . . . Not only do the houses with which he can be connected include some of the most important and impressive of their period; they were also full of ideas, new or newly expressed, which were taken up and developed elsewhere in the country. There is little doubt that Robert Smythson was one of the creators of the Elizabethan style.[28]

Yet Girouard does appear to contradict his own claims for Smythson, for instance when he questions:

> How much was dictated to him [Smythson] by Bess of Hardwick, by Willoughby, by Thynne or Charles Cavendish? How much was left to the initiative of the workmen? The designs he made – perhaps from the start incomplete or lacking in details – were at the mercy of the patron's whim or the inefficiency of independence of the men who carried them out. His employers did not see themselves as consulting a creative genius; they were employing a servant, to give form to their ideas, or provide ideas of his own which they would have no hesitation in adapting or expanding . . . The houses that were erected on the basis of Smythson's plans were exciting and original creations, but it remains something of a problem to what extent he intended to achieve the effects which we admire in them.[29]

My purpose here is not to pick holes in Girourard's excellent book. Rather it is to highlight a more general preoccupation with authorship and the relationship of this to our idea of genius. Indeed, Girouard does signal this but remains determined to create Smythson. The prodigy houses (as Smythson's grand country houses are often called) can cause a problem for historians as they are geographically dispersed, have a range of patrons and each has its own distinct aesthetic. But they are impressive, important, significant works of architecture and it is desirable to be able to ascribe this achievement to an individual architect. But Smythson is up against some very colourful patrons and it is tempting to see the architectural distinctiveness of their houses and representative of their personalities.

The differing accounts of Robert Smythson continue in the writings of Summerson and Pevsner. For instance, Sir Nikolaus Pevsner remarked in his second edition of the volume for the *Buildings of England* series on Nottinghamshire:

> [At Wollaton] Smythson transformed the revolutionary but anonymously devised elevations of Longleat into a very individual statement probably more expressive of Sir Francis' [Willoughby] character and aspirations than his own. At Hardwick where, although the symmetrical plan and towered silhouette are characteristically 'Smythson', the appearance of the building is as hard and uncompromising as its builder, Bess of Hardwick.[30]

Smythson's connection with Hardwick is in fact tenuous. His name appears only once in the documentation relating to the building project. The principal link is made more on stylistic grounds as Pevsner admits in his volume for the same series on Derbyshire which first appeared in 1953

> Hardwick is in the line with these developments [Barlborough and Wollaton] and makes its own contribution. Here lies the principal reason why one is inclined to attribute the design of Hardwick to Robert Smythson, architect of Wollaton.[31]

Here Pevsner gives us a clue as to why there is such a preoccupation with Smythson and his oeuvre. An historian needs to order facts, and for this categories and taxonomic systems are necessary. Authorship is useful in this regard, especially as this adds weight to architectural stylistic classification. This method was used by Sir John Summerson in *Architecture in Britain 1530–1830* which, like Pevsner's volume, was first published 1953. Summerson characterises Smythson thus:

> It is not easy to group the greater Elizabethan houses in an orderly significant way, and any grouping is bound to ignore some cross-current or other which suggests another arrangement but the following grouping is useful for the purpose of exposition;
> I   Sir John Thynne's final rebuilding of Longleat; the work at Wardour Castle; Wollaton; Worksop; Hardwick. With all of these, the name Robert Smythson is associated.
> II   Kirby Hall, Holdenby, the final Burghley. A famous Northants group sharing certain French influences.

Summerson continues by characterising Smythson's approach to design and its significance

> The hall placed on the axis of the main entrance with the contraction of the house into a single pile of complex silhouette was Robert Smythson's chief legacy to his successors . . . This group of Smythsonian houses, all developing in some way from Longleat and thus ultimately from Somerset House, form a great and splendid branch of the tree of English architecture.[32]

The various biographies of Smythson demonstrate the lack of objectivity in this kind of historical narrative. Colvin's *Dictionary*, which first appeared in 1954,[33] takes a more extreme stance in the search for objective empiricism with its alphabetical lists of architects and their known documented buildings and archival sources. These lists are in turn ordered by a heirarchy of building types produced by each architect. Typical headings (and note the order) are public buildings etc.; London domestic architecture; other cities' domestic architecture; country houses; mausolea and monuments; unexecuted designs. Each entry is prefaced by a biographical account of the architect, which varies in length according to the known archive, and a list of bibliographic sources. Colvin's lexical approach to the writing of architectural history stands distinct from the trend in art historical scholarship of the period which ranged between the *Kulturgeschichte* of the Warburgian scholars and connoisseurial preoccupations with stylistic attribution and appreciation. David Watkin has already noted the emphasis placed by Colvin on documentary and archive material which came out of his training as a 'professional academic and medieval historian'. This shift in emphasis and approach, Watkin argued, made architectural history 'academically respectable'.[34] As we have seen this was certainly Colvin's agenda. But it is not the purpose of this volume to assess the validity or strength of the contribution of individual historians to the discipline of architectural history. Rather I am interested in how their different approaches influence our reading of the subject. In the following extracts I want to focus on the broader implications for thinking about architecture in terms of biography and the effect the named author has on this. I have selected Colvin's 'Guide to contents', as this maps out the project of the *Dictionary*, followed by part of his introductory essay 'The Practice of Architecture, 1600–1840' entitled 'The architectural profession'.

Finally, I have included two sample biographical accounts of Robert Adam and Decimus Burton – two successful, productive architects. But the absence of an archive of material on Burton, or publications by him, has pushed him to the sidelines of architectural history in comparison to the well-documented life and work of Adam.

Notes

1 E H Carr, *What is History?*, London, Macmillan, 1961.

2 For a discussion of Burlington's varied interests see J Wilton Ely (ed.), 'Apollo of the Arts', exhibition catalogue, Nottingham University Gallery, 1973 and D Arnold (ed.) *Belov'd by Ev'ry Muse: Richard Boyle, third earl of Burlington and fourth earl of Cork 1694–1753*, London, Georgian Group, 1994.

3 G Darley, *Sir John Soane: An accidental romantic*, New Haven, CT and London, Yale University Press, 1999.

4 A Tinniswood, *His Invention so Fertile: A life of Christopher Wren*, London, Jonathan Cape, 2001.

5 R Barthes, 'Death of the Author', *From Image–Music–Text*, trans. Stephen Heath, 1977, p. 50.

6 Sir Howard Colvin, *A Biographical Dictionary of British Architects 1600–1840*, 3rd edn, New Haven, CT and London, Yale University Press, 1995, pp. 7, 10.

7 For a full discussion of Adam at Kedleston see L Harris, *Robert Adam and Kedleston: The making of a neo-classical masterpiece*, London, National Trust, 1987.

8 Paine's role at Kedleston and his relationship with Adam is discussed in C Webster 'Architectural Illustration as Revenge: James Paine's designs for Kedleston' in M Howard (ed.), *The Image of the Building: Papers from the Annual Symposium of the Society of Architectural Historians of Great Britain 1995*, London 1995, pp. 83–92; P Leach, *James Paine*, London, Zwemmer, 1988; and 'James Paine's Design for the South Front at Kedleston Hall', *Architectural History*, 40, 1997, pp. 159–170.

9 Richardson went on to exhibit one of his designs 'The Ceiling executed in the Grecian Hall at Keddlestone' at the Royal Academy in 1776.

10 For instance, work had been carried out on the west side of the house, including the Gallery, by Sir Francis Child before his death in 1761. For a fuller discussion of Osterley see J Hardy and M Tomlin, *Osterley Park House*, London, Victoria and Albert Museum, 1985.

11 See, for instance, A Appadurai, *The Social Life of Things: Commodities in cultural perspective*, Cambridge, Cambridge University Press 1986.

12 M Brettingham, jnr., *The Plans and Elevations of the late Earl of Leicester's House at Holkham*, 2nd edn, London, 1773.

13 On this point see L Schmidt, 'Holkham Hall' *Country Life* 24 and 31 Jan 1980, pp. 214–217, 298–301 and more recently C Hiskey, 'The Building of Holkham Hall: Newly discovered letters', *Architectural History*, 40, 1997, pp. 144–158.

14 See for instance J Wolff, *The Social Production of Art*, London, Macmillan, 2nd edn, 1981.

15 Sir Howard Colvin, op. cit. p. 31.

16 S Kostoff, *The Architect: Chapters in the history of the profession*, Oxford and New York Oxford University Press, 1977, pp. v–vi.

17 Sir Howard Colvin, op. cit. p. 27.

18 M N Woods, *From Craft to Profession: The practice of architecture in nineteenth-century America*, California and London, University of California Press, 1999, pp. 1–2.

19 M Airs, *The Tudor and Jacobean House: A building history*, Stroud, Sutton, 1995. First published as *The Making of the English Country House 1500–1640* in 1975.

20 M Girouard, *Robert Smythson and the Elizabethan Country House*, New Haven, CT and London, Yale University Press 1983. First published as *Robert Smythson*

and the Architecture of the Elizabethan Era in 1966.

21 See chapter 2.

22 See chapter 5.

23 For instance the Wollaton papers held in Royal Institute of British Architects Library.

24 John Shute is principally remembered for his *First and Chief Groundes of Architecture*, 1563 which was one of the first treatises on architectural design to appear in English. Shute travelled in Europe and was influenced by continental design.

25 See A Friedman, *House and Household in Elizabethan England*, Chicago and London, University of Chicago Press, 1989 and 'Architecture, Authority and the Female Gaze: Planning and representation in the early modern country house', *Assemblage*, 18, August 1992, pp. 41–61. Cited later in this book, pp. 211–216.

26 M Airs, *The Tudor and Jacobean House: A building history*, Stroud, Sutton, 1995, p. 71.

27 Mark Girouard, op. cit. p. 2.

28 M Girouard, op. cit. p. 294.

29 M Girouard, *Robert Smythson and the Elizabethan Country House*, New Haven, CT and London, Yale University Press, 1983, pp. 286, 290.

30 N Pevsner, *Buildings of England: Nottinghamshire*, 2nd edn, 1979, revised by Elizabeth Williamson, London, Penguin.

31 N Pevsner, *Buildings of England: Derbyshire*, 1st edn, 1953, London, Penguin.

32 Sir John Summerson *Architecture in Britain 1530–1830*, Harmondsworth, Pelican first published 1953, revised 1970 and republished by Yale University Press.

33 This first appeared in 1954 as a *Biographical Dictionary of English Architects 1660–1840*, the geographical and chronological scope changed in the second edition in 1974.

34 See D Watkin, *The Rise of Architectural History*, London, Architectural Press, 1980, p. 161.

Biographical Dictionary

Sir Howard Colvin

Guide to contents

The purpose of this book is sufficiently indicated by its title, but there are certain matters of method which require explanation, notably the chronological and topographical scope of the work and the principles upon which individual architects have qualified for inclusion.

My aim has been to include every architect – and by 'architect' I mean anyone, whether amateur, tradesman or professional, who habitually made architectural designs – the major part of whose career falls within the limiting dates. Thus Decimus Burton (1880–1881) has been included because most of his work was done before he was 40, whereas George Edmund Street, who died in the same year, has not because he was active chiefly in the 1850s and 1860s. Inevitably there have been borderline cases, in some of which no doubt another writer would have made different decisions. But I hope that in this as in other respects the element of personal preference has not been sufficiently great to impair the value of this book as a comprehensive record of British architects who practised between 1600 and 1840.

For the purposes of this Dictionary a 'British' architect is one who, irrespective of national origin, practised in England, Scotland or Wales. Architects domiciled in Ireland have been excluded, but many buildings erected in Ireland to the designs of English or Scottish architects have been noted. Architects of British origin whose careers were spent entirely overseas, e.g. in India, have not usually been included, but entries will be found for some who emigrated after an initial period of practice in Britain. Many amateur architects have been given a place, but a man whose architectural activity was limited to designing his own house has not normally qualified for inclusion.

So far as possible the works of each architect have been placed in chronological order. When this has not been practicable they have been listed alphabetically. Whenever it has seemed desirable public and private buildings have been listed separately. The dates printed are normally those of construction (rather than of the whole process of design and construction), but in many cases only an approximate date can be given. No attempt has been made to list unexecuted designs on the same basis as executed ones, but attention has often been drawn to important unexecuted designs either in the body of the biography or in a separate section. Dates of demolition and alteration have been stated so far as it has been possible to ascertain them, and an attempt has been made to indicate the employment of Gothic and other non-classical styles, though in neither case is it claimed that the information given is complete. The county boundaries referred to are those in force before the Local Government Act of 1972 (soon to be rendered obsolete by further legislation) and therefore correspond closely to those in use during the historical period covered by this Dictionary.

The authority for each entry in the lists will be found either at the head the list (where one source is common to all entries) or (more often) within *square brackets* immediately after that entry. References given within *round brackets* are to books and articles which describe or illustrate the building in question but which are not cited as authorities. '*Attributed*' means that the evidence is largely or wholly stylistic. In this edition, as in its predecessors, such purely stylistic attributions have been sparingly made, partly because my purpose has been to provide a body of authentic information uncompromised by speculation and partly because in a dictionary there is no room in which to argue controversial cases of attribution.

[. . .]

The architectural profession

> *You must be aware that Architecture is the profession of a Gentleman, and that none is more lucrative when it is properly attended to.*
>
>   Mrs James Wyatt to her son Philip, 1808 (B.L., Egerton MS. 3515)

The architect as we know him today is a product of the Renaissance. This does not mean that the architect, in the sense of 'one who both furnishes the designs and superintends the erection of buildings',[1] had been unknown in the Middle Ages. But the medieval architect was a master craftsman (usually a mason or a carpenter by trade), one who could build as well as design, or at least 'one trained in that craft even if he had ceased to ply his axe and chisel'.[2] He was a master workman whose skill was based on a technical experience of building rather than on a theoretical knowledge of architecture as an art. The word 'architect' itself, used by the ancients in much the same sense as it is by ourselves, came in the Middle Ages to be regarded as the equivalent of 'master mason' or 'master carpenter'.[3]

It was, then, the mason and the carpenter who were the architects of the Middle Ages. That some of them were men of genius cannot be denied, and even if architecture did not rank as a 'liberal art', there is evidence that those who practised it as masters enjoyed a certain status in the society of their time. The recognition that there were able men in the medieval building world, and that those men deserve the name of 'architect', does not, however, imply that their functions were identical with those of architects in modern times. Architectural practice has evolved together with the society which it serves. A modern architect is a professional man set aside from the building trade by education and specialized training. His architectural expertise is acquired by academic instruction rather than by practical experience, and his approach to design is theoretical rather than empirical. When he designs a building he envisages it as a whole and works it out in detail on paper before transmitting the drawings to the executant builder. The medieval architect, on the other hand, was normally a craftsman by training, and frequently acted as one of the executants of the buildings he himself designed. That he was capable of envisaging a building as a whole we cannot doubt, and there is abundant evidence that he could express his ideas on the drawing-board. But in the Middle Ages the processes of design and construction were much more closely linked than is the case today. Much more was left to be worked out on the spot than is normal in modern architectural practice, and even major churches were sometimes begun without any clear idea how they were to be completed. That the technical achievement of the great Gothic churches was possible at all was due partly to the accumulated experience of the Romanesque age, and partly to the rediscovery of Greek science in the thirteenth century. The science of most utility to architecture was of course geometry, and it was above all a knowledge of geometry that distinguished the medieval master mason or master carpenter from his subordinates. That knowledge might find expression in drawn 'patrons' and 'patterns', of which many examples survive on the continent, though few have been preserved in British archives. But it was also more widely disseminated in the form of simple geometrical formulae which made it possible to develop many of the elevational features of a building from a given plan in accordance with predetermined rules of proportion, without the intervention of working drawings.[4]

Another difference between medieval and modern architectural practice must be emphasized. All that we know of the medieval craftsman suggests that it was very rare for a master mason, however eminent, to dictate to a master carpenter, or *vice versa*. Each was supreme in his own sphere, and solved his own problems in accordance with the traditions of his own craft. Each trade was a distinct 'mistery', understood only by its own practitioners, and applied independently to each new commission. Common patronage, common experience and common artistic conventions enabled one trade to work harmoniously beside another, but it was rare for any one individual to exercise that technical and aesthetic control over every component of a building which modern architects have come to take for granted. In studying the careers of medieval architects it is therefore necessary to think of them as members of a team working in collaboration rather than as architects in the sense in which the term has been understood in modern times.

In Italy – and to a lesser extent in France – the authority of the architect was already asserting itself in the sixteenth and early seventeenth centuries. But in Tudor and Stuart Britain medieval practice was still the norm in architectural matters. The great Elizabethan houses were assembled piecemeal rather than designed as artistically coherent entities. 'The plan might come from one source, the details from a number of others. Designs could be supplied by one or more of the craftsmen actually employed on the building; or by an outside craftsman, or by the employer; or by a friend of the employer; or by a professional with an intellectual rather than a craft background.'[5] Though Renaissance detailing might be one ingredient of the whole it was seen as a decorative dressing rather than as a discipline which pervaded the entire design of the building. So those (often of foreign birth) who purveyed it had not yet usurped the functions of the craftsmen architects who still dominated the British architectural scene at the beginning of the seventeenth century. The way was not yet clear for the genius of a Wren or for the dictatorship of taste of an Earl of Burlington to impose itself on the architecture of an age.

The change, when it came, was the doing, not so much of the builder-architects as of their patrons. The modern architect did not evolve, as if by an involuntary process, out of the traditional master workman. It is true that changing economic conditions were having their effect on the building trades, notably in releasing them gradually from the restrictions of medieval craft-regulation and in encouraging the growth of the contract system that had made its appearance long before.[6] But neither of these developments did anything to modify their functions in the matter of architectural design. The emergence of the modern architect was therefore due less to changing economic conditions than it was to changing tastes, and in Britain it was the more sophisticated taste of the Stuart court that first allowed a man of genius to exercise the full functions of an architect in the modern sense. That man was Inigo Jones, and it was he who first imposed Italian discipline on English architecture, taking his ideas direct from the Italian masters instead of through the indirect medium of French buildings and German and Flemish pattern-books. The Palladian architecture which Inigo Jones introduced into England was based on a highly sophisticated theory of design which could not well be studied outside Italy, and was beyond the intellectual grasp of the average master builder. Moreover, its execution demanded that the craftsman should subordinate himself to a single controlling mind in a way which he had never been required to do before. It demanded, in fact, the employment of someone whose education had included the conscious study of design, and whose functions were to be supervisory rather than executive: in other words, the architect.

As Surveyor of the Royal Works Inigo Jones was paramount for over twenty years. But he was essentially a court architect, and the extinction of court life during the Civil War and Commonwealth meant a serious setback for his personal influence. Nevertheless, the taste for Italian culture had taken firm root even in the minds of those who were of the parliamentary persuasion, and after the Restoration there was a general demand among the English aristocracy for houses in what Roger North called 'the Grand maniere of Jones'. Although there were one or two master builders who were tolerably well versed in the new style of architecture,[7] they were in a minority, and a person who wished his house to be in a correct taste had either to educate his workmen himself,[8] or, as Sir Roger Pratt advised, to

> get some ingenious gentleman who has seen much of that kind abroad and been somewhat versed in the best authors of Architecture: viz. Palladio, Scamozzi, Serlio, etc. to do it for you, and to give you a design of it in paper, though but roughly drawn, (which will generally fall out better than one which shall be given you by a home-bred Architect for want of his better experience, as is daily seen) . . .[9]

The demand thus created was sufficiently general to give employment to a small number of men who specialized in architectural design and supervision. Hugh May, William Samwell and Captain William Winde were architects of the type described by Pratt, gentlemen by birth who supplemented modest private incomes by acting as architects and artistic advisers. In a sense they were the founders of the English architectural profession, but in their lifetimes the conception of such a profession was still in the future, for there was no form of architectural education other than apprenticeship to a building trade, and those who called themselves architects had usually been grounded in some other art or discipline. Inigo Jones himself may have begun life as a painter; so, perhaps, did Hugh May;[10] Balthazar Gerbier was a diplomatist and teacher of aristocratic exercises who merely counted the arts of design among his manifold accomplishments, William Winde a military engineer, and Wren a Professor of Astronomy. Only Webb, who had been 'brought up by his Unckle Mr. Inigo Jones upon his late Maiestyes command in the study of Architecture, as well that wch relates to building as for masques, Tryumphs and the like', could claim to have received a specifically architectural training, and he himself had no disciple. It was the accident of the Great Fire which made Robert Hooke, a practising architect, and there must have been others who, like John Evelyn and Roger North, were equally well versed in architectural matters, but who did not 'pretend either to great publick designes, nor new models of great houses'. Even in the eighteenth century it was still possible for a soldier like Vanbrugh or a painter like Kent to achieve celebrity as an architect, and the century was to be well advanced before the system of apprenticeship to a practising architect provided the established basis of a professional training comparable to that offered by the Law or even the Church.[11]

Most people, indeed, still thought it unnecessary to consult anyone but a master workman when undertaking building operations, and some, like Roger North, preferred to make the designs themselves without professional assistance. 'For a profest architect is proud, opiniative and troublesome, seldome at hand, and a head workman pretending to the designing part, is full of paultry vulgar contrivances; therefore be your owne architect, or sitt still', was his advice.[12] It is not surprising, therefore, that very few seventeenth-century architects lived exclusively upon their earnings. Some, like Samwell and Pratt, had small private incomes; others, like Wren and Hooke, enjoyed academic posts; while for Ryder and Webb (and later for Wren) it was the Office of His Majesty's Works which gave them a basic income in return for official duties which left them ample time for private practice.

The importance of the Office of Works in the history of the English architectural profession cannot easily be over-emphasized. In the seventeenth and eighteenth centuries it provided by far the greatest number of posts open to architects in the form of surveyorships and clerkships of the works.[13] The most famous architects of the day sat on its Board, and it was through the agency of the King's Works that so many skilled master craftsmen became acquainted with the latest ideas in design and decoration – ideas which in due course they incorporated in buildings for their own private clients. The Office of Works was, in fact, a kind of unacknowledged substitute for a royal academy of architecture such as Colbert established in France, and it retained its importance as the focus of English architectural activity well into the latter part of the eighteenth century. So long, moreover, as the clerkships of the Works remained in the gift of the Surveyor-General (which they did at least until 1782), the latter was able to find places for his chosen subordinates, and it is in the exercise of this patronage that the 'school' of Wren or Chambers must be sought, rather than in the idea of private pupilage.[14] It was by capturing the Office of Works in the 1730s that Lord Burlington was able to impose his Palladian formula upon the public buildings of London, and so create a tradition of official architecture which lasted to the Second World War.

The importance of the Office of Works in maintaining the tenuous thread of architectural experience is shown by the number of eighteenth-century architects who were either 'bred up in the King's Works' or held office under the Surveyor-General. But outside the royal palaces there was no body of persons trained in architectural drawing and supervision as there is today, and it was not until about the middle of the century that it became possible for a young man to take up architecture as a career, to enter the office of a practising architect, and to learn to design without previously having learned to build. Fortunes were nevertheless to be made by those who had somehow acquired the requisite knowledge and skill to practise the art. 'Few men who have gained any reputation [as architects] but have made good estates,' declared Campbell in 1747,[15] and George Vertue, writing in 1749, placed architecture at the head of the artistic professions. 'I must own,' he said, '[that] the branch of the art of building in Architecture is much improved and many men of that profession has made greater fortunes . . . than any other branch of Art whatever – their manner of undertakings is so profitable, by their agreements at so much per cent of drawings and direction of works of building. . . . Indeed this profession of building has many profitable advantages which makes it worth while to study, travel and labour.'[16]

The first English architect who was in the habit of taking pupils appears to have been Sir Robert Taylor, of whom it was said that he and James Paine 'nearly divided the practice of the profession between them' until the advent of the brothers Adam.[17] His rival followed his example, and by the third quarter of the eighteenth century it was usual for the London architect to have in his office one or more young men who were at once his pupils and his assistants. Their status was that of articled clerks, unless they had sufficient experience to rank as 'improvers', in which case they would receive a small weekly wage in addition to board and lodging. Such an apprenticeship, commencing at the age of 16, lasted for five or six years,[18] and in the course of it the intelligent pupil had ample opportunity to learn the essentials of architectural draughtsmanship and professional practice. He would, at the same time, seek to attend the lectures of the Professor of Architecture at the Royal Academy, and would show the best of his own essays in design at the annual exhibition under the address of his tutor and master. He might even gain one of the medals (two silver and one gold)[19] offered annually by the Academy for students' work, or gain a 'premium' from the Society of Arts. At the end of his apprenticeship, he aspired to travel – certainly to Rome and northern Italy, if possible to Sicily and Greece, perhaps even to Asia Minor and the Levant. There, for two or three never-to-be-forgotten years, he measured, drew and sometimes excavated the monuments of antiquity, forming a collection of sketches and measured drawings upon which he could draw for inspiration in the future, and some of which he would later work up for future Royal Academy exhibitions. Thus at the age of 25 or 26 the young architect was fully equipped for professional practice. If he was lucky, he obtained a post as surveyor to a corporation, a charity, a fire insurance office or a private estate until such time as, through friends, influence, or success in a public competition, he laid the foundations of a successful private practice and began to take pupils of his own. If he was unlucky – and the indications are that by the beginning of the nineteenth century architecture was attracting more aspirants than it could gainfully employ – he spent his life as an assistant in another architect's office, combined architecture with some other occupation, or gave it up altogether. A good many casualties of this sort will be found in the pages of this Dictionary, but successful careers were open to those in whom creative skill was matched by business ability. The worldly wealth of Sir Robert Taylor, Sir William Chambers or Henry Holland was not derived exclusively from professional fees, but in the next generation Sir John Soane made a fortune strictly by professional activity, and the Probate records show that by the reign of Victoria a leading London architect could expect to leave a substantial estate to his heirs.[20] Architecture had, in fact, become a reputable and remunerative occupation which an ambitious parent could contemplate with favour for his son – one of which no longer depended upon the uncertainties of aristocratic patronage or the doubtful devices of speculative building. The architect had at last taken his place alongside the doctor and the lawyer, and it would not be long before he began to formulate his own standards of professional conduct and to create an organization through which they could be enforced.

In Scotland the development of an architectural profession took essentially the same course. Here, as in England, it was from the ranks of the building tradesmen that the professional architect began to emerge in the course of the eighteenth century. In Edinburgh competence in draughtsmanship had been a necessary qualification for membership of the Incorporation of Masons at least since the early seventeenth century. Thus when James Smith, soon to be Edinburgh's leading architect, applied for admittance in 1680, he was required to draw plans of a large three-storey, double-pile house with four pavilions and a Doric doorway (the last to be drawn to a larger scale). In this way the expertise gained through apprenticeship to an established master was formally tested in a way that was unique to Scotland. On the other hand, the lack after the Union of a Scottish Office of Works meant that there was no established hierarchy of posts to which the leading Scottish architects could aspire, which helps to explain why so many of them chose (like the Adam brothers) to seek employment in England. In Scotland, even more than in England, cultivated gentry played a large part in the formation of architectural taste, but architects like James Smith and William Adam have their place in the history of the Scottish Enlightenment, and by the reign of George III Robert Adam, Robert Mylne and James Playfair were pre-eminent as neoclassical architects in England as well as in their native country. That they thought of themselves very much as professionals is clear from a letter that the Adam brothers wrote to an English client in the 1770s: 'it is of little consequence to us what the practice is, among professional builders. We are not builders by profession, but Architects and Surveyors, & live by those Branches.'[21]

By the accession of George III, there was in Britain the nucleus of an architectural profession, but the implications of professional status had hardly begun to make themselves felt in the minds of architects themselves, still less in those of their patrons. Most architects supplemented their incomes by building speculations, and were thought none the worse of for doing so;[22] nearly all were prepared to contract for the erection of the buildings which they designed;[23] and some acted in the additional capacity of house- and estate-agents. Moreover, there was still no provision for the academic study of design, no place for the exhibition of drawings and models, no forum in which architects could exchange ideas and enjoy one another's society. A few architects had, it is true, been admitted to artists' clubs, like the *Society of Virtuosi of St. Luke*, which counted William Talman, James Gibbs, Christopher Wren, junior, and William Kent among its members; but the activities of such societies were chiefly convivial and their existence was often brief.[24] The 'Society for the improvement of knowledge in Arts and Sciences' to which Robert Morris read his *Lectures on Architecture* in about 1730 was presumably a more serious affair, but seems to have been equally short-lived. Some architects were Fellows of the Royal Society, and the profession has always been well represented in the Society of Antiquaries, but neither body took more than an indirect interest in architectural matters and none in contemporary architectural practice.

In France architecture was catered for by its own Academy, founded by Colbert in 1671, but in spite of frequent pleas for an artistic academy in this country,[25] it was not until 1768 that the idea came to fruition in the Royal Academy of Arts. The truth is, that in the early eighteenth century England was still too dependent upon foreign artists to justify the creation of a national academy, while the political atmosphere was not favourable to the establishment of an institution so closely associated elsewhere with royal absolutism.[26] It was, characteristically, through the agency of a private but highly aristocratic body that England nearly achieved her academy of the arts in the middle of the century. The *Society of Dilettanti* acquired a site in Cavendish Square for the purpose, and in 1755 entered into negotiations with a committee of artists who submitted a detailed plan for the management of the proposed academy. As no less than six of them were architects,[27] it may be presumed that architecture would have been adequately represented in an academy established under the patronage of the Society which sponsored the publication of the *Antiquities of Athens*. But the project came to nothing, partly (as the younger Matthew Brettingham reported)[28] because of the difficulty of raising money, and partly because the Dilettanti demanded a dominant share in the government of the Academy, which the artists were not prepared to concede.[29]

In 1754 architecture received encouragement from a somewhat different quarter. This was the foundation of the *Society for the Encouragement of Arts, Manufactures, and Commerce*, now known as the Royal Society of Arts.[30] Although its primary concern was the encouragement of industrial art, it also sought to promote the 'polite arts' (which included architecture), on the ground that 'the Art of Drawing is absolutely necessary in many employments, trades and manufactures.' So far as architecture was concerned, it did this chiefly by offering small monetary awards for promising designs by student architects. A considerable number of young men received encouragement in this way, and the 'Register of Premiums' includes the names of Edward Stevens, James Gandon, John Plaw, Robert Baldwin and George Richardson.[31]

The Society also provided wall-space for the first public exhibition of paintings in this country, held in April 1760. It was intended to make this an annual event, and to maintain with the proceeds a fund for old and infirm artists. But as the Society would not permit any charge to be made for admission, and also interfered with the hanging of the pictures, the majority of the artists soon seceded and founded their own Society of Artists (incorporated in 1765), which held exhibitions in a room at Spring Gardens from 1761 onwards. Both the *Incorporated Society of Artists* and the rival *Free Society of Artists* (as those who continued to hold exhibitions with the Society of Arts called themselves) had architects among their members, and both admitted architectural drawings to their exhibitions.[32] Architects were, moreover, prominent in the management of the Incorporated Society, and Chambers and Paine both played a leading part in the internal dissensions which led to its eventual dissolution. Paine was one of those who did his best to keep it in being, while Chambers took the initiative in founding a new body to take its place.[33] This was the Royal Academy of Arts (founded in 1768), which in due course rendered both the older societies redundant, the Free Society holding its last exhibition in 1783, the Incorporated Society in 1791.

The *Royal Academy*, with its royal charter and its rooms in Somerset House alongside the Royal and Antiquarian Societies, represented the first official recognition of the place which native artists and architects had created for themselves in the life of the nation. Five of the thirty-six original Academicians were architects,[34] and the post of Treasurer was given to Sir William Chambers, whose successors in office were, for over a hundred years, to be members of his profession.[35] Architectural drawings were hung at the annual exhibitions, and the designs for almost every building of importance erected during the latter part of the period covered by this book were shown at the Royal Academy.[36] Moreover, the Instrument by which the Academy was established provided for the appointment of a Professor of Architecture, 'who shall read annually six public lectures, calculated to form the taste of the Students, to instruct them in the laws and principles of composition, to point out to them the beauties or faults of celebrated productions, to fit them for an unprejudiced study of books, and for a critical examination of structures'.[37] Although these professorial lectures could hardly be said to create a school of architecture, admission to the 'Royal Academy Schools' was eagerly sought by young men serving their time in an architect's office, and for more than fifty years formed a regular part of almost every architect's education. So far as his seniors were concerned, election as A.R.A. or R.A. was the acknowledged recognition of professional eminence.

But the handful of architect R.A.s was inevitably in a permanent minority in a body composed mainly of painters, and even Sir William Chambers, dominant though he was in its counsels for nearly thirty years, showed no wish to increase their number or in any way to associate the Academy with the interests of the architectural profession as such.[38] It was inevitable, therefore, that the first steps towards a professional association should have come from outside the Academy, though it was not until nearly twenty-five years after its foundation that the leading architects practising in London became sufficiently conscious of their mutual interests to form a society composed exclusively of members of their own profession. *The Architects' Club*, as it was called, was founded in 1791 by James Wyatt, George Dance, Henry Holland and S. P. Cockerell, and met once a month at the Thatched House Tavern in St. James's.[39] Its composition was highly select, for no one could be a member who was not an R.A., A.R.A. or Gold Medallist, or a member of the Academies of Rome, Parma, Florence or Paris.[40] Moreover, a single black ball was sufficient to exclude a candidate from admission.[41] Honorary membership was reserved for those whose place of residence was outside London.[42]

Although primarily a dining club, the Architects' Club was not without a sense of its responsibilities as an association of professional men.[43] In 1792 some of its members met in order 'to define the profession and qualifications of an architect',[44] and in 1796 Mylne laid before it a resolution forbidding one architect from interfering in another's commission.[45] In the previous year it had appointed a committee to go into the question of architects' charges. This was a matter upon which Soane held strong views, and his refusal to accept the majority decision to make a measuring charge of 2½ per cent, in addition to the customary 5 per cent for designs and supervision, led to his estrangement from the other members of the Club.[46] This was by no means the only matter over which the Club was divided, and Soane told Farington early in 1796 that he did not think it would last long, 'the members consisting only of persons who are too much in a state of rivalship and frequently crossing each other'.[47] In fact, it survived for at least thirty years.[48] But little more is heard of its activities, and it is clear that so exclusive a body could never adequately represent the interests of a rapidly growing profession.[49]

It is not surprising, therefore, that attempts were made to establish other associations of a more representative character. The first of these was the *Surveyors' Club*, founded in 1792 by sixteen surveyors who met at the Shakespeare Tavern to discuss 'the propriety of forming a meeting of Surveyors on some general and beneficial principles'. But its objects were chiefly of a social and charitable nature, and only three or four of its twenty-four original members were in practice as architects.[50] The rest were District Surveyors appointed under the Act of 1774, or men of the type described in contemporary directories as 'Surveyor and Builder'.[51] More important for the history of the architectural profession was the *London Architectural Society*, founded in 1806. The reason given for its establishment was that 'among the Institutions so liberally established in this city there is not one calculated for the encouragement of Architecture. The feeble protection afforded by the Royal Academy can hardly be deemed an exception.[52] The lectures have long ceased,[53] and medals privately distributed, and the use of a library for a few hours one day in the week, and at a time when it is hardly possible for the student in architecture to attend . . . cannot be deemed of much value', while the 'few clubs which have been formed by persons in the profession, are rather to enjoy the pleasures of good fellowship among men engaged in the same pursuit, than for the advancement of the art'.[54] The method proposed for the advancement of the art was to require every member to produce annually an original architectural design, under forfeiture of two guineas, and an essay, under forfeiture of half a guinea. The Society met once a fortnight in order to discuss these productions, and anyone who was absent from two successive meetings was fined 5s. The designs and essays were to remain the property of the Society, which undertook to publish such as were considered worthy of the honour. The Society attracted some of the more literary members of the profession, such as Joseph Woods, its president, James Elmes and James Peacock, and it published at least two volumes of its essays.[55] But rules of such severity were hardly calculated to attract a large membership, and the life of the Society was earnest but short.

A somewhat more genial association was the *Architects' and Antiquaries' Club*, which was founded in December 1819 by ten gentlemen who, having observed the value of foreign academies of architecture, 'could not resist the mortifying contrast which was presented, in comparing the state of Architecture in those cities with that of this kingdom'. The society was to consist of twenty members, and there were to be six dinners annually at the Freemason's Tavern. Each member was expected 'occasionally to furnish the Society with an Essay on a Subject of Antient Architecture, or some branch of Antiquity connected with domestic economy or the fine Arts'. The members included Edward Cresy, Joseph Gwilt, Augustus Pugin, J. Sanders (its first president) and G. L. Taylor (his successor). The antiquary John Britton acted as Treasurer and Honorary Secretary, and there were two Honorary and Corresponding Members, John Foster of Liverpool and S. T. Whitwell of Leamington.[56]

But, however, profitable this intercourse between the architects and the amateurs may have been, it was no substitute for a professional association, the lack of which continued to be deplored both by those in practice, who needed its protection against inadequate remuneration and unfair competition, and by their pupils, who compared the meagre ration of instruction which they received at the Royal Academy with the life-classes and other facilities enjoyed by the more favoured students of painting and sculpture.[57] Three figures stand out in this period of uncertainty during which the architectural profession was slowly feeling its way towards that Institute of British Architects which all realized was the ultimate goal: Sir John Soane, who by his personal example set a standard of professional conduct which all respected and some emulated; James Elmes, better known as a writer than as a practising architect, who in either capacity lost no opportunity of impressing the need for association both upon his fellow-architects and upon the general public; and Thomas Leverton Donaldson, the leader of the younger generation, who was to live to become President of the Institute of British Architects, and to hear himself hailed as 'father of his profession' by the Prince of Wales.[58]

It was on Elmes's initiative that the first serious attempt to create a professional organization took place in 1810. A meeting of architects was held in his house, in order to take steps to establish a Royal Academy of Architecture, with a Library and a Museum of Models. Details of the scheme were sent to all the leading architects in London, and favourable replies were received from 'Messrs. Nash, Jeffry and Lewis Wyatt, Ware, Gwilt, Hardwick, Porden, Gandy, Tatham, Bond, Beazley, Lewis and other eminent professors'. Elmes afterwards 'drew it out in the shape of a letter' to Thomas Hope, which he published in *The Pamphleteer*.[59] But, as he afterwards confessed, 'little was done, except in private compliments to me, and one Review which noticed it'.[60]

Much the same happened in 1819 when a fresh series of meetings was held in order to discuss a 'Proposed Institution for the Cultivation and Encouragement of Architecture'. Elmes was appointed secretary, and a number of resolutions were passed which were published in *Annals of the Fine Arts*[61] – a periodical which (under Elmes's editorship) consistently championed the cause of architecture.

There, it would seem, the matter rested until 1831, when a renewed attempt to unite the profession resulted in the formation of the *Architectural Society*, whose ultimate ambition was 'to form a British School of Architecture, affording the advantages of a Library, Museum, Professorships and periodical exhibitions'.[62] It began with a membership of over forty, and attracted some eminent Victorian architects.[63] The Duke of Sussex agreed to become its patron, and in 1835 Sir John Soane signified his approval of its aspirations by the gift of £250.[64] But in spite of all that it did to provide improved facilities for architectural students, the Architectural Society did not satisfy the urgent need for an association which would seek to define the obligations of an architect towards his client, and at the same time to gain for its members a status in business and society comparable to that enjoyed by other professional men. It was with these objects that, in 1834, a committee was formed which included the names of P. F. Robinson (its chairman), T. L. Donaldson (its chief organizer), Charles Fowler, J. Goldicutt, H. E. Kendall, James Savage and James Noble.[65] Its purpose was to draw up a scheme for the formation of an institute 'to uphold the character and improve the attainments of Architects'. The result of its deliberations was a prospectus explaining the need for such an institute, defining its objects, and setting out its proposed constitution. There was to be a 'Library of works of every kind connected with Architecture' and a 'Museum of Antiquities, Models and Casts'; there were to be 'periodical meetings of the members for the purpose of discussion and improvement by lecture, essay, or illustration', and provision was to be made for the instruction of students in 'the various branches of Science connected with Architecture in addition to those attainable in an Architect's Office, and not provided by any existing Institution'. Membership was to be divided into two classes – Fellows, who were to be elected from architects who had been established in practice for not less than five years, and Associates, who were to be admitted by examination.[66]

This prospectus was sent to a number of leading architects, who agreed to become original members, and Sir John Soane, the lifelong advocate of professional standards in architecture and the most distinguished member of his profession, was offered the presidency. This he was obliged to decline owing to a rule prohibiting Royal Academicians from becoming members of any other society of artists, but he indicated his approval of the Institute's programme by a gift of £750. At the same time he presented the sum of £250 already mentioned to the Architectural Society, expressing a hope that the two bodies might before long be united – an event which eventually took place in 1842, largely through the efforts of Sir William Tite.

Meanwhile, Earl de Grey had consented to give the Institute the benefit of his social and political influence, and it was under his presidency that the first meeting was held on 3 June 1835. T. L. Donaldson, now Honorary Secretary, was able to announce that the Institute already counted eighty members, that contacts had been established with several foreign academies, and that the nucleus of a library had been formed. In 1836 the Institute began the publication of its *Transactions*, and in 1837 it received the final recognition of a royal charter of incorporation.[67]

With the foundation of the *Institute of British Architects*, architecture had at last achieved its acknowledged place among the professions, and although much remained to be done – both from within the Institute and from without – to work out all the implications of that status, its attainment marks the end of the process which it has been the object of this Introduction to trace. No Victorian barrister would have dared to question a Fellow of the Institute of British Architects in the terms in which counsel is reported[68] to have addressed himself to Daniel Asher Alexander:

'You are a builder, I believe?'
　'No, sir; I am not a builder; I am an architect.'
　'Ah well, builder or architect, architect or builder – they are pretty much the same, I suppose?'
　'I beg your pardon; they are totally different.'
　'Oh, indeed! Perhaps you will state wherein this difference consists.'
　'An architect, sir, conceives the design, prepares the plan, draws out the specification – in short, supplies the mind. The builder is merely the machine; the architect the power that puts the machine together and sets it going.'
　'Oh, very well, Mr Architect, that will do. A very ingenious distinction with a difference. Do you happen to know who was the architect of the Tower of Babel?'
　'There was no architect, sir. Hence the confusion.'

In fact, the Victorian architect, if he were a man of any ability or enterprise, was well able to make a living without maintaining that connection with the building trade which had been the chief resource of so many of his Georgian predecessors. Churches, prisons, town halls, bridges, warehouses and factories were going up apace in the industrial towns of the Midlands and the north, while country houses and suburban villas continued to provide rich commissions for the domestic architect. The improvement in communications meant that the new professional architect, while retaining his London office, could personally supervise the erection of half a dozen buildings at once, in a way that had been quite impossible for his eighteenth-century predecessor, who supplied a plan and elevation, answered queries by letter, and relied on the experience and discretion of his master craftsmen to give satisfaction to his client and observe the established rules of sound building. The Industrial Revolution, which provided the professional architect with so many new opportunities, also provided him with the means to exploit them, and his triumph came in the 1840s and 1850s with the railways, which enabled a Gilbert Scott to rebuild half the parish churches of England in accordance with his own conception of Gothic architecture, and finally destroyed the autonomy of the local builder.

With the fruits of these developments this Introduction is not concerned, for they are part of the history of Victorian architecture, and as such lie outside the chronological scope of this book. Most of the men whose biographies it contains saw England from the road, not from the rail, and there were few of them who had no connection with the building trade in one or other of its forms, from the Smiths of Warwick, who were builders first and architects last, to Sir Jeffry Wyatville, the 'honourable augmentation' of whose name did not conceal the fact that he was descended from a typical eighteenth-century building family, or that he himself was 'taken into a profitable partnership by John Armstrong, a large builder of Pimlico'.[69] Sir William Chambers was the contractor for, as well as the architect of, the houses which he built at Peper Harow and Roehampton, and most architects of his generation were prepared to submit an estimate upon which they obtained advances of money, making contracts with the tradesmen, and not infrequently taking a discount or percentage from them in addition to whatever remuneration they obtained from their employer.[70] But this was a very different matter from the earlier identity of builder and designer which had survived from the Middle Ages. It opened the way for dishonesty and shoddy building, and it made Sir John Soane's definition of an architect's duties, uncompromising in its rejection of the past, the only possible basis upon which the new profession was to achieve the respect of the public:

> The business of the Architect is to make the designs and estimates, to direct the works, and to measure and value the different parts; he is the intermediate agent between the employer, whose honour and interest he is to study, and the mechanic, whose rights he is to defend. His position implies great trust; he is responsible for the mistakes, negligences, and ignorance of those he employs; and above all, he is to take care that the workmen's bills do not exceed his own estimates. If these are the duties of an Architect, with what propriety can his situation, and that of the builder or the contractor, be united?

When this was first published in 1788[71] Soane's was a voice crying in the wilderness, but by 1835, when it was reprinted in his memoirs, he was preaching to the converted. Jeffry Wyatville had found to his mortification that, despite his extensive practice, he was allowed to remain a candidate for admission to membership of the Royal Academy for twenty years, because the 'union of the tradesman with the architect was deemed, by the Royal Academicians, a sufficient bar to the advancement of Mr. Jeffry Wyatt to be one of their society'.[72] When the founders of the Institute of British Architects drew up their prospectus, they had no hesitation in decreeing that divorce between Architecture and Building which subsequent practice made absolute. No architect was to be eligible for membership who received 'any pecuniary consideration, or emolument, from Tradesmen, or who had any interest or participation in any Trade or Contract connected with Building'. Henceforth no architect would be able to supplement his income by speculative building, nor even by measuring and valuing works on behalf of builders. But whatever he may have lost in financial opportunity, he gained in social status and respectability: for henceforth he would rank as a gentleman, a scholar and an artist, clearly distinguished from the 'mechanic' who called himself a builder. For his client the gain was equally great: for now he could entrust his architectural affairs to his architect with the same confidence with which previously he had been accustomed to place his legal affairs in the hands of his lawyer. No longer would he be subjected to the confusion, the expense, above all the exasperation, which (as anyone who is familiar with the minutes of eighteenth-century building committees will know) so often resulted from the haphazard methods and ill-defined responsibilities of the time when the architectural profession was still in the making.

[. . .]

Sample biographical essay

ADAM, ROBERT (1728–1792) was born as Kirkcaldy in Fife on 3 July 1728. He was the second surviving son of William Adam (*q.v.* architect, builder and entrepreneur). In Edinburgh, where he attended the High School, and in 1743 matriculated at the University, Robert met some of the leading figures in Scottish intellectual life, among them William Robertson, the historian (who was his cousin), Adam Smith, the political economist (himself a native of Kirkcaldy), David Hume, the philosopher, and Adam Ferguson, another philosopher who was to become his 'particular friend'. In 1745 or 1746 he left the University prematurely in order to join his father's drawing-office at a time when it was under serious strain. When William Adam died in 1748, Robert and his elder brother John entered into partnership in order to carry on their father's business as an architect and contractor. So lucrative was this that by 1754 Robert had a capital of £5000 – more than enough to enable him to embark on that extended Grand Tour from which he hoped to return with fresh architectural ideas derived from a systematic study of the principal monuments of antiquity.

Robert left Edinburgh in October 1754. In Brussels he joined his travelling-companion the Hon. Charles Hope (younger brother of the Earl of Hopetoun, for whom John Adam was then completing Hopetoun House), whose friendship would automatically give him the entrée to aristocratic society wherever they went. In Florence he persuaded the French architectural designer Clérisseau to join him, thus acquiring the services of a brilliant draughtsman with a strong interest in the neo-classical. He reached Rome in February 1755. There, under Clérisseau's guidance, he studied drawing the antiquity assiduously, acquiring the knowledge and expertise that would enable him to set up in practice as a fashionable architect. Among his Italian acquaintances was another pioneer of neoclassical taste, G. B. Piranesi, who later dedicated his account of the Campus Martius to *Roberto Adam Britann, Architecto Celeberrim*. In the summer of 1757 he set sail from Venice with Clérisseau and two other draughtsmen in order to explore and measure the ruins of the great late Roman palace of Diocletian at Split in Dalmatia. Owing to the difficulties raised by the Venetian governor, it was clear that a prolonged stay was out of the question, and it was only by 'unwearied application' that the task was completed within the space of five weeks. The result was the publication in 1764 of the *Ruins of the Palace of the Emperor Diocletian at Spalatro*, a magnificent volume sumptuously engraved by Bartolozzi and others.

Robert Adam returned to England by way of the Rhineland during the winter of 1757–8, arriving in London in January. He established himself in a house in Lower Grosvenor Street, where he was soon joined by his two sisters and his brothers James and William. The decision to set up practice in London had already been taken while Robert was in Italy, 'Scotland', he wrote in 1755, 'is but a narrow place. [I need] a greater, a more extensive and more honourable scene, I mean an English life.' It was with the object of equipping himself for English practice that, according to his own reckoning, he had spent between £800 and £900 a year in Italy, and the time had now come to realize his ambition to become the leading architect, not merely in Scotland, but in England as well. Henceforth he was to be the principal director of the family firm.[73] There can be no doubt that it was he who made it famous by his brilliance as a designer and his enormous capacity for work: but the less spectacular abilities of James and the business acumen of William also contributed to its success, while John Adam provided capital from his estate at Blair Adam. In addition to these private resources, Robert Adam could count on support from his fellow-countrymen in London, including the Duke of Argyll and Lord Bute, George III's first minister, who, although unfriendly at first, in 1761 procured for Adam one of the two newly created posts of Architect of the King's Works, with a salary of £300 p.a. The other went to Sir William Chambers, the king's architectural mentor and Adam's principal rival. Adam was already a member of the Society of Arts, to which he had been elected immediately after his return from Italy, and in 1761 he became a Fellow of the Royal Society. Thus established in practice, Adam set out to revolutionize English domestic architecture, which for thirty years had followed the pattern laid down for it by Lord Burlington. In place of the strict grammar of the orders as described by Vitruvius and interpreted by Palladio, he substituted a new and elegant repertoire of architectural ornament based on a wide variety of classical sources ranging from antiquity to the Cinquecento. The success of the new style was immediate, and within a very few years it had taken the place of the prevailing Palladianism and become the common property of the London builder. Among architects, only Sir William Chambers remained resolute in his refusal to have anything to do with Adam's 'affectations', and there can be no doubt that it was owing to his disapproval that Robert Adam never became a Royal Academician. Adam, for his part, ignored the Academy, sending none of his designs for exhibition at Somerset House. He did not, however, lack advertisement, for his publication of the *Ruins at Spalatro* was a claim to the archaeological scholarship that was now one of the credentials of a serious neo-classical architect, and in 1773 there appeared the first elegantly engraved volume of the *Works in Architecture of Robert and James Adam*.[74] The second volume followed in 1779, the third posthumously in 1822. By 1773 the Adam manner had already been successfully imitated by others, and the preface to the first volume was intended to assert the brothers' claim 'to have brought about . . . a kind of revolution in the whole system' of English architecture. In particular, they claimed to have brought back the principle of 'movement', which (in their own words) 'is meant to express the rise and fall, the advance and recess with other diversity of form, in the different parts of a building, so as to add greatly to the picturesque of the composition'. This quality they recognized and admired in the works of Sir John Vanbrugh, though at the same time deploring the 'barbarisms and absurdities' which made his bold designs so different from their own refined and polished compositions. The picturesque approach to architectural design revealed by this passage is illustrated by the romantic landscape compositions, of which Robert Adam left a large number executed in pen and was, and even more by the dramatic massing of such castellated mansions as Seton and Culzean Castles, whose picturesque yet always symmetrical grouping, assisted by a minimum of Gothic detail, was to be imitated by a whole generation of Scottish countryhouse architects: but it is also apparent in more orthodox buildings such as Gosford House or Edinburgh University. Here the architectural vocabulary remains strictly classical but effects of surprise or movement are achieved that in other hands or at other periods might be classed as baroque.

It was, however, in interior design that the Adam revolution made its greatest impact. Here ingenious and imaginative planning ensured a progression of varied and interesting shapes in place of the simple rectangular rooms of earlier Georgian architecture, and walls, ceilings, chimneypieces, carpets and furniture – down even to details like door-knobs and candlesticks – were designed as part of an elegant, varied and highly sophisticated decorative scheme incorporating neoclassical and Renaissance motifs such as griffins, sphinxes, altars, urns and putti. Plasterwork, often embellished with panels painted by artists such as Cipriani, Zucchi and Rebecca played a large part in every Adam interior. Joseph Rose (1745–99) wasthe plasterer who gave actuality to many of Adam's designs with unfailing technial skill.

The immense output of the Adam office was made possible only by the employment of a number of highly skilled draughtsmen. Of these the most important were the Scottish George Richardson (*q.v.*), the Liègois Laurent-Benoit Dewez (1731–1812, subsequently the leading Belgian architect), and the Italians Agostino Brunias, Joseph Bonomi, Giuseppe Manocchi and Antonio Zucchi. Manocchi (*q.v.*), who returned to Italy in 1773, considered that he had been badly treated by the Adams, but in the introduction to his *Book of Ceilings* (1776) George Richardson spoke with gratitude of the eighteen years he had spent as an assistant in the Adam office.

Although for nearly thirty years Robert Adam was one of the two or three busiest architects in England, he was given few opportunities for monumental design on a large scale. By the time of his return from Italy, the great country mansions which reflected the ascendancy of the Whig aristocracy had already been built, and in many cases it was left to him only to remodel their interiors in accordance with modern taste. Too rarely was he permitted to design an important house from the foundation up, and it was not until the end of his life that major public commissions were entrusted to him as Cambridge and Edinburgh Universities. The former, however, came to nothing, while the latter, unfinished at the time of his death, was subsequently completed in a very different way from what its architect had intended. Only the Register House remains as the nearest approach to a monumental building in the list of Adam's works.

It is to 'the desire to raise a great building of a semi-public nature in the monumental manner' that the Adelphi scheme is, in part at least, to be attributed. In 1768 the brothers took a ninety-nine-year lease of an extensive area on the north bank of the river Thames, upon which they proposed to erect twenty-four first-rate houses, treated as a single architectural composition and raised on a terrace whose vaulted interior was intended to be let as warehouses. As a development it was admirable, but as a speculation it was unprecedented, and in June 1772 work was halted by a national credit crisis. On 27 June David Hume wrote to Adam Smith:

> Of all the sufferers I am most concern'd for the Adams. . . . But their undertakings were so vast that nothing cou'd support them; they must dismiss 3000 workmen, who, comprehending the materials must have expended above 100,000 a year. They have great funds; but if these must be dispos'd of, in a hurry and to disadvantage, I am afraid the remainder will amount to little or nothing. . . . To me, the scheme of the Adelphi always appeared so imprudent, that my wonder is, how they cou'd have gone on so long.

Having failed to raise sufficient funds by a loan raised on the security of the Blair Adam estate, and by the sale of many of the works of art that they had brought back from Italy,[75] the brothers retrieved themselves from the financial disaster by disposing of the whole property by means of a lottery (1774). Meanwhile in 1773 they had become involved (though not as principals) in another great town-planning venture in Marylebone, where they proposed to build a series of detached private palaces on either side of Portland Place. This time the outbreak of the War of American Independence led to the abandonment of the project in its original form, and blocks of houses took the place of the independent mansions originally proposed. The façades were designed by James Adam, but each house was built as an independent speculation.

A prominent feature of the Portland Place houses was the use of stucco for the central features on either side. Having acquired the patents in two stucco compositions – one invented by a Mr. David Wark of Haddington, the other by a Swiss clergyman named Liardet – the brothers obtained in 1776 an Act of Parliament vesting in the patentees the exclusive right to manufacture what they called 'Adam's new invented patent stucco'. A rival composition was put on the market by John Johnson (*q.v.*), who maintained that it was based on a stucco invented before either Wark or Liardet had come on the scene. The Adams, however, claimed that Johnson had infringed their patent, and went to law (1778). The case was heard before Lord Chief Justice Mansfield, who, as a client and fellow-countryman of the plaintiffs, laid himself open to the charge of partiality when he gave judgement in favour of the Messrs. Adam. The case attracted considerable publicity, and was the subject of two pamphlets.

From about 1760 to 1780 Robert Adam was the most fashionable architect in Britain, but in the 1780s he began to be eclipsed by James Wyatt, and during the last ten years of his life his practice was almost confined to his native Scotland, where Wyatt found no patrons. Here he developed the picturesque castle style – an indeterminate synthesis of Gothic and classical forms – which was characteristic of his later domestic work, and which may be seen as his answer to Wyatt's success as a Gothic designer.

Robert Adam died suddenly on 3 March 1792, and was buried in the south transept of Westminster Abbey. The funeral was 'private', but the pall-bearers were the Duke of Buccleuch, the Earl of Coventry, the Earl of Lauderdale, Viscount Stormont, Lord Frederick Campbell and William Putleney of Westerhall. The only official position which Adam held at the time of his death was the surveyorship of Chelsea Hospital, to which he had been appointed in 1765. He had relinquished the post of Architect of the King's Works in 1769, when he entered parliament as M.P. for Kinross-shire. The death of his brother James in 1794 meant the end of the firm, though William Adam survived to submit designs for the completion of Edinburgh University in 1815. He died in 1822 at the age of 54. He had gone bankrupt in 1801, and in 1815 and 1821 sold all his brothers' pictures, furniture, antiques and other possessions.[76]

In 1833 the bulk of the architectural drawings made by Robert and James Adam, nearly 9000 in number, were purchased from the family by Sir John Soane, and now form one of the principal treasures of the Museum which bears his name. Other drawings are in the collections of the Victoria and Albert Museum, the National Gallery of Scotland and the R.I.B.A., while some remain at Blair Adam and Penicuik houses in Scotland. For those in American collections see John Harris, *A Catalogue of British Drawings for Architecture . . . in American Collections*, 1791. In was apparently in the last years of Robert's life that drawings were made in the Adams' Edinburgh office for a volume of engraved designs for classical villas and castle-style houses. This was never completed, but formed the basis of Alistair Rowan's *Designs for Castles and Country Villas by Robert and James Adam* (Phaidon 1985).

The only certainly authentic portraits of Robert Adam are an ivory plaque at Blair Adam and the portrait in the National Portrait Gallery in London, formerly attributed to Zoffany and now to David Martin. Three medallions in paste-relief by James Tassie are in the Scottish National Portrait Gallery, but two at least are posthumous.

[*Gent's Mag.* 1792 (i), 282–3; John Swarbrick, *Robert Adam and his Brothers: their Lives, Work and Influence on English Architecture*, 1915; A. T. Bolton, 'Robert Adam as a Bibliographer, Publisher and Designer of Libraries', *Trans. Bibliographical Soc.* xiv, 1915–17; A.T. Bolton, *The Architecture of Robert and James Adam*, 2 vols., 1922, with detailed index to the drawings in Sir John Soane's Museum; J. Steegman & C. K. Adams, 'The Iconography of Robert Adam', *Arch. Rev.* xci, 1942; J. Lees-Milne, *The Age of Adam*, 1947; John Fleming, *Robert Adam and his Circle*, 1962: Eileen Harris, *The Furniture of Robert Adam*, 1963; Namier & Brooke, *The House of Commons 1754–1790* ii, 1964, 7–8; Damie Stillman, *The Decorative Work of Robert Adam*, 1966; Clifford Musgrave, *Adam and Hepplewhite Furniture*, 1966; Damie Stillman, 'Robert Adam and Piranesi', *Essays in the History of Architecture presented to Rudolf Wittkower*, ed. D. Fraser, 1967; John Fleming, 'Robert Adam's Castle Style', *C. Life*, 23–30 May, 1968; John Fleming, 'A retrospective View by John Clerk of Eldin, with some comments on Adam's Castle Style', in *Concerning Architecture*, ed. J. Summerston, 1968; Alistair Rowan. 'After the Adelphi: Forgotten years in the Adam brothers' practice', *Journal of the Royal Society of Arts* cxxii, 1974, 659–710; James Macaulay, *The Gothic Revival*, 1975, chap. vi ('Robert Adam's Northern Castles'); A. A. Tait, 'The Sale of Robert Adam's Drawings', *Burlington Mag.*]

[. . .]

Sample biographical essay

BURTON, DECIMUS (1800–1881), was the tenth son of James Burton *(q.v.)*. He was educated at Tonbridge School and received practical training in his father's office. According to a note left by his father, he 'left school in September 1816 and became my assistant in the office'. At the same time he was being taught architectural draughtsmanship by George Maddox, and in 1817 he began to attend the Royal Academy Schools under the professorship of Sir John Soane. He was evidently a precocious pupil, for as early as 1817–18 he appears to have assisted his father to design the latter's villa in Regent's Park, and in 1818–19 he designed South Villa for a private client. Soon afterwards he was allowed by Nash to design Cornwall (1821) and Clarence (1823) Terraces in Regent's Park, of which his father was the builder. He started independent practice in April 1823, 'and found himself, before he had completed his 24th year, in the full tide of professional work'. One of his earliest clients was G. B. Greenough, MP and founder of the Geological Society, for whom he designed another villa in Regent's Park. The wealthy and influential Greenough was to be responsible for bringing him several commissions in later years.

Burton's first public building was the Colosseum in Regent's Park (1823–7). 'A Greek version of the Pantheon', with a dome slightly larger than that of St. Paul's, this was regarded as a remarkable achievement for a young man of 23, and he soon obtained important commissions in the Royal Parks from the Office of Woods and Forests. These included the Hyde Park screen and the arch on Constitution Hill. It was through Greenough that Burton was commissioned to design the Athenaeum Club, of which he was an early member, and where he was to meet many of his future clients. He enjoyed great success both as a designer of villas and small country houses and as a town planner specializing in the kind of picturesque layout of which Regent's Park had been the prototype. Of this the Calverley Estate at Tunbridge Wells was a particularly attractive example. He also had a considerable reputation as an expert in the construction of glass and iron conservatories, of which he designed notable examples at Chatsworth, Regent's Park and Kew.

Although he may be classed as a Greek Revivalist, Burton was by no means an archaeological purist. His knowledge of the principal antique monuments was based on the published works of others rather than on personal investigation and discovery. His use of the orders is always correct, but he showed a lack of pedantry in their application that sets him apart from some of his more doctrinaire contemporaries, such as Hamilton and Smirke. From Nash he had learned to combine the classical and the picturesque, and it is the picturesque that is predominant in much of his later work. For the Gothic Revival he felt no enthusiasm. He did, it is true, design some houses with pointed windows and turrets, and even some Gothic churches, but his lack of sympathy for the style is apparent enough in the arid interiors and coarse detailing of the churches, which are among the least attractive of their period.

Burton travelled extensively both in Europe and in North America. Details of his tours are lacking, but he is known to have visited France and Spain in 1826, Holland in 1846 and Germany in 1850. He was a Fellow of the Royal Society, of the Society of Antiquaries and of the RIBA, of which he was at one time Vice-President, and a member of several other learned societies. He retired in 1869, and lived partly at St. Leonard's, where he had built himself a small house (The Cottage, Maze Hill), and partly in London (1, Gloucester Houses, Hyde Park), where he died unmarried on 14 December 1881. His practice was continued by his nephew Henry Marley Burton (1813–80). John Crake, Henry Currey, George Mair, A. W. Hakewill and George Williams were his pupils. E. J. May (d. 1941) joined his office shortly before he retired. A portrait in oils attributed to Sir William Beechey is known only from a photograph. A photographic portrait taken in 1873 is preserved at the Athenaeum Club and was used as the basis of an engraving in *Illustrated London News* lxxix, 1881, 650. A number of Burton's drawings are in the Victoria and Albert Museum (C. J. Richardson Collection), and there are others in the Hastings Museum, the RIBA Drawings Collection and the Architectural Association's Library.

[Obituaries in *Builder* xli, 1881, 779, and *Jnl. Royal Society* xxxiv, 1882–3, viii–ix; *DNB*; R. P. Jones, 'The Life and Works of Decimus Burton', *Arch. Rev.* xvii, 1905; Philip Miller, *Decimus Burton*, Exhibition Catalogue 1981; information from Mr. Neil Cooke.]

Notes

1 *A.P.S.D., s.v.* 'ARCHITECT'.

2 D. Knoop & G. P. Jones, *The Mediaeval Mason*, 1933, p. 197.

3 N. Pevsner, 'The Term Architect in the Middle Ages', *Speculum* xvii, 1942, pp. 549–62.

4 See P. Frankl, 'The Secret of the Mediaeval Masons', *Art Bulletin* xxvii, 1945, and Lon R. Shelby, 'The Geometrical Knowledge of Mediaeval Master Masons', *Speculum* xlvii, 1972.

5 Mark Girouard, *Robert Smythson and the Architecture of the Elizabethan Era*, 1966, pp. 22–3. See also E. Mercer, *English Art 1553–1625*, 1962, pp. 53–9.

6 D. Knoop & G. P. Jones, 'The Rise of the Mason Contractor', *R.I.B.A. Jnl.* xliii, 1936.

7 E.g. Peter Mills and the sons of Nicholas Stone.

8 As Sir James Pytts had done in 1618 when he lent his mason 'one booke of Architecture . . . which he hath promised to redeliver unto me' ('The Building of the Manor-House of Kyre Park, Worcestershire', in *The Antiquary* xxii, 1890, p. 53), and as Sir Roger Townshend did in 1620 when he took his master mason abroad before setting him to build Raynham Hall (below, p. 330).

9 *The Architecture of Sir Roger Pratt*, ed. R. T. Gunther, 1928, p. 60.

10 His early connection with Lely at least suggests such a possibility: see p. 647.

11 R. Campbell, in his *London Tradesman* (1747), says of architects that 'I scarce know of any in England who have had an Education regularly designed for the Profession.'

12 *Of Building* (B.L., Add. MS. 32540), f. 23.

13 See Appendix C.

14 Thus James Elmes observes that Chambers 'educated no pupils – that is to say, as the word is now understood . . . His only followers or pupils were bred in the office of the Board of Works, in which he held the situation of surveyor-general' ('History of Architecture in Great Britain', in *Civil Engineer and Architect's Jnl.* x, 1847, p. 300).

15 *The London Tradesman*, 1747, p. 157.

16 Walpole Society, *Vertue Note Books* iii, pp. 146, 150.

17 Hardwick's 'Memoir of Sir William Chambers', prefaced to Gwilt's edition of *A Treatise on the Decorative Part of Civil Architecture*, 1825.

18 See the terms of apprenticeship to Sir John Soane, given by A. T. Bolton, *Architectural Education a Century Ago* (Soane Museum Publication No. 12): see also R.I.B.A. *Sessional Papers*, 1855–6, p. 1, for Sir William Tite's statement that a six years' apprenticeship was normal in the early nineteenth century.

19 For a list of the gold medallists, see J. E. Hodgson & F. A. Eaton, *History of the Royal Academy*, 1905, Appendix VII. A travelling studentship was also offered, but as it was tenable for several years, and awarded alternately from those attending the Schools of Painting, Sculpture and Architecture, the chances of obtaining it were small. The architects who held it during the period 1769–1840 were John Soane (1777), George Hadfield (1790), Lewis Vulliamy (1818), Samuel Loat (1828) and John Johnson (1837).

20 Sir Robert Smirke's estate was valued for probate at £90,000. Barry and Blore both left £80,000, Decimus Burton and Lewis Vulliamy £60,000, Burn £40,000 and C. R. Cockerell £35,000.

21 H. Colvin, 'The beginnings of the architectural profession in Scotland', 1986.

22 Wren's Bridgewater Square, Barbican, Paine's Salisbury Street, Strand, Holland's Hans Town, Chelsea, and the Adams' Adelphi Buildings are major examples of speculative building by architects.

23 'The Architect either undertakes the whole work for a certain Sum, or is paid for super-intending the work only' (R. Campbell, *The London Tradesman*, 1747, p. 155).

24 Whitley, *Artists and Their Friends in England, 1700–1799* i, 1928, pp. 68–70, 74–7; ii, pp. 241–4.

25 Cf. Stephen Switzer, *The Nobleman, Gentleman and Gardener's Recreation*, 1715, p. 237; George Vertue, *Note Books* (Walpole Society) ii, pp. 150–5; iii, p. 74; John Gwynn, *An Essay on Design including Proposals for Erecting a Public Academy to be supplied by Voluntary Subscription (until a Royal Foundation can be obtain'd) for Educating British Youth in Drawing*, 1749; Nesbitt, *Essay on the Necessity of a Royal Academy*, 1755. Matthew Brettingham junior's scheme for a British Academy is outlined in a letter, dated 27 May 1753, in Holkham MS. 744, ff. 136–9.

26 N. Pevsner, *Academies of Art*, 1940, p. 126.

27 John Gwynn, Robert Taylor, James Stuart, Isaac Ware, Nicholas Revett and Thomas Sandby.

28 Holkham MS. 744, f. 136.

29 Whitley, *Artists and Their Friends* i, pp. 157–8; L. Cust, *History of the Society of Dilettanti*, ed. Colvin, 1898, pp. 53–5.

30 H. T. Wood, *A History of the Royal Society of Arts*, 1913. Its early members included George Dance, senior, Robert Mylne, James Paine, Sir William Chambers and the three Adam brothers.

31 See the *Register of Premiums* awarded between 1754 and 1776, printed in 1778.

32 See A. Graves, *The Society of Artists of Great Britain and the Free Society of Artists*, 1907, and Horace Walpole's notes printed by H. Gatty in *Walpole Society* xxvii, 1938–9.

33 Whitley, *Artists and their Friends in England* i, 1928, p. 248, where the degree of personal rivalry between Chambers and Paine is, however, greatly exaggerated.

34 Sir William Chambers, John Gwynn, Thomas Sandby, W. Tyler and George Dance, junior.

35 His immediate successors were John Yenn (1796–1820), Sir Robert Smirke (1820–50), Philip Hardwick (1850–61) and Sydney Smirke (1861–74).

36 See A. Graves, *The Royal Academy of Arts, 1769–1804*, 8 vols., 1907.

37 For holders of the Professorship, see Appendix C.

38 Cf. Dr. H. M. Martienssen's unpublished London Ph.D. thesis on *The Architectural Theory and Practice of Sir William Chambers*, 1949, pp. 143–6.

39 The original members, in addition to the four

founders, were Sir William Chambers, Robert Adam, Robert Mylne, Richard Jupp, James Lewis, Richard Norris, John Soane, John Yenn, Thomas Hardwick, Robert Brettingham and James Paine, junior (T. Mulvany, *Life of James Gandon*, 1846, pp. 295–7).

40 The insistence upon foreign travel was abandoned in 1803 owing to the Napoleonic War (*The Farington Diary*, ed. J. Greig, ii, p. 123).

41 George Hadfield, a Gold Medallist of the Royal Academy, was so excluded in 1795, much to the annoyance of James Wyatt, who was one of his proposers (*The Farington Diary*, ed. J. Greig, i, p. 85).

42 John Carr, Nicholas Revett and Thomas Sandby were the first Honorary Members. James Gandon was elected in Dec. 1791.

43 W. L. Spiers, 'The Architects' Club', *R.I.B.A. Jnl.*, 3rd ser., xviii, 1911, p. 240.

44 A. T. Bolton, *Portrait of Sir John Soane*, p. 67.

45 Barrington Kaye, *The Development of the Architectural Profession in Britain*, 1960, p. 59.

46 A. T. Bolton, *Portrait of Sir John Soane*, pp. 76–7. A skit by Soane on the members of the Club and their pretensions is preserved in MS. in the Soane Museum (Envelope F. Div. 14, No. 40). It is in the form of a dialogue between a representative of the Club and a candidate for membership.

47 *The Farington Diary*, ed. J. Greig, i, p. 137.

48 See the lists of members published in the *British Imperial Kalendar* between 1812 and 1824.

49 In 1834 its members were invited to participate in the foundation of an architectural institute, but declined 'altering the character or extending the views of the club' (*A Plain Statement of Facts connected with the Coalition between the Society for the Promotion of Architecture and Architectural Topography and the Society of British Architects*, 1834, p. 11).

50 E.g. William Purser, Edward Mawley and Peter Upsdell. Other members were James Burton, the builder, and Henry Hurle, a carpenter who founded the 'Ancient Order of Druids'.

51 I am indebted to the officers of the Surveyors' Club for their courtesy in allowing me to examine its records.

52 The Academy's attitude towards its architectural responsibilities is strongly criticized in *The Library of the Fine Arts* iv, 1832, pp. 213–19; see also John Britton's complaint in *Portrait of Sir John Soane*, p. 317.

53 Dance, who held the Chair of Architecture

from 1798 to 1805, delivered no lectures.

54 From the preface to *Essays of the London Architectural Society*, 1808.

55 For some account of the Society, see *The Builder* xxi, 1863, pp. 86, 112–13, 140. Other members were James Savage (vice-president), C. A. Busby (secretary), Edmund Aikin, W. H. Ashpitel, Samuel Beazley, J. G. Bubb, the sculptor, Coade, the artificial stone manufacturer, and Josiah Taylor, the architectural publisher.

56 Records of the Society are preserved in the Bodleian Library, Gough Adds. London 8° 405.

57 See an article 'On the Condition of the Architectural Students in the Royal Academy of London compared with those of other Nations' in *Annals of the Fine Arts* ii, 1817, p. 19, and cf. *Monthly Magazine*, July 1809.

58 Donaldson was the founder of the *Architectural Students' Society*, whose members were in the habit of meeting together 'to make a design or a sketch from a given subject, or to discuss a paper'. In 1817, as a young man of 26, he organized a meeting of architectural students in Pall Mall to petition the Royal Academy 'to form a School of Architecture and allow them a further extension of the use of their Library'. The Academicians received this demonstration 'in good part', and agreed to open the Library twice a week in term-time instead of only once. But nothing was done to meet the more important demand that Architecture should be placed on the same footing as Sculpture and Painting in the Royal Academy Schools. (*Annals of the Fine Arts* ii, 1817, pp. 124, 258, 340; *The Farington Diary*, ed. J. Greig, viii, pp. 114, 115; R.I.B.A. *Sessional Papers*, 1855–6, p. 2; R.I.B.A. Library, Pam. Q.11, No. 2.)

59 'A Letter to Thomas Hope Esq. on the insufficiency of the existing establishments for promoting the Fine Arts towards that of Architecture and its Professors', *The Pamphleteer* iii, 1814, p. 330.

60 *Annals of the Fine Arts* ii, 1817, pp. 261–2.

61 Vol. iv, 1819, pp. 348–51.

62 A copy of its printed *Laws and Regulations* is in Sir John Soane's Museum. Its first president was W. B. Clarke, and the members of the committee were T. H. Wyatt, Benjamin Ferrey, A. W. and J. H. Hakewill, T. M. Nelson, Thomas Walker, George Moore and George Mair. Reports of its meetings were published in Loudon's *Architectural Magazine* and in the *Gent's Mag*.

63 Including David Brandon, G. E. Street, Ewan Christian and Sir William Tite (President, 1838–42).

64 A. T. Bolton, *Portrait of Sir John Soane*, 514.

65 Author of a work on *The Professional Practice of Architects*, 1836.

66 The prospectus is printed by Bolton, *Portrait of Sir John Soane*, pp. 509–12. See also the 'Address and Regulations of the Institute of British Architects, explanatory of their Views and Objects', printed in the *Architectural Magazine* ii, 1835, pp. 305–6.

67 It was not, however, until 1866 that the Institute was officially authorized to add the epithet 'Royal' to its title. The Royal Gold Medal had been instituted by Queen Victoria in 1848. For the Institute's subsequent history see *The Growth and Work of the R.I.B.A 1834–1934*, ed. J. A. Gotch, 1934. An *Institute of the Architects of Scotland* was founded in 1840 under the presidency of the 5th Duke of Buccleuch, but collapsed almost immediately owing to a dispute over the eligibility for membership of David Bryce, who was not yet in independent practice. It was refounded in 1850 as the *Architectural Institute of Scotland*, again the Duke of Buccleuch as President.

68 *Builder* xx, p. 795. The interrogator is said to have been Sir James Scarlett (1769–1844), and the case was probably that of Chapman, Gardiner and Upward *v.* De Tastet (1817), reported in *Annals of the Fine Arts* iii, 1818, pp. 560–65, in which Scarlett appeared for the defendant.

69 *D.N.B.*

70 *A.P.S.D., s.v.,* 'ARCHITECT' and 'CONTRACTOR'. Such practices were denounced in vain by Robert Morris in *The Qualifications and Duty of a Surveyor, explained in a Letter to the Rt. Hon. the Earl of* ——, 1752, and in *A Second Letter to the Rt. Hon. the Earl of* —— *concerning the Qualifications and Duty of a Surveyor*, 1752. See also the anonymous article 'On the Present State of the Professions of Architect, Surveyor, and of the Building Trade in England' in Loudon's *Architectural Magazine* i, 1834, pp. 12–16.

71 In his *Plans, Elevations and Sections of Buildings executed in several Counties*, p. 7.

72 *Gent's Mag.* xiii, 1840, p. 546.

73 For the firm of 'William Adam & Co.' set up in 1764 see Alistair Rowan in *Journal of the Royal Society of Arts* cxxii, 1974, pp. 659–78. It was a firm of developers and builders' merchants whose operations included the building of the Adelphi, the management of brickworks in London and Essex, and the quarrying of Aberdeen granite. Despite numerous financial vicissitudes it remained in business until 1801. Robert and James Adam kept a separate account for the profits of their joint architectural practice.

74 There are reprints by Thezard 1902, by Tiranti 1939 and 1959, by Academy Editions 1975, and by Dover Publications 1980. In 1821 a small quarto volume was published by Priestley and Weale entitled *Designs for Vases and Foliage, composed from the Antique*, by Robert Adam, consisting of fourteen engravings without any letterpress.

75 They were sold at Christie's 25–27 Feb. and 1–2 March 1773.

76 The catalogue of the 1818 sale is printed in *Sale Catalogues of Libraries of Eminent Persons* iv, ed. Watkin, 1972, pp. 135–92.

What is an author?

Michel Foucault

The coming into being of the notion of 'author' constitutes the privileged moment of *individualization* in the history of ideas, knowledge, literature, philosophy, and the sciences. Even today, when we reconstruct the history of a concept, literary genre, or school of philosophy, such categories seem relatively weak, secondary, and superimposed scansions in comparison with the solid and fundamental unit of the author and the work.

I shall not offer here a sociohistorical analysis of the author's persona. Certainly it would be worth examining how the author became individualized in a culture like ours, what status he has been given, at what moment studies of authenticity and attribution began, in what kind of system of valorization the author was involved, at what point we began to recount the lives of authors rather than of heroes, and how this fundamental category of 'the-man-and-his-work criticism' began. For the moment, however, I want to deal solely with the relationship between text and author and with the manner in which the text points to this 'figure' that, at least in appearance, is outside it and antecedes it.

Beckett nicely formulates the theme with which I would like to begin: '"What does it matter who is speaking," someone said, "what does it matter who is speaking."' In this indifference appears one of the fundamental ethical principles of contemporary writing (*écriture*). I say 'ethical' because this indifference is not really a trait characterizing the manner in which one speaks and writes, but rather a kind of immanent rule, taken up over and over again, never fully applied, not designating writing as something completed, by dominating it as a practice. Since it is too familiar to require a lengthy analysis, this immanent rule can be adequately illustrated here by tracing two of its major themes.

First of all, we can say that today's writing has freed itself from the dimension of expression. Referring only to itself, but without being restricted to the confines of its interiority, writing is identified with its own unfolded exteriority. This means that it is an interplay of signs arranged less according to its signified content than according to the very nature of the signifier. Writing unfolds like a game (*jeu*) that invariably goes beyond its own rules and transgresses its limits. In writing, the point is not to manifest or exalt the act of writing, nor is it to pin a subject within language; it is, rather, a question of creating a space into which the writing subject constantly disappears.

The second theme, writing's relationship with death, is even more familiar. This link subverts an old tradition exemplified by the Greek epic, which was intended to perpetuate the immortality of the hero: if he was willing to die young, it was so that his life, consecrated and magnified by death, might pass into immortality; the narrative then redeemed this accepted death. In another way, the motivation, as well as the theme and the pretext of Arabian narratives – such as *The Thousand and One Nights* – was also the eluding of death: one spoke, telling stories into the early morning, in order to forestall death, to postpone the day of reckoning that would silence the narrator. Scheherazade's narrative is an effort, renewed each night, to keep death outside the circle of life.

Our culture has metamorphosed this idea of narrative, or writing, as something designed to ward off death. Writing has become linked to sacrifice, even to the sacrifice of life: it is now a voluntary effacement which does not need to be represented in books, since it is brought about in the writer's very existence. The work, which once had the duty of providing immortality, now possesses the right to kill, to be its author's murderer, as in the cases of Flaubert, Proust, and Kafka. That is not all, however: this relationship between writing and death is also manifested in the effacement of the writing subject's individual characteristics. Using all the contrivances that he sets up between himself and what he writes, the writing subject cancels out the signs of his particular individuality. As a result, the mark of the writer is reduced to nothing more than the singularity of his absence; he must assume the role of the dead man in the game of writing.

None of this is recent; criticism and philosophy took note of the disappearance – or death – of the author some time ago. But the consequences of their discovery of it have not been sufficiently examined, nor has its import been accurately measured. A certain number of notions that are intended to replace the privileged position of the author actually seem to preserve that privilege and suppress the real meaning of his disappearance. I shall examine two of these notions, both of great importance today.

The first is the idea of the work. It is a very familiar thesis that the task of criticism is not to bring out the work's relationships with the author, nor to reconstruct through the text a thought or experience, but rather to analyze the work through its structure, its architecture, its intrinsic form, and the play of its internal relationships. At this point, however, a problem arises: What is a work? What is this curious unity which we designate as a work? Of what elements is it composed? Is it not what an author has written? Difficulties appear immediately. If an individual were not an author, could we say that what he wrote, said, left behind in his papers, or what has been collected of his remarks, could be called a 'work'? When Sade was not considered an author, what was the status of his papers? Were they simply rolls of paper onto which he ceaselessly uncoiled his fantasies during his imprisonment?

Even when an individual has been accepted as an author, we must still ask whether everything that he wrote, said, or left behind is part of his work. The problem is both theoretical and technical. When undertaking the publication of Nietzsche's works, for example, where should one stop? Surely everything must be published, but what is 'everything'? Everything that Nietzsche himself published, certainly. And what about the rough drafts for his works? Obviously. The plans for his aphorisms? Yes. The deleted passages and the notes at the bottom of the page? Yes. What if, within a workbook filled with aphorisms, one finds a reference, the notation of a meeting or of an address, or a laundry list: Is it a work, or not? Why not? And so on, ad infinitum. How can one define a work amid the millions of traces left by someone after his death? A theory of the work does not exist, and the empirical task of those who naively undertake the editing of works often suffers in the absence of such a theory.

We could go even further: Does *The Thousand and One Nights* constitute a work? What about Clement of Alexandria's *Miscellanies* or Diogenes Laertius's *Lives*? A multitude of questions arises with regard to this notion of the work. Consequently, it is not enough to declare that we should do without the writer (the author) and study the work itself. The word *work* and the unity that it designates are probably as problematic as the status of the author's individuality.

Another notion which has hindered us from taking full measure of the author's disappearance, blurring and concealing the moment of this effacement and subtly preserving the author's existence, is the notion of writing (*écriture*). When rigorously applied, this notion should allow us not only to circumvent references to the author, but also to situate his recent absence. The notion of writing, as currently employed, is concerned with neither the act of writing nor the indication – be it symptom or sign – of a meaning which someone might have wanted to express. We try, with great effort, to imagine the general condition of each text, the condition of both the space in which it is dispersed and the time in which it unfolds.

In current usage, however, the notion of writing seems to transpose the empirical characteristics of the author into a transcendental anonymity. We are content to efface the more visible marks of the author's empiricity by playing off, one against the other, two ways of characterizing writing, namely, the critical and the religious approaches. Giving writing a primal status seems to be a way of retranslating, in transcendental terms, both the theological affirmation of its sacred character and the critical affirmation of its creative character. To admit that writing is, because of the very history that it made possible, subject to the test of oblivion and repression, seems to represent, in transcendental terms, the religious principle of the hidden meaning (which requires interpretation) and the critical principle of implicit significations, silent determinations, and obscured contents (which gives rise to commentary). To imagine writing as absence seems to be a simple repetition, in transcendental terms, of both the religious principle of inalterable and yet never fulfilled tradition, and the aesthetic principle of the work's survival, its perpetuation beyond the author's death, and its enigmatic *excess* in relation to him.

This usage of the notion of writing runs the risk of maintaining the author's privileges under the protection of writing's *a priori* status: it keeps alive, in the gray light of neutralization, the interplay of those representations that formed a particular image of the author. The author's disappearance, which, since Mallarmé, has been a constantly recurring event, is subject to a series of transcendental barriers. There seems to be an important dividing line between those who believe that they can still locate today's discontinuities (*ruptures*) in the historico-transcendental tradition of the nineteenth century, and those who try to free themselves once and for all from that tradition.

It is not enough, however, to repeat the empty affirmation that the author has disappeared. For the same reason, it is not enough to keep repeating (after Nietzsche) that god and man have died a common death. Instead, we must locate the space left empty by the author's disappearance, follow the distribution of gaps and breaches, and watch for the openings that this disappearance uncovers.

First, we need to clarify briefly the problems arising from the use of the author's name. What is an author's name? How does it function? Far from offering a solution, I shall only indicate some of the difficulties that it presents.

The author's name is a proper name, and therefore it raises the problems common to all proper names. (Here I refer to Searle's analyses, among others.[1]) Obviously, one cannot turn a proper name into a pure and simple reference. It has other than indicative functions: more than an indication, a gesture, a finger pointed at someone, it is the equivalent of a description. When one says 'Aristotle,' one employs a word that is the equivalent of one, or a series, of definite descriptions, such as 'the author of the *Analytics*,' 'the founder of ontology,' and so forth. One cannot stop there, however, because a proper name does not have just one signification. When we discover that Rimbaud did not write *La Chasse spirituelle*, we cannot pretend that the meaning of this proper name, or that of the author, has been altered. The proper name and the author's name are situated between the two poles of description and designation: they must have a certain link with what they name, but one that is neither entirely in the mode of designation nor in that of description; it must be a *specific* link. However – and it is here that the particular difficulties of the author's name arise – the links between the proper name and the individual named and between the author's name and what it names are not isomorphic and do not function in the same way. There are several differences.

If, for example, Pierre Dupont does not have blue eyes, or was not born in Paris, or is not a doctor, the name Pierre Dupont will still always refer to the same person; such things do not modify the link of designation. The problems raised by the author's name are much more complex, however. If I discover that Shakespeare was not born in the house that we visit today, this is a modification which, obviously, will not alter the functioning of the author's name. But if we proved that Shakespeare did not write those sonnets which pass for his, that would constitute a significant change and affect the manner in which the author's name functions. If we proved that Shakespeare wrote Bacon's *Organon* by showing that the same author wrote both the works of Bacon and those of Shakespeare, that would be a third type of change which would entirely modify the functioning of the author's name. The author's name is not, therefore, just a proper name like the rest.

Many other facts point out the paradoxical singularity of the author's name. To say that Pierre Dupont does not exist is not at all the same as saying that Homer or Hermes Trismegistus did not exist. In the first case, it means that no one has the name Pierre Dupont; in the second, it means that several people were mixed together under one name, or that the true author had none of the traits traditionally ascribed to the personae of Homer or Hermes. To say that X's real name is actually Jacques Durand instead of Pierre Dupont is not the same as saying that Stendhal's name was Henri Beyle. One could also question the meaning and functioning of propositions like 'Bourbaki is so-and-so, and so-and-so, etc.' and 'Victor Eremita, Climacus, Anti-climacus, Frater Taciturnus, Constantine Constantius, all of those are Kierkegaard.'

These differences may result from the fact that an author's name is not simply an element in a discourse (capable of being either subject or object, of being replaced by a pronoun, and the like); it performs a certain role with regard to narrative discourse, assuring a classificatory function. Such a name permits one to group together a certain number of texts, define them, differentiate them from and contrast them to others. In addition, it establishes a relationship among the texts. Hermes Trismegistus did not exist, nor did Hippocrates – in the sense that Balzac existed – but the fact that several texts have been placed under the same name indicates that there has been established among them a relationship of homogeneity, filiation, authentication of some texts by the use of others, reciprocal explication, or concomitant utilization. The author's name serves to characterize a certain mode of being of discourse: the fact that the discourse has an author's name, that one can say 'this was written by so-and-so' or 'so-and-so is its author,' shows that this discourse is not ordinary everyday speech that merely comes and goes, not something that is immediately consumable. On the contrary, it is a speech that must be received in a certain mode and that, in a given culture, must receive a certain status.

It would seem that the author's name, unlike other proper names, does not pass from the interior of a discourse to the real and exterior individual who produced it; instead, the name seems always to be present, marking off the edges of the text, revealing, or at least characterizing, its mode of being. The author's name manifests the appearance of a certain discursive set and indicates the status of this discourse within a society and a culture. It has no legal status, nor is it located in the fiction of the work; rather, it is located in the break that founds a certain discursive construct and its very particular mode of being. As a result, we could say that in a civilization like our own there are a certain number of discourses that are endowed with the 'author function,' while others are deprived of it. A private letter may well have a signer – it does not have an author; a contract may well have a guarantor – it does not have an author. An anonymous text posted on a wall probably has a writer – but not an author. The author function is therefore characteristic of the mode of existence, circulation, and function of certain discourses within a society.

Let us analyze this 'author function' as we have just described it. In our culture, how does one characterize a discourse containing the author function? In what way is this discourse different from other discourses? If we limit our remarks to the author of a book or a text, we can isolate four different characteristics.

First of all, discourses are objects of appropriation. The form of ownership from which they spring is of a rather particular type, one that has been codified for many years. We should note that, historically, this type of ownership has always been subsequent to what one might call penal appropriation. Texts, books, and discourses really began to have authors (other than mythical, 'sacralized' and 'sacralizing' figures) to the extent that authors became subject to punishment, that is, to the extent that discourses could be transgressive. In our culture (and doubtless in many others), discourse was not originally a product, a thing, a kind of goods; it was essentially an act – an act placed in the bipolar field of the sacred and the profane, the licit and the illicit, the religious and the blasphemous. Historically, it was a gesture fraught with risks before becoming goods caught up in a circuit of ownership.

Once a system of ownership for texts came into being, once strict rules concerning author's rights, author-publisher relations, rights of reproduction, and related matters were enacted – at the end of the eighteenth and the beginning of the nineteenth century – the possibility of transgression attached to the act of writing took on, more and more, the form of an imperative peculiar to literature. It is as if the author, beginning with the moment at which he was placed in the system of property that characterizes our society, compensated for the status that he thus acquired by rediscovering the old bipolar field of discourse, systematically practicing transgression and thereby restoring danger to a writing which was now guaranteed the benefits of ownership.

The author function does not affect all discourses in a universal and constant way, however. This is its second characteristic. In our civilization, it has not always been the same types of texts which have required attribution to an author. There was a time when the texts that we today call 'literary' (narratives, stories, epics, tragedies, comedies) were accepted, put into circulation, and valorized without any question about the identity of their author; their anonymity caused no difficulties since their ancientness, whether real or imagined, was regarded as a sufficient guarantee of their status. On the other hand, those texts that we now would call scientific – those dealing with cosmology and the heavens, medicine and illnesses, natural sciences and geography – were accepted in the Middle Ages, and accepted as 'true,' only when marked with the name of their author. 'Hippocrates said,' 'Pliny recounts,' were not really formulas of an argument based on authority; they were the markers inserted in discourses that were supported to be received as statements of demonstrated truth.

A reversal occurred in the seventeenth or eighteenth century. Scientific discourses began to be received for themselves, in the anonymity of an established or always redemonstrable truth; their membership in a systematic ensemble, and not the reference to the individual who produced them, stood as their guarantee. The author function faded away, and the inventor's name served only to christen a theorem, proposition, particular effect, property, body, group of elements, or pathological syndrome. By the same token, literary discourses came to be accepted only when endowed with the author function. We now ask of each poetic or fictional text: From where does it come, who wrote it, when, under what circumstances, or beginning with what design? The meaning ascribed to it and the status or value accorded it depend on the manner in which we answer these questions. And if a text should be discovered in a state of anonymity – whether as a consequence of an accident or the author's explicit wish – the game becomes one of rediscovering the author. Since literary anonymity is not tolerable, we can accept it only in the guise of an enigma. As a result, the author function today plays an important role in our view of literary works. (These are obviously generalizations that would have to be refined insofar as recent critical practice is concerned.)

The third characteristic of this author function is that it does not develop spontaneously as the attribution of a discourse to an individual. It is, rather, the result of a complex operation which constructs a certain rational being that we call 'author.' Critics doubtless try to give this intelligible being a realistic status, by discerning, in the individual, a 'deep' motive, a 'creative' power, or a 'design,' the milieu in which writing originates. Nevertheless, these aspects of an individual which we designate as making him an author are only a projection, in more or less psychologizing terms, of the operations that we force texts to undergo, the connections that we make, the traits that we establish as pertinent, the continuities that we recognize, or the exclusions that we practice. All these operations vary according to periods and types of discourse. We do not construct a 'philosophical author' as we do a 'poet,' just as, in the eighteenth century, one did not construct a novelist as we do today. Still, we can find through the ages certain constants in the rules of author construction.

It seems, for example, that the manner in which literary criticism once defined the author – or, rather, constructed the figure of the author beginning with existing texts and discourses – is directly derived from the manner in which Christian tradition authenticated (or rejected) the texts at its disposal. In order to 'rediscover' an author in a work, modern criticism uses methods similar to those that Christian exegesis employed when trying to prove the value of a text by its author's saintliness. In *De viris illustribus*, Saint Jerome explains that homonymy is not sufficient to identify legitimately authors of more than one work: different individuals could have had the same name, or one man could have, illegitimately, borrowed another's patronymic. The name as an individual trademark is not enough when one works within a textual tradition.

How, then, can one attribute several discourses to one and the same author? How can one use the author function to determine if one is dealing with one or several individuals? Saint Jerome proposes four criteria: (1) if among several books attributed to an author one is inferior to the others, it must be withdrawn from the list of the author's works (the author is therefore defined as a constant level of value); (2) the same should be done if certain texts contradict the doctrine expounded in the author's other works (the author is thus defined as a field of conceptual or theoretical coherence); (3) one must also exclude works that are written in a different style, containing words and expressions not ordinarily found in the writer's production (the author is here conceived as a stylistic unity); (4) finally, passages quoting statements that were made or mentioning events that occurred after the author's death must be regarded as interpolated texts (the author is here seen as a historical figure at the crossroads of a certain number of events).

Modern literary criticism, even when – as is now customary – it is not concerned with questions of authentication, still defines the author the same way: the author provides the basis for explaining not only the presence of certain events in a work, but also their transformations, distortions, and diverse modifications (through his biography, the determination of his individual perspective, the analysis of his social position, and the revelation of his basic design). The author is also the principle of a certain unity of writing – all differences having to be resolved, at least in part, by the principles of evolution, maturation, or influence. The author also serves to neutralize the contradictions that may emerge in a series of texts: there must be – at a certain level of his thought or desire, of his consciousness or unconscious – a point where contradictions are resolved, where incompatible elements are at last tied together or organized around a fundamental or originating contradiction. Finally, the author is a particular source of expression that, in more or less completed forms, is manifested equally well, and with similar validity, in works, sketches, letters, fragments, and so on. Clearly, Saint Jerome's four criteria of authenticity (criteria which seem totally insufficient for today's exegetes) do define the four modalities according to which modern criticism brings the author function into play.

But the author function is not a pure and simple reconstruction made secondhand from a text given as passive material. The text always contains a certain number of signs referring to the author. These signs, well known to grammarians, are personal pronouns, adverbs of time and place, and verb conjugation. Such elements do not play the same role in discourses provided with the author function as in those lacking it. In the latter, such 'shifters' refer to the real speaker and to the spatiotemporal coordinates of his discourse (although certain modifications can occur, as in the operation of relating discourses in the first person). In the former, however, their role is more complex and variable. Everyone knows that, in a novel narrated in the first person, neither the first-person pronoun nor the present indicative refers exactly either to the writer or to the moment in which he writes, but rather to an alter ego whose distance from the author varies, often changing in the course of the work. It would be just as wrong to equate the author with the real writer as to equate him with the fictitious speaker; the author function is carried out and operates in the scission itself, in this division and this distance.

One might object that this is a characteristic peculiar to novelistic or poetic discourse, a 'game' in which only 'quasidiscourses' participate. In fact, however, all discourses endowed with the author function do possess this plurality of self. The self that speaks in the preface to a treatise on mathematics – and that indicates the circumstances of the treatise's composition – is identical neither in its position nor in its functioning to the self that speaks in the course of a demonstration, and that appears in the form of 'I conclude' or 'I suppose.' In the first case, the 'I' refers to an individual without an equivalent who, in a determined place and time, completed a certain task; in the second, the 'I' indicates an instance and a level of demonstration which any individual could perform provided that he accepted the same system of symbols, play of axioms, and set of previous demonstrations. We could also, in the same treatise, locate a third self, one that speaks to tell the work's meaning, the obstacles encountered, the results obtained, and the remaining problems; this self is situated in the field of already existing or yet-to-appear mathematical discourses. The author function is not assumed by the first of these selves at the expense of the other two, which would then be nothing more than a fictitious splitting in two of the first one. On the contrary, in these discourses the author function operates so as to effect the dispersion of these three simultaneous selves.

No doubt analysis could discover still more characteristic traits of the author function. I will limit myself to these four, however, because they seem both the most visible and the most important. They can be summarized as follows: (1) the author function is linked to the juridical and institutional system that encompasses, determines, and articulates the universe of discourses; (2) it does not affect all discourses in the same way at all times and in all types of civilization; (3) it is not defined by the spontaneous attribution of a discourse to its producer, but rather by a series of specific and complex operations; (4) it does not refer purely and simply to a real individual, since it can give rise simultaneously to several selves, to several subjects – positions that can be occupied by different classes of individuals.

Up to this point I have unjustifiably limited my subject. Certainly the author function in painting, music, and other arts should have been discussed, but even supposing that we remain within the world of discourse, as I want to do, I seem to have given the term 'author' much too narrow a meaning. I have discussed the author only in the limited sense of a person to whom the production of a text, a book, or a work can be legitimately attributed. It is easy to see that in the sphere of discourse one can be the author of much more than a book – one can be the author of a theory, tradition, or discipline in which other books and authors will in their turn find a place. These authors are in a position which we shall call 'transdiscursive.' This is a recurring phenomenon – certainly as old as our civilization. Homer, Aristotle, and the Church Fathers, as well as the first mathematicians and the originators of the Hippocratic tradition, all played this role.

Furthermore, in the course of the nineteenth century, there appeared in Europe another, more uncommon, kind of author, whom one should confuse with neither the 'great' literary authors, nor the authors of religious texts, nor the founders of science. In a somewhat arbitrary way we shall call those who belong to this last group 'founders of discursivity.' They are unique in that they are not just the authors of their own works. They have produced something else: the possibilities and the rules for the formation of other texts. In this sense, they are very different, for example, from a novelist, who is, in fact, nothing more than the author of his own text. Freud is not just the author of *The Interpretation of Dreams* or *Jokes and Their Relation to the Unconscious*; Marx is not just the author of the *Communist Manifesto* or *Das Kapital*: they both have established an endless possibility of discourse.

Obviously, it is easy to object. One might say that it is not true that the author of a novel is only the author of his own text; in a sense, he also, provided that he acquires some 'importance,' governs and commands more than that. To take a very simple example, one could say that Ann Radcliffe not only wrote *The Castles of Athlin and Dunbayne* and several other novels, but also made possible the appearance of the Gothic horror novel at the beginning of the nineteenth century; in that respect, her author function exceeds her own work. But I think there is an answer to this objection. These founders of discursivity (I use Marx and Freud as examples, because I believe them to be both the first and the most important cases) make possible something altogether different from what a novelist makes possible. Ann Radcliffe's texts opened the way for a certain number of resemblances and analogies which have their model or principle in her work. The latter contains characteristic signs, figures, relationships, and structures which could be reused by others. In other words, to say that Ann Radcliffe founded the Gothic horror novel means that in the nineteenth-century Gothic novel one will find, as in Ann Radcliffe's works, the theme of the heroine caught in the trap of her own innocence, the hidden castle, the character of the black, cursed hero devoted to making the world expiate the evil done to him, and all the rest of it.

On the other hand, when I speak of Marx or Freud as founders of discursivity, I mean that they made possible not only a certain number of analogies, but also (and equally important) a certain number of differences. They have created a possibility for something other than their discourse, yet something belonging to what they founded. To say that Freud founded psychoanalysis does not (simply) mean that we find the concept of the libido or the technique of dream analysis in the works of Karl Abraham or Melanie Klein; it means that Freud made possible a certain number of divergences – with respect to his own texts, concepts, and hypotheses – that all arise from the psychoanalytic discourse itself.

This would seem to present a new difficulty, however: is the above not true, after all, of any founder of a science, or of any author who has introduced some important transformation into a science? After all, Galileo made possible not only those discourses that repeated the laws that he had formulated, but also statements very different from what he himself had said. If Cuvier is the founder of biology or Saussure the founder of linguistics, it is not because they were imitated, nor because people have since taken up again the concept of organism or sign; it is because Cuvier made possible, to a certain extent, a theory of evolution diametrically opposed to his own fixism; it is because Saussure made possible a generative grammar radically different from his structural analyses. Superficially, then, the initiation of discursive practices appears similar to the founding of any scientific endeavor.

Still, there is a difference, and a notable one. In the case of a science, the act that founds it is on an equal footing with its future transformations; this act becomes in some respects part of the set of modifications that it makes possible. Of course, this belonging can take several forms. In the future development of a science, the founding act may appear as little more than a particular instance of a more general phenomenon which unveils itself in the process. It can also turn out to be marred by intuition and empirical bias; one must then reformulate it, making it the object of a certain number of supplementary theoretical operations which establish it more rigorously, etc. Finally, it can seem to be a hasty generalization which must be limited, and whose restricted domain of validity must be retraced. In other words, the founding act of a science can always be reintroduced within the machinery of those transformations that derive from it.

In contrast, the initiation of a discursive practice is heterogeneous to its subsequent transformations. To expand a type of discursivity, such as psychoanalysis as founded by Freud, is not to give it a formal generality that it would not have permitted at the outset, but rather to open it up to a certain number of possible applications. To limit psychoanalysis as a type of discursivity is, in reality, to try to isolate in the founding act an eventually restricted number of propositions or statements to which, alone, one grants a founding value, and in relation to which certain concepts or theories accepted by Freud might be considered as derived, secondary, and accessory. In addition, one does not declare certain propositions in the work of these founders to be false: instead, when trying to seize the act of founding, one sets aside those statements that are not pertinent, either because they are deemed inessential, or because they are considered 'prehistoric' and derived from another type of discursivity. In other words, unlike the founding of a science, the initiation of a discursive practice does not participate in its later transformations.

As a result, one defines a proposition's theoretical validity in relation to the work of the founders – while, in the case of Galileo and Newton, it is in relation to what physics or cosmology *is* (in its intrinsic structure and 'normativity') that one affirms the validity of any proposition that those men may have put forth. To phrase it very schematically: the work of initiators of discursivity is not situated in the space that science defines; rather, it is the science or the discursivity which refers back to their work as primary coordinates.

In this way we can understand the inevitable necessity, within these fields of discursivity, for a 'return to the origin.' This return, which is part of the discursive field itself, never stops modifying it. The return is not a historical supplement which would be added to the discursivity, or merely an ornament; on the contrary, it constitutes an effective and necessary task of transforming the discursive practice itself. Reexamination of Galileo's text may well change our knowledge of the history of mechanics, but it will never be able to change mechanics itself. On the other hand, reexamining Freud's texts modifies psychoanalysis itself, just as a reexamination of Marx's would modify Marxism.

What I have just outlined regarding the initiation of discursive practices is, of course, very schematic; this is true, in particular, of the opposition that I have tried to draw between discursive initiation and scientific founding. It is not always easy to distinguish between the two; moreover, nothing proves that they are two mutually exclusive procedures. I have attempted the distinction for only one reason: to show that the author function, which is complex enough when one tries to situate it at the level of a book or a series of texts that carry a given signature, involves still more determining factors when one tries to analyze it in larger units, such as groups of works or entire disciplines.

To conclude, I would like to review the reasons why I attach a certain importance to what I have said.

First, there are theoretical reasons. On the one hand, an analysis in the direction that I have outlined might provide for an approach to a typology of discourse. It seems to me, at least at first glance, that such a typology cannot be constructed solely from the grammatical features, formal structures, and objects of discourse: more likely there exist properties or relationships peculiar to discourse (not reducible to the rules of grammar and logic), and one must use these to distinguish the major categories of discourse. The relationship (or nonrelationship) with an author, and the different forms this relationship takes, constitute – in a quite visible manner – one of these discursive properties.

On the other hand, I believe that one could find here an introduction to the historical analysis of discourse. Perhaps it is time to study discourses not only in terms of their expressive value or formal transformations, but according to their modes of existence. The modes of circulation, valorization, attribution, and appropriation of discourses vary with each culture and are modified within each. The manner in which they are articulated according to social relationships can be more readily understood, I believe, in the activity of the author function and in its modifications than in the themes or concepts that discourses set in motion.

It would seem that one could also, beginning with analyses of this type, reexamine the privileges of the subject. I realize that in undertaking the internal and architectonic analysis of a work (be it a literary text, philosophical system, or scientific work), in setting aside biographical and psychological references, one has already called back into question the absolute character and founding role of the subject. Still, perhaps one must return to this question, not in order to reestablish the theme of an originating subject, but to grasp the subject's points of insertion, modes of functioning, and system of dependencies. Doing so means overturning the traditional problem, no longer raising the questions: How can a free subject penetrate the substance of things and give it meaning? How can it activate the rules of a language from within and thus give rise to the designs which are properly its own? Instead, these questions will be raised: How, under what conditions, and in what forms can something like a subject appear in the order of discourse? What place can it occupy in each type of discourse, what functions can it assume, and by obeying what rules? In short, it is a matter of depriving the subject (or its substitute) of its role as originator, and of analyzing the subject as a variable and complex function of discourse.

Second, there are reasons dealing with the 'ideological' status of the author. The question then becomes: How can one reduce the great peril, the great danger with which fiction threatens our world? The answer is: one can reduce it with the author. The author allows a limitation of the cancerous and dangerous proliferation of significations within a world where one is thrifty not only with one's resources and riches, but also with one's discourses and their significations. The author is the principle of thrift in the proliferation of meaning. As a result, we must entirely reverse the traditional idea of the author. We are accustomed, as we have seen earlier, to saying that the author is the genial creator of a work in which he deposits, with infinite wealth and generosity, an inexhaustible world of significations. We are used to thinking that the author is so different from all other men, and so transcendent with regard to all languages that, as soon as he speaks, meaning begins to proliferate, to proliferate indefinitely.

The truth is quite the contrary: the author is not an indefinite source of significations which fill a work; the author does not precede the works; he is a certain functional principle by which, in our culture, one limits, excludes, and chooses; in short, by which one impedes the free circulation, the free manipulation, the free composition, decomposition, and recomposition of fiction. In fact, if we are accustomed to presenting the author as a genius, as a perpetual surging of invention, it is because, in reality, we make him function in exactly the opposite fashion. One can say that the author is an ideological product, since we represent him as the opposite of his historically real function. (When a historically given function is represented in a figure that inverts it, one has an ideological production.) The author is therefore the ideological figure by which one marks the manner in which we fear the proliferation of meaning.

In saying this, I seem to call for a form of culture in which fiction would not be limited by the figure of the author. It would be pure romanticism, however, to imagine a culture in which the fictive would operate in an absolutely free state, in which fiction would be put at the disposal of everyone and would develop without passing through something like a necessary or constraining figure. Although, since the eighteenth century, the author has played the role of the regulator of the fictive, a role quite characteristic of our era of industrial and bourgeois society, of individualism and private property, still, given the historical modifications that are taking place, it does not seem necessary that the author function remain constant in form, complexity, and even in existence. I think that, as our society changes, at the very moment when it is in the process of changing, the author function will disappear, and in such a manner that fiction and its polysemous texts will once again function according to another mode, but still with a system of constraint – one which will no longer be the author, but which will have to be determined or, perhaps, experienced.

All discourses, whatever their status, form, value, and whatever the treatment to which they will be subjected, would then develop in the anonymity of a murmur. We would no longer hear the questions that have been rehashed for so long: Who really spoke? Is it really he and not someone else? With what authenticity or originality? And what part of his deepest self did he express in his discourse? Instead, there would be other questions, like these: What are the modes of existence of this discourse? Where has it been used, how can it circulate, and who can appropriate it for himself? What are the places in it where there is room for possible subjects? Who can assume these various subject functions? And behind all these questions, we would hear hardly anything but the stirring of an indifference: What difference does it make who is speaking?

Notes

1 *Ed.*: John Searle, *Speech Acts: An Essay in the Philosophy of Language* (Cambridge, Eng.: Cambridge University Press, 1969), pp. 162–74.

3
On classical ground
Histories of style

Style remains a principal concern of the histories of British architecture from the sixteenth century to the early nineteenth century, if not up to the present day. Architecture and style are interlinked to the point that style can almost be believed to contain the essence of architecture, but if this were the case then style would constitute the subject of architectural history. Quite clearly it does not. Instead, style is one of the many orders of narrative open to the architectural historian. What then is style? We might say that style is the specific organization of form, but the characteristics of a style consist of a repertoire of ornamental components which cannot be confined to a single period, many appear again and again in different configurations. So a style is characterised by the manner in which form is interpreted as the reading of these ornamental components changes according to their context. What changes form – is there a kind of autogenesis or does the historian trace lines of development only possible with the benefit of hindsight? But first of all, where does the idea of style come from, what is its relationship to the aesthetic and how should we read it?

Much has been written on the role and importance of the aesthetic in art where it is used to help set up the distinction of fine art from the everyday. Moreover the aesthetic enables the recognition of a work of art as an object in its own right and ensures that it is intelligible and valuable as such. In this way a work of art has intrinsic properties that are independent of its relation to other things, as well as its creator and viewer. There are several ways of offering explanations or analyses of the aesthetic. We can consider its causal conditions and emotional effects or we can situate the aesthetic within the realm of visual culture, to provide a more materially based explanation. Alternatively, the aesthetic can be reduced to a critique of the visual through either biography or autobiography. The privileging of the aesthetic gives a work of art an autonomous status and this can be employed in the historical analysis of buildings – notwithstanding the obvious pitfall of art for art's sake. But architecture is more than façades; it is a lived experience – a set of spaces which stage social and cultural relationships. The aesthetic is only one element in this complex set of interactions, and although it might offer a framing device for viewing architecture it is not the only explanation. Style is a means of identifying, codifying and interrogating the aesthetic and I want to use it as a way of exploring the taxonomies of architecture and the impact this has on our reading of its histories.

If style is anything more than formal analysis or a description of the ornamentation of a building it must surely offer or represent a specific set of ideals from the moment of its production. We, the viewer, will see this within the context of our own culture – in this way we understand the formal qualities of a building as the product of the convergence of past and present. Thus architecture plays an important ontological role in representing and it is up to us as viewer to be sensitive to the particular statement it is making. It is this secure cultural location of a building that makes it authentic. The phenomenologist Hans-Georg Gadamer in his essay *The Ontological Foundation of the Occasional and the Decorative* shows how architecture fulfils its functional purpose whilst also contributing to its setting though its aesthetic. Importantly, Gadamer asserts that a building is not a work of art in its own right which can exist devoid of context, as we might, for instance, see a painting in a gallery as opposed to its original setting. Instead, a building (or architecture) would not be a work of art if it stood anywhere, and any change of use diminishes its ability to represent. Gadamer sees ornament, what we might call stylistic elements or details, as essential to the ontological role of the building to represent. Ornament is not then applied or extra but intrinsic to our reading of architecture.

> If a building is a work of art, then it is not only the artistic solution of a building problem posed by the contexts of purpose and of life to which it originally belongs, but somehow preserves these, so that it is visibly present even though the present manifestation of the original purposes is strange. Something in it points back to the original. Where the original intention has become completely unrecognizable or its unity destroyed by too many subsequent alterations, then the building itself will become incomprehensible. Thus architecture, the most 'statuary' of all art forms, shows how secondary 'aesthetic differentiation' is. A building is never primarily a work of art. Its purpose, through which it belongs in the context of life, cannot be separated from itself without losing some of its reality. If it has become merely an object of the aesthetic consciousness, then it has merely a shadowy reality and lives a distorted life only in the degenerate form of an object of interest to tourists, or a subject for photography. The work of art itself proves to be a pure abstraction.[1]

We have already seen how the confluence of European academic traditions met British empiricism in the mid-twentieth century to produce a more varied kind of architectural history. One of the principal problems was how to develop a taxonomic system that would enable the historian to group and classify the range of British architectural production. In Chapter 2 Howard Colvin's method, which ignored stylistic attribution and appraisal in favour of named-architect buildings and documentary sources produced a distinctive analysis and archive of the architecture of our period. In Colvin's own words in his *Biographical Dictionary of British Architects 1600–1840*:

> '*Attributed*' [Colvin's emphasis] means that the evidence is largely or wholly stylistic. In this edition, as in its predecessors, such purely stylistic attributions have been sparingly made, partly because my purpose has been to provide a body of authentic information *uncompromised* [my emphasis] by speculation and partly because in a dictionary there is no room in which to argue controversial cases of attribution.[2]

But if the architectural history of the British Isles was to have the same academic weight as its continental counterparts it required recognisable formal qualities which gave it distinction and allowed it to be read as signifying sets of social and cultural ideals of its builders, users, historians and its many publics past and present. It would also be preferable for these formal qualities to relate to the European canon of architecture – namely the classical style. (Here I use classical to mean any style that draws on the architecture of antiquity.) The influx of European scholars into Britain in the mid-twentieth century opened up the possibilities for placing British architecture in its cultural and aesthetic context and seeing it a part of a broader intellectual history of culture. Not least here Rudolph Wittkower and Fritz Saxl's *British Art and the Mediterranean* first published in 1948 which, in the Warburgian tradition, presented a cultural and iconographic survey of the use of classical motifs across a broad chronological span. The typological approach adopted by Wittkower comprised the study of specific stylistic details or elements and provides an illuminating set of connections. His discussion of a type of window and door frame, with blocked quoins at regular intervals and a compact mass of three or five voussoirs in its lintel, demonstrates Wittkower's innovatory method of analysis of a motif that was extensively used in seventeenth- and eighteenth-century British architecture. Examples include Campbell's Houghton (Figure 3.1), Lord Burlington's house for Lord Montrath, Henry Flitcroft's west porch of St Giles-in-the-Fields. James Paine's Axwell Park and Sir William Chamber's Pembroke House in Whitehall. Wittkower offers this examination of a specific classical ornamental form:

> How does this motif fit into the pattern of Palladian and Neoclassical architecture? Does it correspond to our conception of classical poise and is it – an *a priori* demand of classical architecture – easily 'readable'? Doubtless, we are faced with a highly complex motif, and the reason why we accept it without any disturbing reaction is not only that we take it for granted from having seen it too often, but also that in its English interpretation the conflict which it originally held is blotted out . . .
>
> Was the important motif really taken from Palladio? The answer is no. A shrewd observer like Sir William Chambers in his *Treatise on Civil Architecture*, published such a window with the comment: 'It is, I believe, an original invention of Inigo Jones,

Figure 3.1 Houghton Hall, Norfolk, entrance façade, begun 1722 (photo, author).

which has been executed in many buildings in England' . . . English architects could indeed quote Inigo Jones as their authority for the use of the motif. Not only were such drawings among Jones's collection, bought by Lord Burlington [and] published by Kent in *The Designs of Inigo Jones,* but it was found that Jones himself had favoured this treatment of doors and windows . . .

The question arises whether, as Sir William Chambers believed, this treatment of doors and windows originated in the circle of Inigo Jones or whether it has an older pedigree. Although very rare, a few buildings with the same peculiarity exist in Italy. Jones, who was in Rome in 1614, may have seen Ottavio Mascheroni's entrance door to the Palazzo Ginnasi in Piazza Mattei. The door is dated 1585, i.e. it was modern in Jones's days and may have attracted his attention as the last word in architecture . . .

The form of the motif used in England was, of course, far removed from the highly personal interpretations of Guilio Romano, Serlio and Giacomo del Duca [the architects of other examples cited by Wittkower]. It was legalized and academically petrified. France was the junction whence the standardized type went on to its further travels . . .

. . . [it] reached England in the beginning of the seventeenth century, [the motif was also found in the Low Countries Belgium and Austria] . . .

What is the conclusion to be drawn from these observations? Although originating in Italian mannerism and cherished in France for a short period, the motif was never absorbed into the countries of 'functional' architecture. The pedigree of the motif has revealed its *unorthodox* [my emphasis] origin, and now it should be mentioned that there were men in England [Vanbrugh and Hawksmoor] who understood its original meaning . . .

. . . it remains to inquire what it was about it that fascinated English academic architects. The answer is that they had no eye for the intricacy of the motif and saw in it a decorative pattern which could be advantageously employed to enliven a bare wall . . .

In English academic architecture flat surface patterns replace Italian functional element.[3]

Wittkower's cultural analysis of Lord Burlington and Palladianism emphasised the meaning of stylistic elements as cultural symbols which found its apogee in Wittkower's seminal work *Architectural Principles in the Age of Humanism,* first published in 1949. For the first time in these works, British architecture was linked with the architecture of Europe in formal and intellectual terms. This made a significant break with the inward-looking, insular empirical surveys of previous decades. But, importantly, whilst placing British architecture in its European context in formal terms, Wittkower did recognise that it is a *repertoire* of classical ornament that he identifies rather than a coherent self-consciously constructed style.

Wittkower's typological approach is only one of the many different methods used in architectural histories to trace and account for stylistic changes, some of which rely more heavily on philosophical or theoretical models than others. Perhaps more than any other order of narrative, style invites the tracing of lines of progression and development, the movement of architectural ornament from point A to point B through a set of teleologically observed processes. To this end the Hegelian notion of the Spirit of the Age, together with the thesis-antithesis-synthesis model of analysis of movement or change, has informed many narratives of style where style is seen as an indicator of the spirit. Sir Nikolaus Pevsner perhaps sums up one way of using Hegel to narrate the stylistic history of architecture and the importance of the aesthetic to architecture in the introduction to his *An Outline of European Architecture,* first published in 1943:

An age without architecture is impossible as long as human beings populate this world . . . .

That does not, however, mean that architectural evolutions are caused by function and construction. A style in art belongs to the world of the mind, not the world of matter. New purposes may result in new types of building, but the architect's job is to make such new types both aesthetically and functionally satisfactory – and not all ages have considered, as ours does, functional soundness indispensable for aesthetic enjoyment. The position is similar with regard to materials. new materials make new forms possible, and even call for new forms. Hence it is quite justifiable if so many works of architecture (especially in England) have emphasized their importance. If in this book they have been deliberately kept in the background, the reason is that materials can become architecturally effective only when the architect instils into them an aesthetic meaning. Architecture is not the product of materials and purposes – nor by the way of social condition – but of the changing spirits of changing ages. It is the spirit of an age that pervades its social life, its religion, its scholarship, and its arts. The Gothic style was not created because somebody invented rib vaulting; the Modern movement did not come into being because steel frame and reinforced concrete construction had been worked out – they were worked out because a new spirit required them.[4]

Pevsner is concerned with a macro-history of European architecture where a clearly defined method of analysis and selection of examples gives a coherence to the narrative presented. This approach also presents a possible route through the history of British architectural production as the thesis-antithesis-synthesis model of Hegelian dialectic transposes itself well, for instance, to the juxtaposition of the severity of early eighteenth-century Palladianism and the mid-century frivolity of the rococo, which can be seen to result in the neo-classical style of the end of the century. But throughout this period in British architecture different styles coexisted and their dominance or otherwise can be as much a product of the historian's aims and interests as any quantification of contemporary preference or spirit. Despite Pevsner's bold claims, style is usually linked to the social and cultural context of its production, and here we find the classical privileged over the non-classical as it is seen as representative of a set of superior values. This linear view of stylistic development is made more complicated when we remember that architects sometimes worked in different styles and some of these styles are more closely identified with particular architectural credos than others. Moreover, the emphasis on the classical – in the broadest sense – and its dominance has resulted in the side-lining of other kinds of architectural production, for instance the gothick, chinoiserie and the primitive, all of which manifested themselves in significant ways in the architectural production of the period under discussion in this book. (Figures 3.2, 3.3 and 3.4). What is important here is that disparate styles in the same period indicate a lack of public unanimity in issues of taste, so implying that different formal elements represent the distinct ideologies of social classes. Thus an architectural style can become representative of a class ideology through its users, producers and historians.[5] This has special relevance for a study of the styles of domestic building, an area in which individual taste can perhaps most obviously manifest itself. Yet, the role of the individual in the macro-stylistic histories of British architecture is generally subjugated to the larger historical and cultural forces explored by the narrator/historian. As we have seen in Chapter 2, biographical histories of architecture facilitate the grouping of buildings into stylistic categories based on a perceived consensus in the process of design. But this becomes more problematic when astylar architecture, here I mean vernacular (outwith the established canon of stylistic classification), is considered. This is by

Figure 3.2 'Gothick' folly, Stowe, Buckinghamshire by James Gibbs (photo, author).

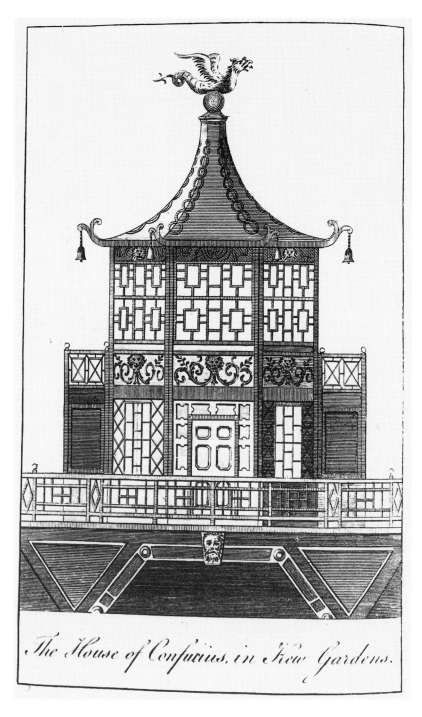

The House of Confucius, in Kew Gardens.

Figure 3.3 The House of Confucius in Kew Gardens; illustrated in the *Gentleman's Magazine*, June 1773 (private collection).

Figure 3.4 Essai sur l'Architecture, Marc-Antoine Laugier. Frontispiece to his influential essay on the primitive origins of architecture, Paris 1753 (private collection).

definition idiosyncratic and localised and here the expression of individuality, human agency, is a core part of the style. We will return to the resonance between vernacular and high architecture later on. At this point I wish to raise the question of the relationship between style and human agency and the impact this has on the stylistic categories used in architectural history. In particular here I am concerned with urban environments, especially their domestic architecture, which often evade classification in the established range of styles used to formulate macro-histories. These histories group disparate large-scale buildings, not least country houses, by their use of stylistic motifs. Urban vernacular architecture is impor- tant as cities remain a nexus of social and cultural forces, and certainly in the period under review in this book, cities became increasingly significant in this regard. In addition, owners, occupants and patrons, through the link between individuals and their environ- ments, subvert the predominance of style and the various readings of it as an effective tool of architectural historical analysis. As Ernst Bloch points out, human environments are made by humankind just as humankind is made by its environment and they are dialectically related. In this way architecture and the objects within it tell a story of the occupant as they reveal taste and class:

> Of course, these matters never depend solely on the taste of the individual . . . The most appropriate posture in the chair, as well as that of the chair itself, is determined by the social habitus of an entire era, i.e. by its fashion-determining class and, not least, by the petty bourgeoisie's imitation of the taste of the ruling class, by the latter perhaps most revealingly. This relationship is most visible in the visible, in the exterior and interior architecture, both of which dominate by imposing the forms of those who dominate. This relationship, then, is what is called style.[6]

This helps to vivify what might otherwise appear to be a set of ossified social and cultural values in the interior and exterior architectural ornament of past centuries. In order to explore the full resonance of these encoded cultural messages let's project them into the pre- sent day and think about a more accessible form of visual culture: television sitcoms and how we read the representation and use of style in them. Here we know instantly the class and social aspirations of the characters through the briefest glimpse of their living room (or is it front room, sitting room, lounge or drawing room?) with its sofa (or settee or three-piece suite) and polished wood floors and rugs (or fitted carpets). As for the house, we can ascer- tain the same information from a period property (or suburban semi or inner-city high rise) and, importantly, the authenticity of any 'period' stylistic features and garden design. And as for the three flying ducks. . . .[7]

Two themes which emerge from this brief consideration of style comprise the main sub- stance of this chapter. First the dominance of the classical tradition the formation of the yardstick against which to measure British architectural production from the late sixteenth to the early nineteenth century. The second theme is the predominance of classical styles of building in architectural histories, how the preference for this relates to the question of taste and the formation of class ideologies through the perceived uniform use of style, and within this the role of human agency.

The dominance of the classical tradition

The range of stylistic labels and categories appears to offer a great deal of choice to the architectural historian. But there are fundamentally two classifications of architectural design in the period under discussion in this book – classical and non-classical. And it can be argued that this division continues into current architectural theory and criticism. The predilection for the classical can be traced back perhaps unsurprisingly to the architectural criticism of antiquity. Vitruvius's treatise *De Architectura* (*The Ten Books of Architecture*) concentrates solely on the classical style of building. This supplied a ready-made taxonomic apparatus with which to discuss architectural design.[8] Vitruvius (*c.* 90–20 BCE) codified the classical orders of architecture and instilled into them a language and grammar which made them intelligible. The anthropocentric proportions and associations of the different orders – for instance, Doric being based on the masculine body and Ionic the feminine body – strengthens the relationship of classical architecture to a human-based appreciation of style (Figure 3.5). The reading of the orders went well beyond these binary gender divides to give a more nuanced meaning to style. As Vitruvius remarks:

> Propriety is that perfection of style which comes when a work is authoritatively constructed on approved principles . . . The temples of Minerva, Mars, and Hercules, will be Doric, since the virile strength of these gods makes daintiness entirely inappropriate to their houses. In temples to Venus, Flora. . . the Corinthian order will be found to have peculiar significance, because these are delicate divinities . . . The construction of temples of the Ionic order to Juno, Diana, father Bacchus . . . will be in keeping with the middle position which they hold; for the building as such will be an appropriate combination of the severity of the Doric and the delicacy of the Corinthian.[9]

The narratives around the orders found in Vitruvius's text embellished further their role as transmitters of ideas and ideals based in part on Greek history. Vitruvius explains the caryatid, a draped female form which takes the place of columns (Figure 3.6), in this charming history:

> . . . among the ornamental parts of an architect's design for a work, there are many underlying ideas of whose employment he [the architect] should be able to explain . . . the marble statues of women in long robes, called Caryatides . . . [can be explained thus]. Caryae, a state in Peloponnesus, sided with the Persian enemies against Greece; later the Greeks, having gloriously won their freedom by victory in the war, made common cause and declared against the people of Caryae. They took the town, killed the men, abandoned the State to desolation, and carried off their wives to slavery, without permitting them, however, to lay aside the long robes and other marks of their rank as married women, so that they might be obliged not only to march in the triumph but to appear forever after as a type of slavery, burdened with the weight of their shame and so making atonement for their State. Hence, the architects of the time designed for public buildings statues of these women, placed so as to carry a load, in order that the sin and punishment of the people of Caryae might be known and handed down even to posterity.[10]

Vitruvius's reinforcing of classical architecture with these associated values enabled the construction of an enduring canonical style imbued with a set of social and cultural beliefs

Figure 3.5 The orders of architecture, additional engraving by Giacomo Leoni to his translated edition of A. Palladio, in *I Quattro Libri Dell'Architettura* (private collection).

Figure 3.6 Erechtheon, Acropolis, Athens (detail of caryatid porch), fourth century BCE (photo, author).

expressed through a human-based system of proportions. Obviously, Virtuvius operated solely within the architecture and design of the classical world, but we can see how his appraisal of 'irregular' design, in this case wall painting, could influence the judgement on non-classical styles made by later generations of writers:

> Such things neither are, nor can be, nor have been. On these lines the new fashions compel bad judges to condemn good craftsmanship for dullness. For how can a reed actually sustain a roof, or a candelabrum the ornaments of a gable, or a soft slender stalk a seated statue, or how can flowers and half statues rise alternatively from roots and stalks? Yet when people view these falsehoods, they approve rather than condemn.[11]

This introduces the idea of truth and morality into the classical style of building. This was adopted by Giorgio Vasari in his *Lives of the Artists* which appeared in the latter half of the sixteenth century in Italy but remained a benchmark of aesthetic criticism for several centuries. The Vasarian concepts of *regola, ordine, misura, disegno a maniera* (rule, order, measure, drawing and style) drew on the Vitruvian ideal and remain touchstones of academic formal criticism and the benchmark of perceived perfection against which other indigenous traditions were always to be found wanting – not least the Gothic. Vasari's criticism is severe and has resonance with Vitruvius's misgivings expressed above:

> There is another kind of work called German . . . which could well be called Confusion or Disorder instead, for their buildings – so numerous they have infected the whole world – they made doorways decorated with columns slender and contorted like a vine, not strong enough to bear the slightest weight; in the same way on the facades . . . they made a malediction of little tabernacles one above the other, with so many pyramids and points and leaves that it seems impossible for it to support itself, let alone other weights.[12]

The concentration on stylistic elements is important here and there is no regard for the technical achievements of such structural illusionism; for Vasari it is not classical, therefore, it is not good.

The judgements of Vitruvius and Vasari were handed down through subsequent generations of writers and influenced, for instance, Winckelmann's account of the history of art which privileged the classical ideal. The veneration of classical architecture was also promoted through the academies where design was taught through rules and formulae. Academic architecture relied heavily on these textual sources for the formulation of its classical style, moreover, many architects and cognoscenti also used them as guides to the buildings of antiquity and renaissance Italy. The confluence of the verbal and the visual produced potent manifestos for classical architecture as seen in Palladio's *I Quattro Libri dell'Architettura* first published in 1570, which was used across Europe as a guide to the architecture of antiquity as well as Palladio's own buildings (Figures 3.7 and 3.8). This was translated into English in the early eighteenth century so widening the accessibility of its textual analysis of the buildings.[13] At about the same time Colen Campbell began his survey of British architecture *Vitruvius Britannicus* which ran to several volumes[14] (Figures 3.9 and 3.10). Although much less academic and analytical, the popularity of this kind of survey underscores the enduring preoccupation with the associative values of these stylistic formulae.[15]

Figure 3.7 Pantheon, Rome section and elevation as illustrated in A. Palladio, *I Quattro Libri Dell'Architettura*, 1570, book IV ch XX (private collection).

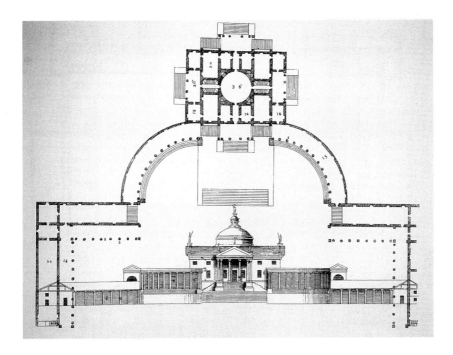

Figure 3.8 Villa Trissino at Meledo, elevation and plan as illustrated in A. Palladio, *I Quattro Libri Dell'Architettura*, 1570, book II, plate 43.

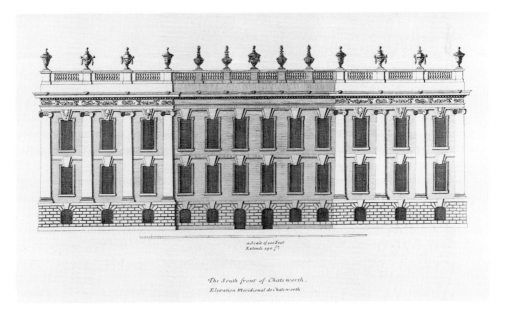

Figure 3.9 Chatsworth, Derbyshire south front as illustrated in *Vitruvius Britannicus*, Volume I, plate 76, 1715 (private collection).

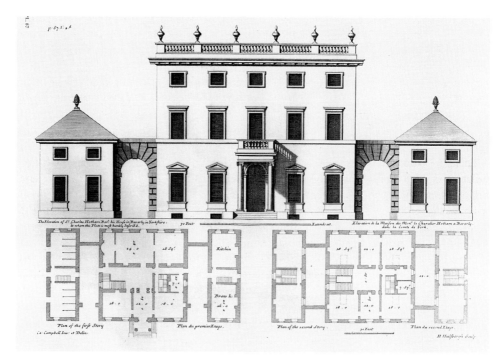

Figure 3.10 House of Sir Charles Hotham, Yorkshire as illustrated in *Vitruvius Britannicus*, Volume II, plate 87, 1717 (private collection).

Classicism, taste and the formation of class ideologies

One of the most important developments concerning the study of style was the realisation that architectural history could also be the history of ideas. But we have to consider whose ideas. Returning to Gadamer we see how architecture functions in this regard:

> Hence the comprehensive situation of architecture in relation to all the arts involves a twofold mediation. As the art which creates space it both shapes it and leaves it free. It not only embraces the decorative aspects of the shaping of space, including ornament, but is itself decorative in nature. The nature of decoration consists in performing that two-sided mediation; namely to draw the attention of the viewer to itself, to satisfy his taste, and then to direct it away from itself to the greater whole of the context of life which it accompanies.[16]

Although there had been studies made of British architecture from the eighteenth century onwards, as we have seen, the convergence of continental academics and new archives and interest led to a much wider field of investigation with far greater possibilities and with thorough attention paid both to the form of buildings and their social and cultural contexts. Now the form or style of British architecture was being scrutinised in the same way as its European counterparts and the taxonomic system of stylistic classification was grafted onto its architecture. As a result, sensitivity to the aesthetics of architecture became more refined. Previously, British architecture from Inigo Jones to Sir John Soane was simply referred to as 'renaissance' by such writers as Reginald Blomfield[17] who wished to keep a substantial distance between Britain and Europe by celebrating the divergent traits in design on either side of the Channel. Now style became subject to closer scrutiny, allowing micro-histories based on such classifications as mannerism, baroque and neo-classical, although the homogeneity of these different groupings is questionable – a point I discuss later in this chapter. The balance of analysis also shifted from the originality of a vernacular tradition based loosely on classical design as stressed by Blomfield *et al.* to the manifestation of different styles all within the classical canon and all of which borrowed heavily from European traditions.

This raises the question of a national style or school of architecture, or at least the formulation of such an idea by historians. British architecture could be seen as derivative and lacking in originality and certainly without influence in the European arena, the emphasis being on the import rather than the export of ideas. And it is difficult to find examples of the export of either British architectural styles or the employment of British architects on the continent.[18] But usually the derivative nature of British architecture has not been presented quite so unfavourably. Instead, the adoption of classical motifs has been seen as essential to the formulation of a national style of architecture, which in turn represented distinct social and political ideologies. This perception of a more uniform classical architectural vocabulary superseded the celebration of individuality and idiosyncracy in design that had been the mainstay of British architectural histories in the decades before the Second World War. Consequently one set of nationalistic aesthetic principles was replaced with another. This latter set of classical architectural formulations was at once more established within the canon of architectural design but yet more alien to indigenous traditions. In this way the presentation of histories around classical norms subjugated the taste of the individual to bigger historical forces that could account more generally for the *evolution* of style and give a sense of coherence and intellectual purpose to the architectural production of the long eighteenth century. This did not mean, however, that the political symbolism of a national architectural style was completely lost. Alongside the newly adopted taxonomies which described nuances of 'classicism' a parallel system based national political history evolved, and is still in use today. We refer to the architecture of the period covered in this volume as Tudor (sixteenth century) through Stuart, Georgian to Victorian. The teleologically imposed categories subjugate the aesthetic and instead privilege the political dominance of the monarch during the period in question. British architectural history becomes then a subnarrative of political history, so enforcing the imperialistic and nationalistic agendas at work in its production and consumption.

The architecture of antiquity remains of fundamental importance to our understanding of western culture and society, if not by its familiar presence then by its conspicuous absence. It is helpful to see classicism as a more general sign and to unpick its meaning beyond perceived stylistic homogeneity or correctness. This enables us to explore why classicism would appeal when it is not an indigenous style at times of such heightened nationalistic sentiment in Britain, as for instance in the long eighteenth century and the mid-twentieth century. This enquiry may also provide some clues as to why classicism became such a dominant narrative in so many histories of architecture. The move towards 'classical' formulae in art, architecture and literature gave British culture an appropriate pedigree and intellectual basis. The nation's belief in its cultural superiority over the rest of Europe meant it saw itself as the inheritor of the mantle of ancient Rome. This self-conscious construction of culture makes a classical past out of current beliefs and values. Classicism, in its broadest sense, is used according to its utility in a contemporary ideological system. In this way the re-use of antiquity is an invented memory with an ideological end.[19] This helps define what the use of classical motifs means in a broader historical context. The adoption of building types unsuited to the British climate such as the villa, which was in effect more of an eighteenth-century fashion accessory with a limited shelf life, is a case in point.[20]

The history of the idea of a national style which privileges configurations of classical elements helps to explain the architectural production in Britain, *c.* 1600–1840. And the identification of classicism as a primary expression of English culture helped to underpin the imperialist[21] nature of British society whilst allowing historians to credit its architecture with appropriate gravitas to hold its own in the arena of European architectural design. The diversity of classical formulae was rationalised by the selection of one strand as the progressive element. Indeed, stylistic histories that offer an evolutionary view of architecture impose a notion of continuity and progress which might not necessarily be there. But discontinuity is not a problem if the historian recognises the limitations of teleological methodologies. Palladianism might appear to be the inevitable style for the Augustan era but is this really the case (Figure 3.11)? Does something become Palladian in this era because it is no longer Baroque? And can the Baroque of architects like Vanbrugh be seen as part of the repertoire of classical elements rather than a break with the Palladian tradition (Figure 3.12)? Ultimately the repertoire of motifs, as Wittkower has suggested, is the same, but he attributes Vanbrugh and Hawksmoor with an understanding of these in contrast to those architects who used them subsequently, albeit in a more academic style.[22] Furthermore, in the absence of large numbers of replica Palladian buildings[23] it is possible that the classical style is telling a different story which remains partly unread. This is especially the case when it is remembered that the importance of classicism as an expression of cultural ideologies has been recognised in other fields of cultural production – most notably literature.[24]

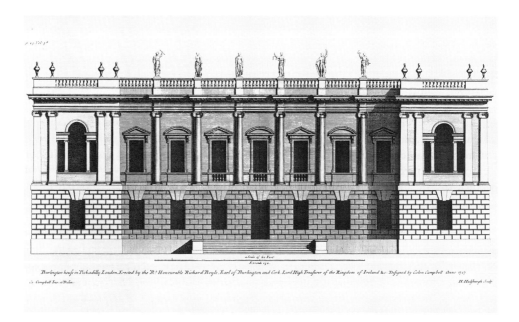

Burlington house in Piccadilly London Erected by the R.[t] Honourable Richard Boyle, Earl of Burlington and Cork, Lord High Treasurer of the Kingdom of Ireland &c. Designed by Colen Campbell Anno 1717

Figure 3.11 Burlington House, Piccadilly, London seen as the beginnings of Palladianism in Britain with its Palladian window comprising an arch flanked by two rectangles, as illustrated in *Vitruvius Britannicus*, Volume III, plate 76, 1722 (private collection).

Figure 3.12 Grimsthorpe, Lincolnshire by Sir John Vanbrugh, 1722–1726. The Palladian window motif (see Figure 3.11) also appears here despite its 'Baroque' stylistic label. As illustrated by Sir John Soane.

So far I have concentrated on an imported architectural aesthetic and its role in the production of a national style. But we have seen that it is difficult to find instances of British architecture and architects being influential outside their own country, especially in Europe. Yet if we consider architecture in a colonial context, where it represented an idea of empire, we do see the exportation of nationalistic ideals. This does not necessarily mean grand architecture, as vernacular domestic architecture was the most prevalent 'export' and in this way was an effective communicator of such ideologies. I want first to look at how British architecture is interpreted as a colonial presence and then to think about how this exterior view of it might reconfigure our interpretations and shed new light on the histories discussed in this volume.

James Deetz discusses the exportation of a national style as seen in a colonial context in his analysis of the Georgian architecture of the American colonies.

> The Georgian style, which so influenced the form of Anglo-American building . . . was introduced into the colonies at that century's end. Strictly formal in its adaptation of classical architectural detail, the Georgian was rigidly symmetrical and bilateral, both in facade and floor plan . . . The entire configuration is profoundly different from that of the houses built before its advent.
>
> . . . The wealthier men in the cities, often trained to some extent in architecture in England, were both conversant with the style and had the means to have it created in America. The number of skilled craftsmen required to create such houses was steadily

increasing in the eighteenth century . . . Perhaps the most important single factor in the introduction of the Georgian style into America was the large number of architectural books that appeared on the scene from the late seventeenth century onward . . . Volumes on the classical orders of architecture and carpenters' handbooks . . . enabled a man of means to work with experienced help to construct such a grand edifice. The fact that the houses' forms were derived from books rather than from the mind of a folk builder is what probably sets the academic Georgian apart from the vernacular tradition so clearly.

. . . it is not surprising that we see an increasing similarity in houses over all of Anglo-America as the eighteenth century progresses. Such broad similarity, with its origin among the urban élite, is one more hallmark of the re-Anglicized popular culture of America on the eve of the Revolution.

The distinction between vernacular and academic building traditions is a critical one, since each reflects different aspects of the culture that created the buildings. Vernacular building is folk building, done without benefit of formal plans. Such structures are frequently built by their occupants or, if not, by someone who is well within the occupant's immediate community. Vernacular structures are the immediate product of their users and form a sensitive indicator of these persons' inner feelings, their ideas of what is or is not suitable to them. Consequently, changes in attitudes, values, and world view are very likely to be reflected in changes in vernacular architectural forms. Academic architecture proceeds from plans created by architects trained in the trade and reflects contemporary styles of design that relate to formal architectural orders. It is much less indicative of the attitudes and life styles of the occupants of the buildings it creates. Vernacular building is an aspect of traditional culture, and academic architecture of popular culture. The change in Anglo-American building from the early seventeenth century to the end of the eighteenth century is essentially a picture of the slow development of vernacular forms under an increasing influence of the academic styles that were their contemporaries.'[25]

Deetz suggests that style, here he means academic architecture, makes distant the social and cultural conditions of production and importantly, the role of human agency. Stepping back from this we can see how perceived stylistic uniformity and readily identifiable, classifiable elements and/or architects enable historians to construct macro-histories where human agency, as expressed in this case in vernacular traditions, is subjugated to larger forces. Indeed, the emphasis on the uniformity of the town house and urban planning in the long eighteenth century as a stripped-down form of the classical ideal means individuality in design is subsumed into meta-narrative which privileges academic architecture (Figures 3.13, 3.14 and 3.15). In the case of colonial architecture the style can be seen as representing the intentions of its builders and users.

The divide suggested by Deetz between vernacular and academic architecture can be explored further if we ignore style or the aesthetic and formulate alternative classificatory schemes. The anthropologist Alfred Gell has made the contentious suggestion that art objects are the equivalent of social agents and, therefore, a system of action intended to change the world instead of encoding or symbolising it.[26] Art, then, is 'about' social relations and how primary agents, which may be users, producers or objects, make their agency effective through objects which are indices of intention and efficacy. I want briefly to see what this brings to our consideration of style. Gell's theory destabilises the importance of style both as a taxonomic historical tool and as a symbol. Instead of one

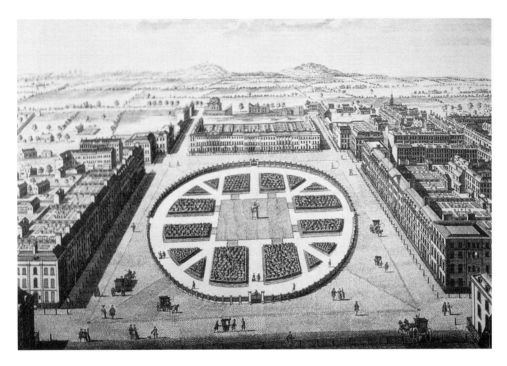

Figure 3.13 View of Grosvenor Square showing the uniform rows of eighteenth-century town houses. Engraving by Nicholls, published 1747 (private collection).

style encroaching on another we might see new building types as indices of different sets of social relations and as agents in the process of change. In this way we can take issue with Deetz's claim that '[academic architecture] is much less indicative of the attitudes and life styles of the occupants of the buildings it creates' because it is of that society and is a primary agent in changing uses of space. If we apply Gell's ideas more widely, the architectural history of Britain in the period covered in this book becomes at once liberated from the constraints of an imposed stylistic homogeneity yet fragmented into the specificity of individual agencies. But we are as a result able to consider patrons, architects, viewers and architecture as equally important agents and establish dynamic relationships between these groups.

The map of the history of British architecture is still identified as that drawn up by Sir John Summerson in his seminal work *Architecture in Britain 1530–1830.* It is important to consider how this canonical text has shaped subsequent views of architecture with particular reference to style. The choice of examples made by Summerson as a set of stepping-stones through the architecture of the Georgian period have become the benchmark of greatness. But the development of architecture in the period is presented as some kind of autogenesis where a repertoire of ornamental components re-appear. This is seen, for instance, in the diagrammatic grouping of buildings which share common stylistic elements to present some kind of formal coherence or development (see Figure 3.16 Summerson's in text). Here Summerson is concerned principally with classicism. And it is the classical country house which dominates – the 'purer' the style the better. This constructs categories of quality

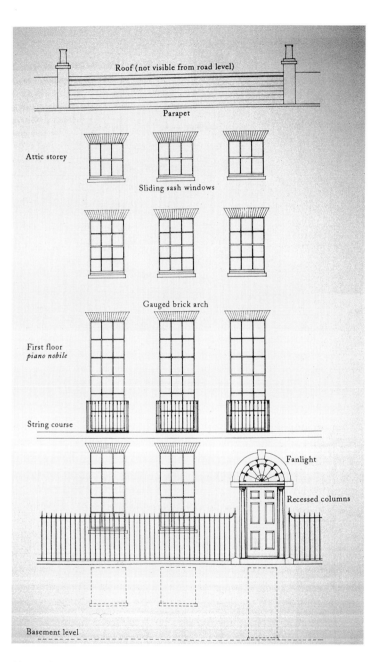

Figure 3.14 Diagrammatic representation of an eighteenth-century town house.

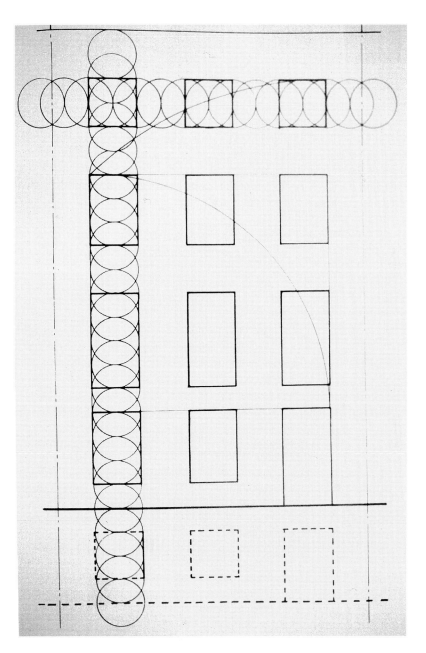

Figure 3.15 Diagram showing proportional system of an eighteenth-century town house based on the classical idea of the circle, square, and the proportional relationship of the square to the half square.

determined only by twentieth-century criteria based on a knowledge of what we know to have happened and our fuller understanding of classical systems of design. This system must embody political, economic, cultural and philosophical beliefs of the dominant ruling class. The deviations in styles, whether Palladian, neoclassical or baroque, matter less than the persistent use of this repertoire of classical elements. And on closer inspection the distinctiveness of these categories is further eroded.[27]

The purpose here is to demonstrate the diversity of classical formulae which appeared in architectural design, and if we look at classical architecture as a repertoire of forms rather than statements of specific design credos we can challenge teleological constructions of stylistic histories. The method of grouping the architecture from given periods of time under general stylistic labels has, without doubt, been the backbone of the discipline of architectural history.[28] And when used skilfully and carefully it can provide useful punctuation marks in the lengthy and complex narrative that is the subject-matter of the history of western building. Yet it is only one of many tools with which to explore social and cultural contexts.

It is not only Summerson's stylistic preoccupations which have coloured our view of the country house but also his choice of examples. The Anglocentric focus of Summerson's architectural survey results in the architecture of Scotland and Ireland being marginalised.[29] This runs contrary to and distorts the stylistic preoccupations of the survey, as architects like William Adam[30] and Edward Lovet Pearce who perhaps showed a greater architectural sensitivity to the ideas of Andrea Palladio and the baroque than the some of those more fully discussed by Summerson. But the purpose here is not to criticize Summerson. Any survey presents fundamental choices of inclusion and exclusion of material. Nor is the aim to provide a supplement to the examples Summerson discusses or to reconfigure his material or arguments. It is intended more to present and prompt an awareness of the consequences of this seminal and pioneering work for architectural history as a whole.

I have juxtaposed extracts covering Palladianism, the villa and urban architecture from *Architecture in Britain* with the work of a Marxist art historian Nicos Hadjinicolaou. His study *Art History and Class Struggle*[31] has proved a contentious but stimulating text. It presents and explores the relationship between art and class – not least the importance of style in this dynamic. I use Hadjinicolaou partly as a critique of Summerson and partly of the society that desired the architecture Summerson discusses. But his work is also a way of examining our acceptance and indulgence of the stylistic, social and cultural hegemonies that are represented in *Architecture in Britain* and the many texts which follow its lead.

Notes

1 H-G Gadamer, 'The Ontological Foundation of the Occasional and the Decorative' in *Truth and Method*, trans. William Glen Doepel, ed. John Cumming and Garrett Bardez, London, Sheed and Ward, 1979, pp. 140–142.

2 H Colvin, *A Biographical Dictionary of British Architects 1600–1840*, 3rd ed London and New Haven, CT, Yale University Press, 1995, p. 18.

3 R Wittkower, *Palladio and English Palladianism* (1945), London, Thames and Hudson, 1974.

4 Sir Niklaus Pevsner, *An Outline of European Architecture*, Harmondsworth, Penguin, 1st edn 1943, reprinted 1990, pp. 23–25.

5 For a provocative, if flawed, discussion of the relationship between style and class ideology see N Hadjinicolaou, *Art History and Class Struggle*, trans. Louise Asmal, London, Pluto, 1978: extracts cited at the end of this chapter.

6 E Bloch 'Formative Education, Engineering Form, Ornament', trans. Jane Newman and John Smith, *Oppositions*, 17, Summer 1979, pp. 45–51.

7 Pierre Bourdieu presents a sociological study

of the class implications of taste and style in, for instance, *Distinction: A social critique of the judgement of taste*, trans. Richard Nice, London, Routledge and Kegan Paul, 1984. and *The Field of Cultural Production: Essays on art and literature*, ed. Ronald Johnson, Cambridge, Polity, 1993.

8 On the point of language and criticism see the full discussion in M Baxandall *Giotto and the Orators*, Oxford, Clarendon, 1971.

9 Vitruvius, *The Ten Books of Architecture*, Book I, ch. 2, paragraph 5, trans. Morris Hickey Morgan, New York, Dover, 1960, pp. 14–15.

10 Vitruvius, *The Ten Books of Architecture*, Book I, ch. 1, paragraph 5, trans. Morris Hickey Morgan, New York, Dover Publications, 1960, p. 6–7.

11 Vitruvius, *The Ten Books of Architecture*, Book VII. ch. 5, paragraph 4, trans. Morris Hickey Morgan, New York, Dover, 1960, p. 211.

12 G Vasari *The Lives of the Artists* (1550 and 1568), trans. George Bull, Harmondsworth, Penguin, 1965.

13 It first appeared in translation (from a French version) by Giacomo Leoni in 1712 with a dedication to the new king, George I. The text was inaccurate and the plates rather crude. Better versions appeared later in the eighteenth century.

14 Campbell produced three volumes in 1715, 1717 and 1725 but the project was taken on and republished in expanded form by Woolf and Gandon later in the century.

15 Sir John Summerson's series of lectures for radio published as *The Classical Language of Architecture* (Thames and Hudson, London 1980) shows how the Vitruvian ideal seeped into architectural criticism and the choices made in selecting the visual stepping stones of architectural history.

16 H-G Gadamer, op. cit. pp. 141–142.

17 Reginald Blomfield, *A History of Renaissance Architecture in England 1500–1800*, London, George Bell and Sons, 1897.

18 In the latter half of the eighteenth century there are isolated examples of the influence of English academic architecture (i.e. that which followed the strict rules of classicism) on European architects. For instance Ange Jacques Gabriel drew on this tradition in his designs for the Ministère de la Marine and the Petit Trianon. See Fiske Kimball, *The Creation of the Rococo Decorative Style*, Philadelphia, Philadelphia Museum of Art, 1943, p. 216.

19 On this point see my discussion of the effect of the Grand Tour on architectural design and appreciation in D Arnold, *The Georgian Country House: Architecture, landscape and society*, Stroud and New York, Sutton, 1998.

20 For a full discussion of the significance of the villa in the long eighteenth century see Dana Arnold (ed.) *The Georgian Villa*, Stroud and New York, Sutton, 1996.

21 The historical background to British Imperialism and mercantilism which underpinned the choice of Augustan Rome as an imperialistic and cultural model is discussed in C Hill, *The Century of Revolution 1603–1714*, London, Oxford University Press, 1966 and W Speck, *Stability and Strife in England, 1714–1760*, Cambridge MA, Harvard University Press, 1977.

22 Wittkower makes an important distinction between the use of classical elements that shows an understanding of their function and purpose in Italian architecture and their reiteration as part of a tradition of design taught by rules in academies where these elements were divorced from their original context and subsumed into a classical repertoire. See his essay 'Pseudo-Palladian Elements in English neo-Classicism' in *England and the Mediterranean Tradition: Studies in art, history and literature*, R Wittkower (ed.), London and New York, Warburg Institute and Oxford University Press, 1945.

23 Alongside the obvious examples of Chiswick Villa and Mereworth, Nostell Priory was based on Villa Mocenigo and other Palladian villas. See P Leach *James Paine*, London, Zwemmer, 1988 p. 29. Moreover, it has been argued that Lord Burlington quickly moved away from Palladio to other expressions of classical form. On this point see J Harris 'Lord Burlington The Modern Vitruvius' in D Arnold (ed.) *The Georgian Villa*, Stroud and New York, Sutton, 1996, pp. 41–47 and C Sicca 'The Architecture of the Wall: Astylism in the Architecture of Lord Burlington, *Architectural History* 33, 1990, pp. 83–101.

24 A useful discussion of the writings of Alexander Pope in this context can be found in L Brown, *Alexander Pope*, Oxford and New York, Blackwell, 1985.

25 J F Deetz, 'Cultural Dimensions of Ethnicity in the Archaeological Record', Keynote Address, 28th Annual Meeting of the Society for Historical Archaeology, Washington, DC, 1995.

26 A Gell, *Art and Agency: An anthropological theory*, Oxford, Clarendon, 1998.

27 Summerson admits that the name Palladianism is inaccurate but nevertheless a useful taxonomic tool '. . . the whole output

of English building [from the period 1710–1750], has long ago become labelled "Palladian", a description not wholly accurate (as no such labels can be), but accurate enough and secure in acceptance.' J Summerson, *Architecture in Britain 1530–1830*, New Haven, CT and London, Yale University Press, 1993, p. 317.

28 For a fuller discussion of trends in the writing of architectural history in Britain see D Watkin, *The Rise of Architectural History*, The Architectural Press, London, 1980.

29 For instance, brief sections on 'Palladianism in Scotland' and 'Palladianism in Ireland' appear on pp. 376–380 of the 1977 edition.

30 For a fuller discussion of the work of William Adam see J Gifford, *William Adam 1689–1748: A life and times of Scotland's universal architect*, Edinburgh, Mainstream 1989.

31 N Hadjinicolaou, op. cit.

Architecture in Britain, 1530–1830

Sir John Summerson

The Palladian movement: Campbell, Burlington, and Kent

About the time that Blenheim was finishing and the Queen Anne churches were rising, when Wren was very old, Vanbrugh and Hawksmoor past their prime, and Archer in affluent retirement, English architecture entered a period during which it became increasingly subject to what has appropriately been called the Rule of Taste. During that period, which lasted for about forty years, a set of distinct ideas as to what was good in architecture became widely held, and standards, based on the acknowledged excellence of certain architects and authors, were widely endorsed. This period of consolidation, during which the influence of a small group of architects and amateurs became impressed on the whole output of English building, has long ago become labelled 'Palladian', a description not wholly accurate (as no such labels can be), but accurate enough and secure in acceptance.

How and among whom this Palladian taste became formed it will be our business presently to inquire. The first point to note is that it had nothing to do with Wren, Vanbrugh, Hawksmoor, or Archer except in so far as, by excluding the works of these architects from salvation, it was better able to distinguish its own particular sort of grace. The second point to note is that, once formulated, the Palladian taste became the taste of the second generation of the Whig aristocracy, the sons of that Whiggery which dated its accession to power from 1688 and to which, in Anne's time, artistic and intellectual leadership, once centred at the Court, had passed. This second Whig generation had strong beliefs and strong dislikes, conspicuous among the latter being the Stuart dynasty, the Roman Church, and most things foreign. In architectural terms that meant the Court taste of the previous half-century, the works of Sir Christopher Wren in particular and anything in the nature of Baroque.

As spokesman of that generation, we cannot do better than lend our ear to the Earl of Shaftesbury who, writing from Italy in 1712, expressed himself forcibly concerning English architecture of the age of Wren.[1] 'Thro' several reigns we have patiently seen the noblest publick Buildings perish (if I may say so) under the Hand of one single Court-Architect; who, if he had been able to profit by Experience, wou'd long since, at our expence, have prov'd the greatest Master in the World. But', he continues, 'I question whether our Patience is like to hold much longer', and he consoles himself with the reflexion that a new Whitehall and a new House of Parliament are opportunities still unspoilt. 'Hardly . . . as the Publick now stands, shou'd we bear to see a *Whitehall* treated like a *Hampton-Court*, or even a new Cathedral like St Paul's.' Shaftesbury was the complete Whig and, according to him, the British people, having solved the fundamental problem of government, were now in the best possible position to develop the arts. To this end, an Academy should be established; and it is with a general plea for such an institution that the letter concludes.

It is noteworthy that Shaftesbury gives no hint as to the character of the reformed archi-tecture of Whig Britain, and although, in another of his writings, he says that it should be 'founded in truth and nature' and 'independent of fancy', he is merely restating an already worn platitude. Shaftesbury's intuition, however, was correct. At the moment he wrote, an architectural movement in Britain was beginning to stir and it did ultimately permeate the whole building capacity of the nation with astonishing thoroughness. Moreover, his notion of an Academy was taken up, as we shall see, almost at once and never quite lost sight of until finally realized in the Royal foundation of 1768. How and when did the new taste begin to appear? To answer this question we must take our bearings from two important books, the first volumes of which appeared in 1715.

The first of these books was the first volume of *Vitruvius Britannicus*, a folio of 100 engravings of classical buildings in Britain. Volume 2 appeared in 1717 and a supplementary volume in 1725. The author was Colen Campbell (?1676–1729).

The second book was a translation of Palladio's *I Quattro Libri Dell'Architettura*, in two folio volumes with plates specially redrawn by Giacomo Leoni (1686–1746) and engraved in Holland, and the text translated by Nicholas Dubois (*c*. 1665–1735), who also supplied an introduction. Publication was spread over several years.[2]

These two books have certain things in common. Both are dedicated to George I and thus stamped as Whiggish products. Further, both evince the same distinct architectural loyalties namely, to Palladio and Inigo Jones as the two modern masters to whom the British architect is to look for guidance, to the exclusion of all others. Further, both books show that their authors knew of the large collections of drawings left by Jones and fully appreciated their importance. That there was no rivalry between the two projects is shown by the fact that Dubois quotes appreciatively from Campbell's introduction in his own.

Here, then, we have two books and three persons Campbell, Leoni, and Dubois con-cerned in the inauguration of a Palladian movement coupled with the name of Inigo Jones. A careful analysis of the contents of Campbell's first volume justifies us in adding a fourth name and an influential one, that of William Benson (1682–1754), the man who was very shortly to succeed Wren as Surveyor of the Works and whose brief occupancy of that office we noted earlier. The reason Benson comes into the picture is that in 1710 (according to *Vitruvius Britannicus*) he built for himself Wilbury House, Newton Toney, Wilts. Campbell illustrates the design and distinguishes it as being 'in the style of Inigo Jones'. It derives largely from Amesbury, a house built by John Webb from a Jonesian design and only a few miles from Newton Toney. Wilbury as designed represents, so far as we know, the earliest evi-dence of anything in the nature of an Inigo Jones revival.[3]

Benson was certainly the most influential of the group. He was Sheriff of Wiltshire in 1710, a prominent Whig writer, and M.P. for Shaftesbury in 1715. He spent some years before 1714 at the Electoral Court of Hanover where, by devising the mechanical parts of the fountains at Herrenhausen, he no doubt prepared his future sovereign's mind for his ele-vation to the Surveyorship. Giacomo Leoni, a Venetian by birth, had been employed by the Elector Palatine. Nicholas Dubois was probably the oldest of the group, having been born about 1665. William III had sent him to Holland as tutor to the son of the Prince of Orange. In 1715 he described himself as one of George I's 'engineers', and in 1719 became (perhaps through Benson's influence) Master Mason.[4] As for Campbell, he was a Scotsman and a lawyer. He launched his *Vitruvius Britannicus* under the patronage of the Scottish nobility in general and the clan Campbell in particular.[5] He had built a house in Glasgow for one of the clan in 1712 and had perhaps come south in pursuit of the large number of

Scottish notables who had made for London after the Union of 1707. In 1718 Benson succeeded Wren as Surveyor-General and brought in Campbell as his deputy. Both were obliged to retire in the following year but their brief authority enabled Campbell to design Rolls House and Benson to insist upon the addition of a Jonesian balustrade to the parapets of St Paul's Cathedral. The relations of this group of architects cannot be precisely determined, but it looks as if Campbell, Dubois, and Benson between them initiated both the Palladian movement and its counterpart, the Inigo Jones revival.

Why, and under what inspiration, did these people seek so energetically the diversion of English taste from the French, Dutch, and Italian models of Wren, Hawksmoor, Vanbrugh, and Archer? The motive probably has some connexion with that search for absolutes with which the French Academy had for many years been concerned and which had given rise to much painful argument between 'ancients' and 'moderns', between those who believed that the architecture of antiquity comprehended a *complete* rational system of architecture and those who held that innovation was to a certain extent permissible. Those quarrels, by 1710, had become quiescent in France, but the search for absolutes was open to anybody to resume and in England it had some flavour of novelty, while Vanbrugian Baroque offered a wonderful target for polemics. Moreover, the dawning philosophy of Whiggism was extremely propitious to a thesis which embraced, at one and the same time, a devotion to antiquity, a flexibility authorized jointly by Palladio and common sense, and a strong national loyalty in the figure of Inigo Jones.

One further point. Not only the reputation (and the drawings) of Inigo but that of Palladio were ready to be exploited here in England, for as far back as 1665 Evelyn had published his translation of Roland Fréart's *Parallèle*, a book of pronouncedly Palladian prejudice. The new Palladians had but to select threads from the English past and draw them together. The exposition of the new pattern required a master and it found one – in Colen Campbell. It required an ascending phase of building activity and it found one – in the country house boom of the 1720s.

[. . .]

Wanstead was a key building of its age. It looked back to Castle Howard, but by virtue of its purity of detail superseded that house as a model. In its designing there were three stages. Wanstead I is a simple 'double pile' with hall and salons on the main axis and six rooms interconnecting on each side, providing as many rooms *en suite* as there are at Castle Howard though not (as there) in one long vista, but doubled back. The elevation is an unbroken rectangle and there is an obvious revulsion from the mobile and plastic character of Castle Howard.

Wanstead II, the executed design, approaches a little nearer to Castle Howard. It is lengthened from 200 ft to 260 ft and is made to consist of a centre and lower wings. Furthermore, in the design (though not as it was executed) there is a cupola over the hall, an equivalent in silhouette to the dome of Castle Howard. Finally, in Wanstead III Campbell added towers (never built) to this elevation thus reproducing the Castle Howard composition pretty completely, though now without the cupola. All three designs were to prove classic statements by which English country houses were influenced, directly or indirectly, for half a century. Wanstead was tremendously admired and, being near London, much visited. Its size and the lavish splendour of its grounds impressed all. To the connoisseur the beautiful novelties will have been (*a*) the horizontal divisions of the façade, detailed on the basis of a thorough study of Inigo Jones and wholly devoid of fancies and affectations; and (*b*) the portico – 'a just Hexastyle, the first yet practised in this manner in the Kingdom'. The portico was not merely an applied effect; the roof behind the pediment rode right across the house and the

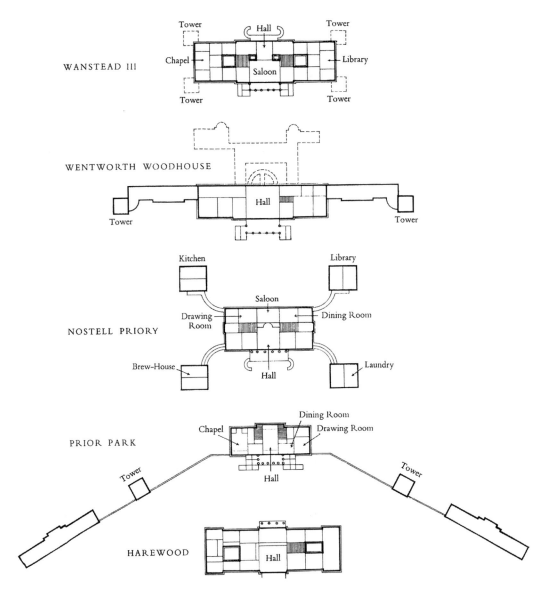

Figure 3.16 Plans of Wanstead III and four derivatives as shown in *Architecture in Britain, 1530–1830.*

interior Corinthian order of the hall was nearly identical in size and nearly ranged with that of the portico, so that the temple idea was pretty forcibly implanted. No previous English house had displayed such spectacular and rational loyalty to Rome.

The main derivatives of Wanstead are found within the twenty years ahead from 1715. Almost immediately there was a crop of grand porticos and of these Benjamin Styles's at Moor Park, Herts, designed probably by James Thornhill, is the one survivor. But Moor Park does not show a true appreciation of Campbell and it was not till round about 1733–5 that three houses were begun which were conscious and studied derivatives. The earliest of the three is Wentworth Woodhouse, Yorks. This house had been under reconstruction since soon after 1716 in a mildly Baroque style by Thomas Watson–Wentworth, who became Lord Malton in 1728. By 1733 he had started the eastern block which is a building in itself, extending right across and concealing the older parts and continuing in long outlying wings to a total length of 606 ft. In the centre of this enormous range is a very close imitation of Wanstead II. Next to it, on either side are blocks of offices with pedimented centres, and these blocks are linked by short curved portions to towers suggested by those belonging to Wanstead III. The total composition carried the idea of an extended Wanstead just about as far as it could be taken without a collapse of architectural coherence.

Begun almost at the same time as the great east range of Wentworth Woodhouse was Nostell Priory, built by Sir Rowland Winn. Here the main block of the house is a derivative, both in plan and elevation, of Wanstead I but curtailed, with thirteen windows instead of seventeen to the principal floor, and the portico (here Ionic) flattened against the house. Here the appendages were originally intended to take the form of four square pavilions linked to the house by quadrant passages in the manner of Palladio's design for a Mocenigo villa; but only one was built.

[. . .]

The villa

Turning now from the great practitioners to the field in which they practised, it becomes necessary to investigate what, in the middle of the eighteenth century, was happening to the English country house. We have seen that Colen Campbell, within the decade 1715–1725, set forth a number of important new models. These were of two distinct kinds: (i) The great 'house of parade', exemplified in Wanstead and Houghton and based on seventeenth-century types, and (ii) The 'villa', after Palladio, exemplified in Stourhead, Mereworth, Newby, and Lord Pembroke's house at Whitehall. Of the two sorts of models, it was the 'house of parade' which had, at first, the most resounding success; the derivatives of Wanstead and the derivatives of Houghton make up the grand succession of country houses of the thirties and forties. In the fifties, however, there are signs that these huge fabrics are losing their appeal and by 1760 they have manifestly lost it. The Wanstead type and the Houghton type are being superseded – by the villa.

In using the word 'villa' we must be careful about its meaning in the eighteenth-century context. Palladio himself, from whom the English villa idea ultimately derives, does not call his country houses villas; he calls them *case di villa*, which allows to *villa* the meaning of a country estate as distinct from the owner's house. Throughout the three volumes of *Vitruvius Britannicus* Campbell uses the word villa once only and then with the exact Palladian meaning of a country estate – not just a house. When Kent, in 1727, published plans and elevations of Lord Burlington's villa at Chiswick he did not call it a villa but simply Lord Burlington's 'building' at Chiswick. Gibbs, on the other hand, in his *Book of Architecture* of 1728, calls two of his designs *villas* (italicizing the word) and they happen to be designs for houses in the

Thames Valley intended for the Duke of Argyll and his brother, Lord Islay, so that Gibbs seems to recognize the villa both as a nobleman's secondary seat and as more or less suburban – a meaning it certainly possessed later on. By 1750 its diminutive character was established, for Robert Morris alludes in a book of that year to 'the cottage or plain little villa' and Horace Walpole uses villa as a diminutive in 1752. It may well be that Lord Burlington's Chiswick villa – small in size and tiny in scale – did more than anything to reduce the villa image from the amplitude it had acquired through the pages of Pliny.

The Earl of Burlington's seat at Chiswick is properly a villa and by much the best in Britain', wrote Sir John Clerk of Penicuik after a visit in 1727,[6] and there is no doubt that the house made a great impression. So did Marble Hill. So did Stourhead. But if we look round for imitations of these in the thirties and forties there are not so very many. Bower House, Havering, Essex (1729), by Flitcroft is a plain version of the Marble Hill type. Frampton Court, Gloucestershire (1731–3), is an ornate distortion of Stourhead by a Bristol architect, John Strachan. Linley Hall, Shropshire (1742–3), is a fascinating interpretation of the villa idea by Henry Joynes, still using his old master Vanbrugh's vocabulary. But these are curiosities and it is only with the 1750s – a generation after the prototype statements – that we find the villa idea really breaking through. Then it certainly does, to the extent that one is tempted to speak of a 'villa revival'. This revival – if we may so call it for the moment – took as its patterns the villa designs of Campbell, Burlington, and Morris. Its course is most easily traced by considering the houses built by two architects already mentioned – Isaac Ware and Sir Robert Taylor – and a third whose career in the main belongs to a later chapter – Sir William Chambers.

Ware's first work in the villa style was Clifton Hill House, built for a Bristol merchant in 1746–50, though the plan is quite commonplace and not what one would expect from the exteriors. Before 1756, he had built two villas in Scotland, both with service wings linked to the houses by passages. In 1755 Sir Robert Taylor built Harleyford Manor, Bucks, in 1756 Danson Hill, Kent, and in 1758–67 Asgill House, Richmond, all on the outskirts of London

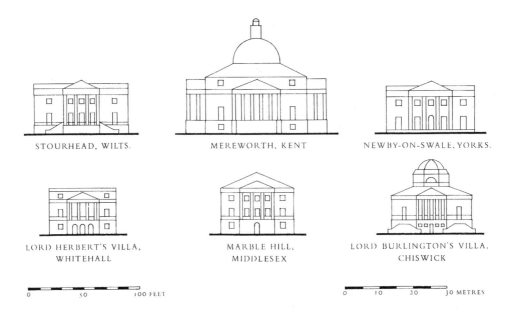

STOURHEAD, WILTS.   MEREWORTH, KENT   NEWBY-ON-SWALE, YORKS.

LORD HERBERT'S VILLA,   MARBLE HILL,   LORD BURLINGTON'S VILLA,
WHITEHALL   MIDDLESEX   CHISWICK

0   50   100 FEET

0   10   20   30 METRES

Figure 3.17 Anglo-Palladian villa prototypes as shown in *Architecture in Britain, 1530–1830.*

and all for wealthy City men. Asgill House (already mentioned) introduced the half-pediments of Palladio's church-fronts, probably following the example of Kent in a design for a garden building at Chiswick. More striking evidence of the revival is the building of two further imitations of Palladio's Rotonda – one being Nuthall Temple, Notts (destroyed), for Sir Charles Sedley and the other Foot's Cray Place, Kent, for Bourchier Cleeve, the financier. Both belong around 1754 – a generation after Campbell's Mereworth – and the architect of Foot's Cray was probably Ware; it almost certainly prompted Sir William Chambers' design for Lord Bessborough's villa at Roehampton to which we shall come presently.

To 1754 also belongs what is perhaps the most significant house of the decade Ware's Wrotham, Middlesex, for Admiral John Byng. Here we have a composition consisting of a centre which is palpably a villa (strongly marked by Chiswick influences) to which wings terminating in pavilions are added, the whole thing from end to end being, however, a single continuous house. Nothing could mark more emphatically the ascendancy of the villa idea than this new handling of an arrangement which in outline goes back to Wanstead III but is now re-assessed to introduce the fashionable villa element at its centre. If we compare Wrotham with Carr's Harewood, built four years later, we see the crossing of ascendant and descendant types. Harewood is arrived at by telescoping the plan of Wanstead III; Wrotham by expanding a villa into a house of parade.

It is obvious that the works of Ware and Taylor were creating a new situation in country-house design. It is obvious, too, that the villa had been taken up by the new-rich – from 1750 it has strongly mercantile patronage. So that when a newcomer, William Chambers, arrived on the scene fresh from Italy in 1755 it was the villa theme which offered itself as the obvious path for an aspiring talent. But Chambers' work belongs to a later chapter.

Palladianism in Scotland

On the death, in 1710, of Sir William Bruce, Scotland's last Court architect, the architecture of the country was in a condition of remote provincialism from which it was not to emerge for half a century. Colen Campbell's respectably classical house for a Glasgow merchant was exceptional, and it was perhaps inevitable that its gifted architect should seek fame and fortune in London. In his *Vitruvius Britannicus* Campbell mentions a Mr James Smith as being 'the most experience'd architect of' Scotland and illustrates a rather grim, plain house built by him in 1697. Smith had, in fact, been to Italy and was a student of Palladio, though this hardly emerges in the few designs known to have been executed, all of which seem to have English affiliations.

After 1715 and much more after 1745, opportunities for architecture did gradually increase in Scotland, thanks to those noblemen and lairds who began to enclose land and enrich themselves and the country by adopting English methods of agriculture. A large proportion of these opportunities fell to William Adam (1688–1748), a man of some property and standing who held an important official post as Master Mason in North Britain to the Board of Ordnance. Adam enlarged and reconstructed Smith's house for the Duke of Hamilton and succeeded Smith at other great houses. At Hopetoun he transformed Bruce's house into a grandiose pile, owing much to Winde's Buckingham House, London. Most of his houses reflect the mixed influence of Wren, the Palladians, and Gibbs, and Adam showed no desire to discriminate between them. His interiors have rich Rococo plaster-work. In a general way, he adopted Palladian plan arrangements, while Wren's motif of a pediment against a high attic was a favourite, and heavily rusticated architraves of the Gibbs type give some of his houses a quaintly barbaric richness. Latterly, his eldest son John brought a purer Palladianism into the business. Adam had his works engraved, with those of a few other

Scottish architects, and sets of these engravings were eventually (*c.* 1810) published under the rather presumptuous title of *Vitruvius Scoticus*.

Scotland, shorn in 1707 of Court and Parliament, had not the need nor the means for much public architecture. At Edinburgh William Adam built the Royal Infirmary (destroyed), with its square French dome, in 1738. The Royal Exchange (now the Burgh Hall), by J. Fergus, followed in 1753–61. To William Adam again is due the Town House, Dundee (demolished), a roughly Palladian mass, on a traditional Scottish plan, surmounted by a Gibbsian steeple. But these are the best of a period in Scottish history when architecture cannot be said to have flourished.

Palladianism in Ireland

In contrast to the economic and cultural poverty of Scotland, Ireland presents the picture of a country poverty-stricken indeed but supporting an alien aristocracy of great wealth and cultural vitality. At Dublin the Parliament and the Vice-regal Court provided the focus for a metropolitan life scarcely less lavish and varied than that of Westminster, and with architectural opportunities more obvious because less obstructed by an inheritance of old buildings. Here Palladianism flourished exuberantly for thirty years, contributing to the movement two or three at least of its finest monuments.

The most interesting Palladian building in Ireland is the old Parliament House, Dublin, now the Bank of Ireland, built in 1728–39 and comprising a House of Lords and House of Commons, behind an imposing colonnaded approach. The Surveyor-General for Ireland in 1728 was Thomas Burgh (d. 1730), whose Trinity College Library (finished 1732) is a simple three-storey mass showing Gibbsian rather than Palladian influence. Burgh, however, appears to have delegated the Parliament building wholly to a younger man, Edward Lovet Pearce (*c.* 1699–1733), and it was Pearce who was responsible for the provision of drawings and the expenditure of funds.

Pearce was a man of good family, whose father was first cousin to Sir John Vanbrugh. Like Vanbrugh, he started his career soldiering, but in 1723 was in Italy and France and in 1724 in Geneva. Again like Vanbrugh, his period of architectural tutelage is a blank. However, by the time he had begun to deputize for Burgh he was a fair draughtsman and had mastered the Palladianism of Campbell; while the designs for the Parliament House strongly suggest that he was in the counsels of the Burlington group. The octagonal House of Commons (burnt in 1792), with its dome showing externally, recalls the octagon of Chiswick House; its internal treatment, with an Ionic order raised on a high plinth, is prophetic of the hall at Holkham.

The colonnaded approach to the Dublin building is strikingly original. Lateral colonnades, entered from arches, return along the main front and meet in the portico, which breaks forward without the intermediacy of piers. This and Pearce's other works, which include the south front of Drumcondra House (1727) and Cashel Palace (*c.* 1731), show him to have been one of the most interesting figures in the whole Palladian school. In 1730, he succeeded Burgh as Surveyor-General but three years later he died.[7]

The influence, no doubt through Pearce, of the Burlington group on Irish architecture extends to the mansion which Speaker Conolly built for himself at Castletown, Kildare, in 1725–30. This has a three-storey, thirteen-window front of stupendous monotony, recalling Burlington's Westminster Dormitory (fifteen windows) begun three years earlier. The actual authorship of Castletown is doubtful – Alessandro Galilei appears at one stage to have been consulted.[8]

[. . .]

The house and the street in the eighteenth century

Such variations as these vanish with the onset of Palladian influence; for the movement rapidly established a new formula for the London house. This derived from the old houses in Lincoln's Inn Fields and Queen Street (generally supposed, at the time, to be by, or connected with, Inigo Jones) and insisted on a major emphasis at the level of the first floor. It did not insist on the application of pilasters. It involved not an applied but an *implied* order, standing (with or without pedestal) at first-floor level. This idea, of course, is implicit in any part of a Palladian design (e.g. the sides of a villa) where the order is not expressed; and its application to the ordinary London house is perhaps too obvious a move to be accounted a stroke of genius. Yet the success of the formula makes its introduction important. From about 1730 till well after 1830 the façade of the London house was loyal to this Palladian *schema*. Where there is an order, it rises at first-floor level through two or three storeys to the entablature, above which there may be an attic. Where there is no order, a broad band marks the first-floor level and there is room between the lintels of the top windows and the cornice for the architrave and frieze which are not there. Sometimes an additional (narrow) band runs under the cills of the first-floor windows in token (as in many Palladian villas) of an absent pedestal under the order.

It is impossible definitely to locate the first London houses in which this formula was introduced, but one naturally looks towards the streets around Burlington House, where building began soon after 1717 and where there are houses of the older type adjacent to others of a more Palladian character which must reflect the influence of Burlington himself. In Burlington Gardens we find Queensberry House, now the Bank of Scotland, with a noble Composite façade by Leoni based on Lindsey House, Lincoln's Inn Fields. This façade [9] not only resurrects in a splendid way the theme of 1630, but controls the proportions of the houses in Old Burlington Street, where they meet its return façade. Now the date of Queensberry House is given by Leoni as 1721, so here is the probable birthplace of the Palladian town house. In Old Burlington Street a broad stone band, continuing from Queensberry House, emphasizes the primacy of the first-floor level. In the next street, Savile Row, the *schema* is independently introduced and the narrow stone band at cill level is added – perhaps for the first time in a street of plain houses.

Palladian houses of the Burlington Gardens and Savile Row kind are still common in London and we mentioned a few in dealing with Flitcroft, Ware, and Vardy. Representing the later Palladian phase, there are several fine examples by Sir Robert Taylor.

The London house naturally led the way in design throughout the country, and there is little to add concerning the provincial town house except that it developed, all along, much later than its prototype and often with much greater elaboration. There are Palladian town houses in York, Norwich, Bristol, Derby, Nottingham, and many smaller places, which in the London of their time would have ranked as very conspicuous and even pretentious residences. Usually they overlap in date the next phase of innovation in the capital, but in design and execution they are often equal to the best London work.

[. . .]

Bath and John Wood I

With the completion of Shepherd's Grosvenor Square houses, about 1730, the development of urban design in London ceases, for a time, to be of much interest. The story, however, continues and reaches its climax in Bath where street design developed in a most important way for a matter of forty years.

Bath in the first quarter of the eighteenth century was still a small town dependent on a moribund wool industry, but with an extraneous attraction in the qualities of its famous waters. That attraction had drawn royal health-seekers and, in their train, a section of London society in search of a summer centre of amusement, when the Court was out of town. By 1720 the city's social reputation was already high, and its architecture, hitherto indistinguishable from that of any moderately thriving west-country town, began to receive distinguished additions. Of these, one of the earliest and most important was a house in Abbey Church Yard (*c.* 1720) built for General Wade and closely imitating the 'Inigo Jones' façade in Lincoln's Inn Fields. We do not know who designed it, but a local mason with *Vitruvius Britannicus*, Volume I before him would fill the rôle.

The great period, however, of Bath's expansion began in 1725. In that year, 'Beau' Nash as Master of Ceremonies was at the height of his influence, while the brains and capital of Ralph Allen were exploiting the capabilities of Bath stone. In that year also John Wood (1704–54) drew the first plans of those parts of the city with which his name will always be associated.

Now these plans were drawn by Wood not in Bath but in Yorkshire, a country where he enjoyed the patronage of Lord Bingley, whose seat was at Bramham, near Tadcaster. The house at Bramham was built in 1710, possibly by Archer. Wood came on the scene about fifteen years later and was certainly engaged on the lay-out of the Park at Bramham, for there is an engraving bearing his name which shows an ambitious design in the Le Nôtre manner; one feature of this plan is highly important (as we shall see) in view of Wood's later planning activities in Bath.

In 1725–7, however, Wood was mostly in London, where he was employed by the Duke of Chandos on some trifling work in Cavendish Square and where he may also have been associated with building activities on the Grosvenor Estate. It was in London that Wood approached two owners of land near Bath with the development schemes he had prepared in Yorkshire. One of these landowners, Robert Gay, accepted his proposal and employed him as his agent. Almost at the same time (1727) Wood undertook a considerable rebuilding scheme in Bath for the Duke of Chandos and was also involved in other projects there, including a Hospital, for Humphrey Thayer.

In 1727, Wood moved to Bath and lived there until his death twenty-seven years later. He soon found himself not only architect and builder but lease-holder of much of Gay's land, on which, at his own risk, he started to build Queen Square (1729–36). In view of Wood's London experience, it is not surprising to find that Queen Square is directly related to the great west London estates of the time. Its north side, with its rusticated ground floor and attached portico, is, in fact, a fulfilment of Edward Shepherd's thwarted intentions in Grosvenor Square, while the original arrangement of the west side, with a house set back and two more as salient wings, echoed a proposal (not executed) by the Duke of Chandos for the north side of Cavendish Square. In short, Wood's first work in Bath is the direct outcome of the most recent architectural experiments in London.

But if Queen Square is, for that reason, important in the history of architecture, John Wood's further works at Bath are much more so. He had a curiously original mind, fundamentally unlearned, but steeped in amateur erudition. As his *Origin of Building* shows, he had read a great deal, and out of this reading had come the conception of an expanded Bath with something of the character of its ancient Roman predecessor. Wood never lived to see the rediscovery of the ancient Baths, but he knew the city had been Roman, and was determined to re-endow it with Roman monuments, including a Forum, a Circus, and what he called an Imperial Gymnasium. This quixotic ambition he partly achieved. In the South

Parade (1743 onwards) and the open space in front of it, we see the relics of Wood's Forum; had it been completed according to his desires, it would have consisted of houses with classical palace façades facing on to sunk gardens with rusticated retaining walls related in design to the houses – an original and striking conception. As it stands it is a rather tame composition standing above an extensive car park.

But if the Forum misfired, the Circus was a considerable success. Although Wood first conceived his Circus as a place 'for the exhibition of sports', the fantastic impracticability of such a project in eighteenth-century Bath must soon have dawned on him. The conception became practicable only when he merged the Circus idea with the idea already embodied in Grosvenor Square and Queen Square – that is to say, the treatment of a row of ordinary town-houses as a monumental unity.

The Circus at Bath was ridiculed by Smollett as a toy Colosseum 'turned outside in' and Soane likewise thought of it so. Its origins however are a good deal more abstruse and Professor Piggott has even suggested with some probability that Wood's historical fantasies, in which 'druidical' civilization played a prominent part, induced him to think of Stonehenge as a prototype.[10] Inigo Jones's restoration of Stonehenge, published by Webb in 1655, does indeed show three entries in the outer bank of the monument and triple entry is one of the special features of the Circus. An alternative and more prosaic explanation may be that the plan is that of a *rond-point* in the tradition of French garden lay-out of the Le Nôtre school, and we only have to glance at Wood's engraving of the gardens at Bramham to see where, in fact, this important element in the design comes from. Nor should it be forgotten that J. H. Mansart had built his circular Place des Victoires in 1686.

One of the streets leading into the Circus is Gay Street, the first Bath street planned by Wood on the Gay estate. The other two are short streets leading to the two major works of Wood's son and successor who bore the same name. One of these is the Assembly Rooms: the others is the Royal Crescent.

John Wood II: the invention of the crescent

The elder Wood lived only to see his Circus begun. He died in 1754, and it was completed by his son. In 1766 the younger Wood acquired, in partnership with another person, a piece of land westwards of the Circus and on this he built the Royal Crescent (1767–75). This great semi-elliptical block, comprising thirty houses, is of very special importance in the history of English architecture, for it introduced a type of urban composition which was employed over and over again, with innumerable variations, until well into the nineteenth century.

The creation of this type was a remarkable stroke. Probably it developed out of the Circus by way of the notion of an elliptical 'circus' following, more or less, the true curvature of the Roman Colosseum. That conception was split into two 'demi-colosseums' by the need for a road passing through the structure. The omission of one of the 'demi-colosseums' leaves the Crescent.[11] The younger Wood, however, did not retain in his 'demi-colosseum' the ordonnance his father used in the Circus, but adopted the simpler canon which had first appeared in London in Lindsey House. The result is a noble sweep of Ionic columns, raised on a high base. The scale is much greater than that of the Circus, the monumentality more effective.

Taken together, the Circus and the Royal Crescent with Gay Street and Queen Square form a highly original complex of urban architecture. Nowhere in Europe had anything with quite this same freedom and invention been executed. In England the influence of these things was naturally very great, Bath having become, by the middle of the eighteenth century, nearly as important a centre of artistic leadership as London. The idea of blocks of town-houses presented as monumental unities was immediately accepted. The Circus, it is true, was rarely imitated until Dance, followed by Nash, took up the theme for its merits as a way of dealing with a traffic-crossing. But the Crescent had a glorious career.

The first important imitation of the Bath crescent was at Buxton, Derbyshire, where the 5th Duke of Devonshire employed (1779–81) John Carr of York to build a structure comparable in many ways to Royal Crescent, Bath. But Carr went back to another famous classic of the Inigo Jones period – the Piazzas of Covent Garden, giving his crescent a round-arched loggia on the ground floor. At Bath, Camden Crescent, by John Eveleigh, was built in 1788, to be followed at once by John Palmer's Lansdown Crescent, and by Somerset Place, again by Eveleigh. The fashion soon spread about the country. In London a miniature crescent and circus, joined by a short street, were laid out off the Minories by the younger Dance as early as 1768, before the Bath crescent was complete; and Dance's later planning schemes introduced the feature frequently, though few of his projects were executed. The crescent arrived at the seaside before the end of the century, and Royal Crescent, Brighton, was built in 1798. Here the theme of a 'demi-colosseum' is quite forgotten. There is no order, nor even the token of one; angular bay windows to each house are introduced and here, too, the verandah makes one of its first appearances in this country.

Street design: later developments

Street design up to the time of the Regency will be found to be loyal, in principle, to what had been developed in Bath. The two most important names in English planning during the period are those of Robert Adam and George Dance II, whose careers will be dealt with in the chapters which follow. Both of them recognized the principle of the monumentally treated block of ordinary houses, with centre and wings emphasized, as the proper solution of the urban street problem. We shall find Adam using this theme at the Adelphi (1768), Portland Place (1774), and Fitzroy Square (1790), London, and Charlotte Square, Edinburgh (1791). For William Pulteney's Bathwick estate at Bath, Adam prepared plans one of which has features recalling Wren's London project of 1666. Adam built the bridge (Pulteney Bridge, 1769–74) which links the estate to the city, but it was Thomas Baldwin (*c.* 1751–1820) who, basing himself on Adam, laid out the 100-foot wide Great Pulteney Street (1788). Baldwin also designed the charming Bath Street, Bath (1791), where the fronts of the houses are supported on slim Ionic columns so that a covered promenade is formed behind them.

George Dance II's planning schemes prepared for the Corporation of the City of London exist mostly on paper, but show that he was bent on developing the discoveries of the two Woods. Among other things, he planned Alfred Place (1790) off Tottenham Court Road, London, with two facing crescents joined by a broad street, the fronts of the houses (all rebuilt) being designed by him.

The square, the crescent, and the circus, alone and in combination, formed the basic elements in English town-planning till the end of our period, and in a later chapter we shall discuss their architectural development in the hands of John Nash in London and by other architects elsewhere in Britain.

Notes

1 *A Letter concerning the Art or Science of Design.*
2 Leoni's versions of Palladio's designs are so free as almost to amount to Baroque re-interpretations. R. Wittkower, 'Giacomo Leoni's Edition of Palladio, etc.', *Arte Veneta* (1954), suggests that Leoni lost Burlington's favour on this account.
3 The present house does not correspond at all closely with Campbell's illustration, but there is no mistaking its architect's intention to imitate Jones.
4 He designed the remarkable circular staircase at Chevening and a large house at Stanmer, Sussex (1722–7), which, while free from any Baroque taint, is not notably Palladian.
5 Campbell has been identified, though not securely, as Colin Campbell of Boghole who graduated in Edinburgh in 1695 and practised as a lawyer in Edinburgh and London. *Architectural Review*, August 1966 and February 1967.
6 For this extract from the Penicuik papers I am indebted to Mr John Fleming.
7 I am grateful to Dr Maurice Craig for drawing my attention to the significance of the Pearce drawings in the Proby Collection at Elton Hall and for expounding them to me.

In previous editions I concluded on stylistic evidence, combined with a contemporary imputation, that Pearce merely fathered the designs of another architect, and that the real authorship of the Parliament House belonged to one or another of the Palladian group[s] in London. The Elton drawings, however, leave no doubt as to the legitimacy of Pearce's claim as established by Curran [C. P. Curran, 'The Architecture of the Bank of Ireland', in F. G. Hall, *The Bank of Ireland, 1783–1946*, Dublin and Oxford, 1949].

8 The Knight of Glin, 'New Light on Castletown', *Quarterly Bulletin of the Irish Georgian Society*, January–March, 1965.
9 Altered in 1792. J. B. Papworth in *Britton and Pugin, Public Buildings of London* (1825), implies that it was wholly rebuilt, but Malton, in his *Picturesque Tour* (1792), makes it clear that this is an exaggeration.
10 S. Piggott, *The Druids* (London, 1968), 149–53.
11 The adoption of this word requires explanation, but none has so far been proposed. The invention of this form may well be related to the elder Wood's plan of Prior Park, originally designed on three sides of a dodecagon.

Art history and class struggle

Nicos Hadjinicolaou

I. Ideology and Class Struggle

Any scientific treatment of the history of art must encompass not only the concepts of 'social class' and 'class struggle', but also all the terms which describe particular social groups such as social category, autonomous fraction of a class, fraction of a class, and social stratum.[1] It is not proposed to define these here, but it must be stressed that any concrete analysis of a picture from a historically determined period requires a knowledge of them so that the art historian can recognise them in their historical reality.

It is, however, necessary to pay close attention to one concept, ideology, which is of vital importance for the discipline of art history.

1. Ideology

Just as people take part in economic and political activity, so they take part in religious, moral, aesthetic and philosophical activities, and their ideology is the relatively coherent system of ideas, values and beliefs that they develop. Ideology is concerned with the world in which they live, their links with nature, society, other people, and their own activities, including their political and economic activities. In fact people express in their ideology not their actual relation to their situation in life, but the way in which they see this relation – which implies a dual relation to reality, one real and one imagined. Thus ideology signifies their relation to 'their world'. It expresses the inevitable coalescence of their actual and their imagined relation to the true conditions of their existence. In ideology, the actual relationship is determined by the imagined relationship, which expresses a will (conservative, conformist, reformist or revolutionary), a hope or a nostalgia, rather than describes a reality.

On the one hand it follows that ideology must be an illusion, because it is so interwoven with an imaginary view of life. Its social function is not to provide people with a real understanding of the structure of society, but to give them a motive for continuing the practical activities which support that structure. In a class-ridden society, the structure ensures that class exploitation is not conducted nakedly. Its operations are veiled so that society can function in an acceptable way, and this of necessity impedes human vision of it. Thus even when ideology contains elements of knowledge,[2] it is still inherently flawed and of necessity only partially equates to reality.

On the other hand it follows that the internal workings of ideology are not apparent. This bring us to the question of the inner coherence of the ideological level, that is to say of its structure and its relation to the ruling class. The very function of ideology, as opposed to science, is to hide the contradictions in life by fabricating an illusory system of ideas which shapes people's views and gives them a perspective on their experience of life. Since this system has a relationship with human experience in society, ideology does not cover just the rudiments of knowledge, ideas, and so on, but also extends to myths, symbols, taste, style, fashion, and the whole 'way of life' of a particular society.

However, each ideology can only function within the limits of a particular society and the predominant mode of economic production. The contradictions which are contained within that society and which, taken together, form its unity, are the raw materials which ideology shapes into an imaginary coherence. The structure of the ideological level derives therefore from the system of society, and its specific role is to reflect unity in the imaginary system it builds.

It should now be clear that ideology – the ideological level – is an organic part of every society. Human societies need these systems of ideas and beliefs in order to survive, and they secrete ideology as if it were an essential nourishment for their being and for their historical continuance.

2. Ideology and the ruling class

If the relation of the ideological level of society to social classes and the ruling class is considered more closely, it is clear that in societies divided into classes the fundamental function of ideology is determined by class relations. Dominant ideology corresponds to the politically ruling class because the ideological level is constituted within the overall structure of a society which has as an effect the domination of a particular class in the field of class struggle. The dominant ideology, while it ensures that people keep their place within the social structure, at the same time aims at the preservation and cohesion of this structure, principally through class exploitation and dominance. It is in this precise sense that in the ideological level of a society the prevailing ideas, values, opinions, beliefs and so on are those that perpetuate class domination; thus this level is dominated by what may be called the ideology of the ruling class.

It follows that if the function of ideology in general is to conceal contradictions, then the function of the dominant ideology, the ideology of the ruling classes, is *a fortiori* the same. This is bound to have serious consequences for all historical disciplines which are concerned with the various forms of ideology, including art history.

This is a crucial point for understanding ideology and the ideological class struggle. Ideology's positive or affirmative character is shown in the very way in which it works, making the struggle appear as a struggle without opponents, or a combat without combatants. It is paradoxical that, in spite of what the word 'struggle' seems to suggest, participation in the class struggle does not only involve the propagation, defence, condemnation or glorification of the political or social ideas of a class (this is only one aspect of the struggle and necessitates a certain degree of class consciousness), but requires the affirmation of class values which apparently have nothing to do with politics or the division of society into classes. These values are concerned with the unity of society, with the successes and misfortunes of mankind as a whole, and with the provision of a positive world view. Their affirmative character is a fundamental aspect of ideology. This explains why I have thought it necessary to introduce the term 'positive ideology' for all those ideologies which manifest this affirmative character, and 'critical ideology' for those ideologies which are more or less openly opposed to particular class practices or class ideologies (usually ruling-class ideologies).

The distinction between 'positive visual ideology' and 'critical visual ideology' that I make later in order to clarify the concept of 'style' is based on this fundamental aspect of ideology.

The way in which the ruling ideology is expressed often borrows features from ways of life which differ radically from that of the ruling class, and which may even belong to the exploited classes. In any society one may also find whole sub-systems, functioning by themselves with relative autonomy in regard to the ruling ideology (for example, in a capitalist society one can find feudal and petit-bourgeois sub-systems, and so on).

We have just considered the role of the ruling ideology as the decisive element in ideological social relations. The second important element which is characteristic of the ideological level is its division into spheres, of which one always dominates the others.

[. . .]

Style as visual ideology

If we substitute this last term for style in the definition arrived at in the preceding chapter, it would then read: 'Visual ideology is the way in which the formal and thematic elements of a picture are combined on each specific occasion. This combination is a particular form of overall ideology of a social class.

[. . .]

Visual ideology and social classes

The sense of visual ideology can be further elucidated by linking it with the concept of ideology in general. It will be recalled that 'in ideology the real relation of men to their real conditions of existence is inevitably invested in the imaginary relation, a relation that expresses a will (conservative, conformist, reformist or revolutionary), a hope or a nostalgia, rather than describing a reality'[3] and also that

> every ideological representation is in a way a representation of reality, it somehow makes *allusion* to reality, but equally produces only an *illusion*. We understand too that ideology gives men some kind of *cognition* of their world – or rather, by allowing them to *recognise* themselves in their world, gives them some *recognition* while at the same time leading them to a misappreciation of their world. Ideology, considered from the point of view of its relation to reality, yields only an allusion to reality which is always accompanied by an illusion, a comprehension* accompanied by a misapprehension.[4]

This allusion-illusion or comprehension-misapprehension of reality that characterises ideology differs according to social class. The place that a social class occupies in society enforces a specific view of social reality that no other class possesses. Dominant classes and dominated classes (even though the latter may, as has been pointed out earlier, be impregnated with the ideology of the dominant classes), cannot have the same ideology. Even within each class, there are sections or layers which have their own individual features at the ideological level.

It would seem therefore that this two-way allusion-illusion feature which characterises ideology in general is also a feature of visual ideology. Each style makes allusion to reality, to one particular reality which is the combination of the consciousness a class has of itself and its view of the world. This allusion to reality goes together with an illusion about the objective place the class occupies within class relations in a society. Historical analysis of each visual ideology is needed to reveal this two-way allusive-illusory process which characterises the production of pictures in general.

One may therefore conclude that the production of pictures constitutes a sphere of the ideological level, since every picture belongs to a visual ideology even when it can in some way be considered as inaugurating a new one. However one must not forget that this sphere has specific features and some autonomy even though it is not independent. Its autonomy is shown by the fact that the elements of which it is composed do not exist as such, or certainly not all of them, in other types of ideology. Its dependence is shown by the fact that it is always determined by other types of spheres of the ideological level, according to the mode of production and the social formation. Thus, to give an example, between the fourth and fourteenth centuries within the ideological level the sphere of visual ideology was determined by the sphere of religious ideology.

If the production of pictures is defined as one sphere of the ideological level, it follows necessarily that what is valid for ideology in general is equally valid for visual ideology. Thus neither social classes nor different layers or sections of different classes can have the same visual ideology. From an abstract point of view each class or layer or section of a class 'ought' to have at each historical 'moment' its own visual ideology, given the particular vision each has of itself, of other classes and of society in general. In reality however things are a great deal more complex, for in the first place some classes have never historically had a developed visual ideology of their own. In some cases they did not produce a certain type of picture, for example paintings, at all. This comes from the fact that the need to produce some types of image presupposes a specific ideology, and a particular social position.[5] In the second place, the visual ideology of the dominant classes[6] strongly permeates the visual ideologies of the dominated classes, to the point where the latter may be totally distorted. It has a kind of monopoly over the whole of society.[7] So if I speak of class struggle in the context of the arts, and say that it appears in this domain through the existence of styles, and even sometimes through the struggle between styles, it must be recognised that *this 'struggle' takes place more often between the visual ideologies of layers or sections of the same class or of the ruling classes than between the visual ideologies of the ruling classes and the dominated classes*. It is not far from the truth to affirm, even in this exaggerated form, that in all societies up to our times the history of the production of pictures is the history of ruling class visual ideologies. Pictures are often the product in which the ruling classes mirror themselves.

The question of an artist's style

On three occasions already I have rejected the thesis according to which it is necessary to have recourse to a picture's producer in order to explain the work itself: the first time when the concept of art history as the history of artists was criticised, the second when the usual conception of a monograph on an artist was rejected, and the third when the artist's aesthetic and political ideologies were distinguished from the visual ideology of his pictures.

Now that some light has been thrown on 'style' and what it is, it is time to pursue this thesis into its last refuge: the idea that each artist has his own style. This idea complements art history as the history of artists, or even art history as the history of styles. The conception that 'every artist has his own style', which is an integral part of the bourgeois ideology of the unique character of the individual, is expressed in art history by the two following variants:

1. If an artist espoused several styles in succession, the historian tries to show that in reality only one of these is consistent with his personality and has the right to be called his 'style *par excellence*'. Styles preceding the one considered to be typically his are called 'early' or 'precursory', and those that followed his 'mature period' are referred to as

'later' or 'styles of old age', and so on (as an example of this, one could quote David).

2. If an artist espoused several styles simultaneously during the greater part of his life, then the bourgeois art historian concerns himself with the style that is considered essentially his, disregarding the other coexisting styles, though he may laud the artist's 'variety of talent' (for example, Rembrandt).

Obviously the rare case of an artist who virtually never changes his style adds apparent weight to this thesis, which cannot separate the style from the man because it considers that 'the style is the man'.

However, in the opinion of this writer there is no such thing as 'an artist's style'; pictures produced by one person are not to be centred on him. The fact that they have been produced by the same artist does not link them together, or at least not in any way that is important for the purposes of art history.

[. . .]

Notes

1   Nicos Poulantzas, *Political Power and Social Classes*, London, New Left Books and Sheed Ward, 1973, pp. 77–98.

2   This is important: when one leaves the stage of theoretical research with its rigorous conceptual distinction between ideology and science and proceeds to concrete historical research, it should be unthinkable to treat 'ideological' investigations with contempt and ignore them instead of making use of the insights they contain. The distinction between ideology and science can be as mechanical as that between theory and history.

3   Louis Althusser, *For Marx*, Allen Lane: Penguin Press 1969, p. 233.
   * The word 'comprehension' is used in this instance to translate 'connaissance', which elsewhere is rendered as 'knowledge', in order to keep the flavour of the original 'connaissance-méconnaisance'. (Translator's note)

4   Louis Althusser, 'Théorie et formation théorique – Idéologie et lutte idéologique', in *Casa de las Americas*, no. 34, Havana.

5   This point has more validity for pictures than it does for the graphic arts since the fifteen century, or even for the so-called 'decorative arts', 'minor arts', 'folk art' and so on.

6   Dominant does not necessarily mean politically dominant.

7   From 1830 onwards, but only indirectly before that date, it is possible to discern visual ideologies which belong to the dominated classes, though they are still impregnated with ruling class visual ideologies. Lenin's article, 'Party organisation and party literature', of 13 November 1905, his articles on Tolstoy, and also Mao's contribution to the 1942 forum 'On literature and art', mark a new phase in history, in so far as they demonstrate a sharpened awareness of the role of literary and artistic work in the class struggle.

4

A class performance
Social histories of architecture

I am interested in how we interrogate architecture in terms of its social functions and meanings. Architectural historians writing on eighteenth and early nineteenth century Britain have tended to see social history as the answer to this question. But the social history of architecture or the histories of specific social groups which operated in and around the architecture or building(s), or indeed the spaces created by them or for them, provide only a backdrop or loose historical context. And this kind of social history of architecture offers little in the way of explanation. The focus remains firmly on the function in terms of use rather than, for instance, the symbolic meaning of architecture. There is no doubt that studies like those made by Mark Girouard have made important connections between architecture and the world outside its stylistic or authorial categories. At the time Girouard's work was first published in the early 1970s this approach appeared to be revolutionary, and in terms of British architectural history it was. But now it has entered the canon and it is hard to see what all the fuss was about. I will return to Girouard later on in this chapter but first I want to talk about different kinds of social theory and the ways in which our reading of architecture and its histories can be shaped by these paradigms. Here I consider architecture particularly in relation to the following: gender/other; space and spatial practices and hegemonies, and more generally the notion of performance.

The narrative structures of architectural history present a kind of dialectic between different epistemologies – here specifically I mean the Enlightenment project of knowledge and post-structuralist theory. These are not considered in terms of a chronological progression as I want to see how they coexist and converge in our reading of architecture as social history. First it is important to consider the Enlightenment project of knowledge which asserts that there is an underlying order to the social world.[1] Humankind, according to Immanuel Kant, is able to know the truth of this order through the exercise of reason which, he claimed 'operates identically in each subject and it can grasp laws . . . that are equally knowable and binding on every person'. This led to a belief in the relationship between reason and freedom whereby increased rationality will produce increased freedom. The kind of social science or theories of society that developed out of the Enlightenment project were built on the assumption that the rational human subject is the basis of society which is governed by a set of laws or rigid systems and will bring about greater freedom and progress. This epistemological stance connects with architecture as a social history. The rational human subjects remain with few exceptions the white male élite and the system of laws is that of the white male patriarchal society based on immutable and uncontestable rationality that will lead to a better lot for all.

This practice of constructing and narrating the social experience of the inhabitants of buildings has been extremely successful. It is seen as enlarging the picture and in a limited way righting imbalances in terms of which social groups remain the focus of the historian's attention. In this way a cultural icon such as the English country house is presented as an emblem of a set of social, economic and political values, which no matter how remote they may appear from the present day remain unquestioned and venerated. Moreover, this architectural expression or embodiment of these values is presented and accepted as something we might want to both revere and preserve because of its *value*. Any curiosity we might have about the alternative social rituals and cultural practices that also took place in or were given spatial expression by the country house, or any other building, remain unasked and unanswered (for instance the role of profits from slavery in the enabling of large building projects) or pre-empted and contained by, for instance, the presentation of often fabricated 'servants' room' in country house visitor circuits and guidebooks. This kind of social history of architecture is perhaps so readily acceptable and easy to follow because it stays within the traditional framework of the kinds of historical enquiries made into architecture from at least the sixteenth century right up to the end of our period. It stays safely within the epistemological frame of orthodox history whilst appearing to be more inclusive than previous narratives. The historical 'truth' of these kinds of enquiries is usually based on a reconstructed experience of those social groups under scrutiny, based on diaries, letters and household accounts, which inevitably privileges the literate classes and the property-owning élite. These kinds of histories often assume that the facts of these anecdotal accounts can speak for themselves and offer no questioning of the kinds of social categorisation these sorts of historical enquiries endorse. Nor do they prompt an interrogation of the systems of repression which are evident in the absence of certain voices from the archive. So if we were to look at architecture from the point of view of let's say the female struggle for equality we might see it in teleological terms as a progression throughout the centuries towards female emancipation. But it would not fundamentally challenge our historical frame for architecture as we would not be asking why or how the mechanisms of repression, either in terms of the lives of the female subjects or the methods of historical enquiry that perpetuate it, came into being.[2]

How then does post structural social theory help? As I mentioned in Chapter 2, theory has been criticised over the last decade by feminist and gay scholars for being a smokescreen behind which western white males hide. As they can no longer control the production of knowledge and, therefore, no longer define the *truth*, their response is to say that there is no *truth* to be discovered. Post-structuralism's rejection of social and cultural structures and of theories to explain wide-ranging phenomena have been dismissed as meaningless and reactionary demonstrating an obsession with text and language. But post-structuralist discourse does encourage less-exclusive views which recognise that rationality is not innate but culturally constructed, and as we have seen in Chapter 1, historical knowledge is never complete or objective. Returning then to architecture we see that there are a range of social histories or means of interrogating architecture using social theory. Architecture is not just about the élite, it is about all users and consumers and, importantly, about ourselves as authors and active recipients of its various narratives. These ideas go against the subject/object divide as social theory must be part of what it analyses and seeks to explain. In other words, we can move towards a more fluid and overlapping relationship between the subject and the object, or between the theory and the archive. This enables us to move away from those rigid frameworks that establish structures within the social history of architecture as a way of explaining it. These epistemological systems, in the case of the period of architecture in question in this book, relate strongly to the dominant social groups. We look at the architecture in our period as evidence of the white male hegemony rather than accepting this as the history of only one of the range of social groups who interacted in the built environment.

Moreover, the social histories of architecture have been written largely by those in whose interest it is to ensure the continued veneration for the perceived *value* of the hegemony of this social group.

Gender/other

The final chapter in this book is concerned with the question of gender in relation to reading architectural history. But it is important to consider it briefly here as it is one of the dominant traits of social histories of architecture where the biographical narratives of subjects are used as a means of exploring the built environment. As we have seen in Chapter 2, biography is an essential part of human memory. We think about ourselves in terms of what we have done – our identity is constructed around our past and this has had a considerable impact on the narrative structures of architectural history. But the cult of the personality – the named protagonist – is only one aspect of biography. Society mostly comprises anonymous subjects who exist only within categories of people described by patterns in the historical record. The focus here is then the relationship between these anonymous objects and subjects and how specific biographies of these or biographical narrative techniques are used, or not, as a means of explaining or articulating sets of social, cultural and spatial relationships. These biographical methods bring the authentic voice of subjects, revealing personal meanings and strategies and their relationship to society and the contexts in which individual lives are played out.

My aim is to highlight an increasing fluidity and interaction between theory, methods and history. The particular focus here is issues of gender and categories of 'other' in respect of architectural space. The questions raised offer a re-evaluation of the relationship between biographical objects and subjects which is of significance to the analysis and construction of social histories of architecture. This allows an exploration of the ways in which narratives of the subject and the object/subject can be constructed within paradigms that stand outwith those of the canon or the 'other'.[3]

One of the most obvious categories that has been 'managed' within the canon of British architectural history is that of women.[4] The work of Judith Butler[5] is important here as she has argued that feminism had made a mistake by trying to assert that 'women' were a group with common characteristics and interests – replacing one hegemony with another and setting up binary oppositional epistemologies. Butler notes that feminists rejected the idea that biology is destiny, but then developed an account of patriarchal culture which assumed that masculine and feminine genders would inevitably be built, by culture, upon 'male' and 'female' bodies, making the same destiny just as inescapable. That argument allows no room for choice, difference or resistance, instead Butler prefers 'those historical and anthropological positions that understand gender as a relation among socially constituted subjects in specifiable contexts'. In other words, rather than being a fixed attribute in a person, gender should be seen as a fluid variable which shifts and changes in different contexts and at different times. Butler points out that the experience of a gendered cultural identity is considered an achievement and prompts a kind of gender performance, a point she clarified in an interview about her first book *Gender Trouble*.[6]

> RP: A lot of people like *Gender Trouble* because they liked the idea of gender as a kind of improvisational theatre, a space where different identities can be more or less freely adopted and explored at will. They wanted to get on with the work of enacting gender, in order to undermine its dominant forms. However, at the beginning of *Bodies That*

Matter you say that, of course, one doesn't just voluntaristically construct or deconstruct identities. It's unclear to us to what extent you want to hold onto the possibilities opened up in *Gender Trouble* of being able to use transgressive performances such as drag to help decentre or destabilise gender categories, and to what extent you have become sceptical about this.

Butler: [. . .] It is important to distinguish performance from performativity: the former presumes a subject, but the latter contests the very notion of the subject. The place where I try to clarify this is toward the beginning of my essay 'Critically Queer', in *Bodies that Matter*, I begin with the Foucauldian premise that power works in part through discourse and it works in part to produce and destabilise subjects. But then, when one starts to think carefully about how discourse might be said to produce a subject, it's clear that one's already talking about a certain figure or trope of production. It is at this point that it's useful to turn to the notion of performativity, and performative speech acts in particular – understood as those speech acts that bring into being that which they name. This is the moment in which discourse becomes productive in a fairly specific way. So what I'm trying to do is think about the performativity as that aspect of discourse that has the capacity to produce what it names. Then I take a further step, through the Derridean rewriting of Austin, and suggest that this production actually always happens through a certain kind of repetition and recitation. So if you want the ontology of this, I guess performativity is the vehicle through which ontological effects are established. Performativity is the discursive mode by which ontological effects are installed. Something like that.

Butler is not without her critics and her argument is not without flaws, but it is important here as it summarises much of the thinking on gender roles and provides a sharp lens through which to view social histories of architecture that offer a reading of the role of women. Martha Nussbaum's critique of Butler inadvertently endorses my point:[7]

Butler's main idea, first introduced in *Gender Trouble* in 1989 and repeated throughout her books, is that gender is a social artifice. Our ideas of what women and men are reflect nothing that exists eternally in nature. Instead they derive from customs that embed social relations of power.

This notion, of course, is nothing new. The denaturalizing of gender was present already in Plato, and it received a great boost from John Stuart Mill, who claimed in *The Subjection of Women* that 'what is now called the nature of women is an eminently artificial thing.' Mill saw that claims about 'women's nature' derive from, and shore up, hierarchies of power: womanliness is made to be whatever would serve the cause of keeping women in subjection, or, as he put it, 'enslav[ing] their minds.' With the family as with feudalism, the rhetoric of nature itself serves the cause of slavery. 'The subjection of women to men being a universal custom, any departure from it quite naturally appears unnatural . . . But was there ever any domination which did not appear natural to those who possessed it?'

. . . In work published in the 1970s and 1980s, Catharine MacKinnon and Andrea Dworkin argued that the conventional understanding of gender roles is a way of ensuring continued male domination in sexual relations, as well as in the public sphere. They took the core of Mill's insight into a sphere of life concerning which the Victorian philosopher had said little . . . Before Butler, they stressed the ways in which male-dominated power structures marginalize and subordinate not only women, but also

people who would like to choose a same-sex relationship. They understood that discrimination against gays and lesbians is a way of enforcing the familiar hierarchically
ordered gender roles; and so they saw discrimination against gays and lesbians as a form
of sex discrimination . . . [T]he psychologist Nancy Chodorow gave a detailed and
compelling account of how gender differences replicate themselves across the generations: she argued that the ubiquity of these mechanisms of replication enables us to
understand how what is artificial can nonetheless be nearly ubiquitous . . . Gayle Rubin's
important anthropological account of subordination, *The Traffic in Women* (1975), provided a valuable analysis of the relationship between the social organization of gender
and the asymmetries of power.

My interest here is not in the debates around Butler but in the epistemological systems discussed and how they relate to the way we look at the material world, and it is at this point
that we locate the connectivity between the architectural historical archive and its interrogation and explanation through the biographical subject/object. As a result we impose our
expectations of gender performance on the social readings of architecture. Inherent in this
reading of architecture and its archives is an epistemological gender bias in our social and cultural formulation of the biographies of objects in relation to the human subject. In this way
architecture can become part of the gender performance. We see this is images of the female
'architect', or 'lady' designer (Figure 4.1) who *must* be an amateur. It is also evident in

Figure 4.1 Lady Kildare, later Duchess of Leinster, was a keen architect and designer (courtesy of
the Irish Architectural Archive).

interiors design by women such as print rooms or other *non-canonical* styles of design (Figure 4.2). These demonstrate a feminine *ergo* inferior/other approach to design.[8] But what do we then make of spaces where we might want to see femininity performed but the form of the building suggests otherwise? The name Hamels Dairy (Figure 4.3) might prompt an expectation of female grace but its ground plan perhaps owes more to Ledoux's *architecture parlante* in his design for a *House of Sexual Instruction* and the elevation remains firmly in the rustic doric/tuscan (masculine) idiom. By choosing to be different about it, we might work to change gender norms and the binary understanding of the narrative biographical structures of masculinity and femininity as read through architecture. Moreover, the notion of performance can be used to investigate other culturally determined identities and social hegemonies as we see later in this chapter.

Figure 4.2 Chinese room at Carton, Co. Kildare. Lady Kildare was actively involved with the design of her own house. Chinoiserie is considered a non-canonical style, often with feminine associations (courtesy of the Irish Architectural Archive).

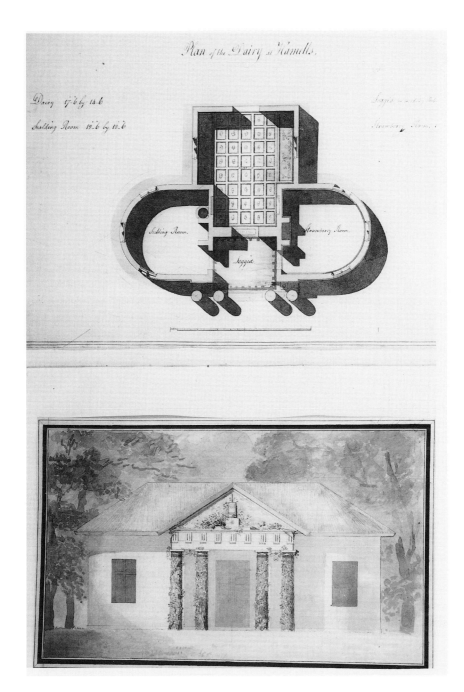

Figure 4.3 Hamels Dairy, Hertfordshire by Sir John Soane, 1781–1783, plan and elevation. Dairies often have feminine associations but the ground plan resembles a truncated phallus and the order is a distinctly masculine doric. C. N, Ledoux had used a phallic-shaped ground plan for his design for a *House of Sexual Instruction*, an example of *architecture parlante* (courtesy of the Trustees of Sir John Soane's Museum).

Space and spacial practices

One of the ways in which we might avoid a culturally predetermined reading of the social histories of architecture is to think about the built environment as space rather than focusing on the architecture that surrounds space. The work of Henri Lefebvre concentrated on the idea of lived experience of architecture in terms of space and spacial practices. He shows how an awareness of the complexities of post-modern analysis, which he recognises as a 'strategic hypothesis' situated in its own transient cultural and temporal milieu. Although principally concerned with urban environments, Lefebvre's methods of analysis can be used to equal effect when looking at other kinds of buildings – including the country house which was a dominant building type in the period under review. Here in his *The Production of Space* Lefebvre argues that the primacy of the image in terms of architectural design and our understanding of it subjugates the role of social space:

> Let us now turn our attention to the space of those who are referred to by means of such clumsy and pejorative labels as 'users' and 'inhabitants'. No well-defined terms with clear connotations have been found to designate these groups. Their marginalization by spatial practice thus extends even to language. The word 'user' (*usager*), for example has something vague – and vaguely suspect – about it. 'User of what?' one tends to wonder. Clothes and cars are used (and wear out), just as houses are. But what is the use value when set alongside exchange and its corollaries? As for 'inhabitants', the word designates everyone – and no one. The fact is that the most basic demands of 'users' (suggesting 'underprivileged') and 'inhabitants' (suggesting 'marginal') find *expression* [Lefebvre's emphasis] only with great difficulty, whereas the signs of their situation are constantly increasing and often stare us in the face.
>
> The user's space is *lived* [Lefebvre's emphasis] – not represented (or conceived). When compared with the abstract space of the experts (architects, urbanists, planners), the space of the everyday activities of users is a concrete one, which is to say, subjective. As a space of subjects rather than of calculations, as a representational space . . . It is in this space that the 'private' realm asserts itself . . . against the public one.
>
> It is possible . . . to form a mental picture of a primacy of concrete spaces of semi-public, semi-private spaces, of meeting-places, pathways and passageways. This would mean the diversification of space, while the (relative) importance attached to functional distinctions would disappear . . .
>
> . . . the reign of the facade over space is certainly not over. The furniture, which is almost as heavy as the buildings themselves, continues to have facades; mirrored wardrobes, sideboards and chests still face out onto the sphere of private life, and so help dominate it . . . In as much as the resulting space would be inhabited by *subjects*, it might legitimately be deemed 'situational' or 'relational' – but these definitions or determinants would refer to sociological content rather than to any intrinsic properties of space as such.[9]

The loaded meaning of space is a common concern in many theoretical writings. Importantly for our interests here Theodore Adorno makes the following observation on the relationship between space and purpose:

> One speaks, with good reason, of a sense of space (Raumgefuehl) in architecture. But this sense of space is not a pure, abstract essence, not a sense of spaciality itself, since

space is only conceivable as concrete space, within specific dimensions. A sense of space is closely connected with purposes. Even when architecture attempts to elevate this sense beyond the realms of purposefulness, it is simultaneously immanent in the purpose. The success of such a synthesis is the principal criterion for great architecture. Architecture inquires: how can a certain purpose become space; through which forms, which materials? All factors relate reciprocally to one another. Architectonic imagination is, according to this conception of it, the ability to articulate space purposefully. It permits purposes to become space. It constructs forms according to purposes. Conversely, space and the sense of space can become more than impoverished purpose only when imagination impregnates them with purposefulness.[10]

In this way we can see that the users, producers and interpreters of space all play equally important roles in the understanding of it. Space is encased by architecture which as a result gives some kind of static, physical frame to the diverse social rituals and cultural practices performed in and around it. The interaction of architecture and social history and/or theory must then also be about spaces. We can see this in the way in which space is represented in the case of the Assembly Rooms in York (1731–2), a nexus of social activity and performance of a range of social and cultural roles (Figures 4.4, 4.5 and 4.6). The social activities which took place in the rooms dominate a perspectival, pictorial image of the interior and provide a narrative whilst the plate from Palladio's *I Quattro*

Figure 4.4 Grand Assembly Room, York, a perspective view of the interior. Engraving by William Lindley, 1759 (private collection).

Figure 4.5 An Egyptian Hall as illustrated in A. Palladio, *I Quattro Libri Dell'Architettura*, 1570, was a likely source for the design of the York Assembly Rooms.

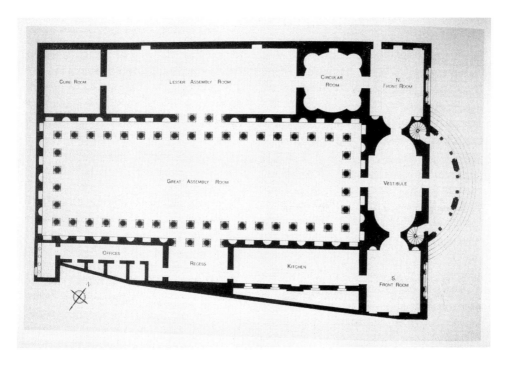

Figure 4.6 Ground plan of the Assembly Rooms, York.

Libri shows the likely source of the design based firmly in the tradition of antique architecture and its veneration and use as a social marker in the eighteenth century. Alongside this a groundplan of the building shows a complex layout of differently shaped spaces ranged around the central hall which fill the irregular site and provide a range of spaces for different kinds of social activities. At the same time this plan shows how the building deviates from the regularity and order which is often presented as dominating architecture and society at that time.

Hegemonies

It is important also to consider the relationship between social structure and social consciousness. In this way the experience of architecture can be conjectured as the interaction between subjective feeling and external influences. E P Thompson was one of the first to consider this relationship between the structural and the psychological. 'People do not only experience their own experience as ideas, within thought and its procedures . . . they also experience their own experience as feeling.'[11] According to Thompson experience is the beginning of a chain of events that moves towards a social consciousness which might be a class identity and which provides a uniform identity based on material circumstances. In the *Poverty of Theory*, as elsewhere in his writings, Thompson is concerned with the working class and his construction of this class identity causes other subjects such as race or gender to take second place. Thompson remains preoccupied with class structures and how they operate in a capitalistic society. But his enquiries do open the way to an awareness and sensitivity to the experience of architecture as being shaped by structural and psychological factors. This control was, according to Thompson, 'located primarily in the cultural hegemony and only secondarily in an expression of economic or physical (military) power'[12] Moreover, Thompson recognises that defining control in terms of cultural hegemony does not signify an abandoning of any kind of analysis. Rather it allows analysis to be made at the point where power and authority manifest themselves to create a mentality of subordination within the populace. In other words, the role of architecture, specifically here the country house, as a symbol of patrician authority is paramount in this context. This is seen in the relationship between the style of architecture and the style of politics and in the rhetoric of the ruling élite. Architecture is then a microcosm of the social, political and cultural trends in Britain and had a crucial role in maintaining the status quo in the face of increasing adversity. Nevertheless the ruling class maintained a controlling influence on the lives and expectations of the lower orders. To this end architecture functioned as a space for the performance of highly visible paternalistic displays, which is certainly the case for the country house, where these included the hunt and the celebration of marriages or national festivals (Figure 4.7). All these elements were used to exact deference from the lower orders and reinforce the social system.

There might, at first, appear to be little connection between the theatricality of the rituals of the ruling élite and their authority. But once pre-eminence is established and

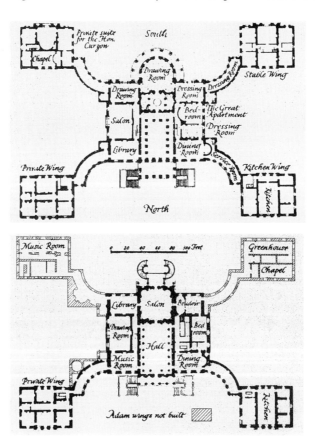

Figure 4.7 Ground plans of Kedleston Hall, Derbyshire showing the array of public and private spaces where a range of social rituals and cultural practices took place.

the rules are set there is little need to enforce them except to show they are there. In this way the performative elements of the display of power were important and architecture functioned as the spatial focus for these. Parallel to this is the formidable presence of the country house in the rural environment as both a representation of the ruling class and the lynchpin of country life. The country house functioned to moderate, preserve and represent the status quo.[13]

The notion that domestic architecture, here I mean lived-in spaces, is the physical embodiment of governmental and social systems is evident in the important role private mansions in rural and urban settings, rather than public buildings or even royal palaces, played in the architectural production of the period (Figure 4.8). Architecture (and its spaces) is therefore an ordered physical structure that acts as a metonym for other inherited structures – this encompasses the make-up of society as a whole, a code of morality,

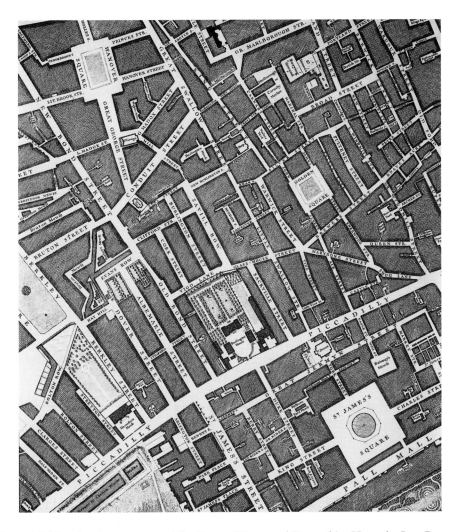

Figure 4.8 Map showing area around Burlington House and Devonshire House by Jean Rocque, published 1737–1746 (private collection). This shows the dominance of private mansions in London's urban landscape.

a body of manners system of language and the manner in which an individual relates to their cultural inheritance. And here I want to briefly mention style as opposed to space and means of enabling these kinds of performances. In Chapter 3 we saw how an appreciation of architecture based on the buildings of antiquity was seen as a marker of social rank and how this practice continues into the present through the appreciation of historic architecture. If we then consider the 'classical splendour' of the Georgian town house or country house in terms of the social readings discussed in this chapter we might see something rather different. I have talked about architecture as an instrument of hegemonies but so far only in terms of patriarchal social systems at a national level. If we step back and consider the economic basis for the development of Georgian cities, for example Liverpool or Bristol, or how the building of many country houses was funded, for example Harewood in Yorkshire, we see how the repressive systems inherent in these buildings operated at a global level as the exploitation of Britian's colonies and profits from slavery provided the economic impetus and support for these projects. The relationship between social history and architecture goes beyond spaces and performance to include an aesthetic expression of these values – classicism – which both legitimised them and enabled a feeling of inclusivity. Raymond Williams identified this as

> a lived hegemony is always in process . . . [it] does not passively exist as a form of dominance. It has continually to be renewed, recreated, defended and modified. It is also continually resisted, limited, altered, challenged by pressures not all its own.[14]

The changing relationship between the aristocratic and bourgeois classes is part of the performance of these rituals and architecture provides both the space and the aesthetic for this ongoing process.

Whose life in the English country house?

The introduction of social history as a method of analysing architecture has signalled an important move away from these tropes of biographical (author genius) or stylistic surveys. This approach was pioneered by Mark Girouard in his study *Life in the English Country House*. Here, social life is used as a way of examining a building. Girouard himself was aware of the possible pitfalls of such a survey. In his preface to the first edition he writes;

> The range of sources for an approach of this kind is almost infinite and I cannot pretend to have done more than sample it. Moreover, instructive and enjoyable though it is for an architectural historian to adventure outside his own discipline, he is bound to make gaffes in doing so. I can only ask for indulgence in what is essentially a pioneering work.

Girouard's critics picked up on this but the value of his contribution to the broadening of the nature of architectural history justly outweighed the reservations. Lawrence Stone observed

> . . . as is inevitable in any pioneering venture, this endeavour . . . has many weaknesses. He [Girouard] knows his architectural history better than his social and economic history and therefore makes a number of mistakes of detail and a number of grand and unsubstantiated assertions . . . But [it is] . . . a learned, entrancing and stimulating book which ought to start a new range of studies on the neglected interface between culture and architecture.[15]

Similarly, David Watkin in *The Rise of Architectural History* recognised Girouard's achievement:

> [the book] is a brilliant and stimulating study which, as its author would be the first to admit, marks only the beginning of our understanding of this complex and curiously ignored subject. Naturally, some of his historical and social assumptions have been questioned by social and political historians but this has not involved any serious undermining of his achievement.[16]

Such praise perhaps gives some clue as to the kind of 'life' which is the focus of the book. Little attention is paid to women, children, servants or the many tenants and labourers occupied in and around the house and its estate. Life in the country house means here the country house as a spatial container for patriarchal values and the hegemony of this ruling élite. And it is questionable whether this approach gives us any kind of broader cultural meaning as it pins down the function of a building to the notion of how it was used by a specific social group for the range of social activities pertaining to them which took place in and around it. This understanding of function is doubtlessly an essential part of the history of the country house. But if this area of study is taken less literally the notion of the function of a country house can be discussed in both metaphorical and actual terms. These associative values are another part of the process of interpretation which gives the country house its meanings.

The metaphorical function of the country house can be identified as it being a symbol of the power and wealth of the landowner and more broadly the social, cultural and political hegemony of the ruling classes. In no way is this metaphorical function opposed to the physical function of the country house. Rather it reinforces the physical function of the building. This is at once the focal-point of the estate and the primary residence of the landowner – the family seat. The house was a place of business, whether political or to do with the estate, and it provided a backdrop both to the extensive collections of fine and decorative art owned by the aristocracy and to the social rituals performed in and around it. The metaphorical and physical aspects combine to make an embodiment and reinforcement of a distinctive social system enhanced by a set of cultural values, some of which were based on indigenous traditions and others borrowed from antiquity. In this way the country house functioned as a symbol of social control and the supremacy of the ruling class and its social histories serve to perpetuate these hegemonies.[17]

But architecture is more than a stage for the acting out of these performances. It offers a space for other social groups and kinds of social interactions. It is also important to remember that in examples such as the country house it was home to a large number of residents representing a variety of interests. Gaston Bachelard in his *Poetics of Space* identifies how closely we relate to the architecture of the home – where we live or can identify with the practice of living within that space:

> The house, quite obviously, is a privileged entity for a phenomenological study of the intimate values of inside space, provided, of course, that we take in both its unity and complexity, and endeavour to integrate all the special values in one fundamental value. For the house furnishes us with dispersed images and a body of images at the same time. In both cases, I shall prove that imagination augments the values of reality.
>
>   . . . it is not enough to consider the house as an 'object' on which we can make our judgments and daydreams react. For a phenomenologist, a psychoanalyst or a psychologist (these three points of view being named in the order of decreasing efficacy), it is not a question of describing houses, or enumerating their picturesque features and

analyzing for which reasons they are comfortable. On the contrary, we must go beyond the problems of description – whether this description be objective or subjective, that is, whether it gives facts or impressions – in order to attain the primary virtues, those that reveal an attachment that is native in some way to the primary function of inhabiting. A geographer or ethnographer can give us descriptions of varied types of dwellings. In each variety, the phenomenologist makes the effort needed to seize upon the germ of the essential, sure, immediate well-being it encloses. In every dwelling, even the richest, the first task of the phenomenologist os to find the original shell . . . We therefore have to say how we inhabit our vital space, in accord with all the dialectics of life, how we take root, day after day, in a 'corner of the world'.[18]

The following extracts from *Life in the English Country House* demonstrate the range and coverage given to such a rich subject. The text can be re-read using the categories I suggest in this chapter, and there are many other possible readings which relate to the themes of the other chapters in this volume. Here I juxtapose Girouard with Sir Ernst Gombrich who discusses another way of writing about the broader contexts for the production and consumption of the visual in his essay *In Search of Cultural History*.

Notes

1 I Kant, *What is Enlightenment?* in *The Works of Immanuel Kant*, trans. Paul Gruyer and Allen W Wood, Cambridge, Cambridge University Press, 1998.

2 There have been some moves to re-evaluate the role of certain social groups in other disciplines. See for instance C Hall 'Gender Divisions And Class Formation in the Birmingham Middle Class, 1780–1850' in R Samuel (ed.), *People's History and Socialist Theory*, London, Routledge, 1981, pp. 164–175.

3 On this point *inter alia* see J Scott, 'Women's History' in P Burke (ed.), *New Perspectives on Historical Writing*, Cambridge, Cambridge University Press, 1992 and J Kelly, *Women, History and Theory: The essays of Joan Kelly*, Chicago, University of Chicago Press, 1984.

4 See for instance J Lummis and J Marsh, *The Woman's Domaine*, London, Viking, 1990 and A Vickery, *The Gentleman's Daughter*, New Haven, CT and London, Yale University Press, 1999.

5 See J Butler, *Gender Trouble: Feminism and the subversion of identity*, London and New York, Routledge, 1990.

6 P Osborne and L Segal, 'Gender as Performance: An interview with Judith Butler' conducted in London 1993, in *Radical Philosophy*, 67, Summer 1994.

7 M Nussbaum 'The Professor of Parody', *New Republic*, March 1999.

8 On these points see my essay 'Defining Feminity: Women and the country house' in D Arnold, *The Georgian Country House: Architecture, landscape and society*, Stroud and New York, Sutton, 1998.

9 Henri Lefebvre, *The Production of Space*, trans. David Nicholson-Smith, London, Blackwell, 1991, pp. 362–336.

10 T Adorno, 'Functionalism Today', trans. Jane Newman and John Smith, *Oppositions*, 17, Summer 1979, pp. 30–41.

11 E P Thompson 'The Poverty of Theory or an Orrery of Errors' in *The Poverty of Theory and Other Essays*, London, Merlin, 1978, p. 170.

12 E P Thompson, 'Patrician Society, Plebian Culture' *Journal of Social History*, 7, 4, Summer 1974, pp. 382–405.

13 I discuss this point more fully in my book *The Georgian Country House: Architecture, landscape and society*, op. cit.

14 R Williams, *Marxism and Literature*, Oxford, Oxford University Press, 1978, p. 112.

15 L Stone, 'On the Grand Scale': Review of *Life in the English Country House*, *TLS*, 10 November 1978, p. 298.

16 D Watkin, *The Rise of Architectural History*, London, Architectural Press, 1980, p. 185.

17 See my book *The Georgian Country House: Architecture, landscape and society*, op. cit.

18 G Bachelard, *Poetics of Space*, trans. Maria Jolas, Boston, Beacon, 1969 Part One, p. 387.

Life in the English country house

Mark Girouard

The formal house 1630–1720

Both and France and England had started in the Middle Ages with the basic system of hall
and chamber (in France *salle* and *chambre*), but the system had developed differently in the
two countries. In England some of the functions of the hall had been hived off into the
chamber, and the chamber had been subdivided into a great chamber for state, and a relatively private chamber for living and sleeping. No such development had taken place in
France; nor had anything resembling the further subdivision of the chamber into withdrawing chamber and bedchamber. In the mid seventeenth century a *chambre* was still
basically a bed-sitting room – even if, in a big house, a very grand bed-sitting room. It was
used for the reception of visitors and for private meals as well as for sleeping. Its combination of functions was sometimes expressed by putting the bed in an alcove, like a room
within a room. In a royal *chambre* the bed was separated from the rest of the room by a
balustrade, like an altar rail in a church, and only courtiers above a certain rank were
allowed behind it.

The rooms before and beyond the *chambre* accordingly had functions rather different
from those of their English equivalents. The *antechambre* was, as its name implies, essentially
a waiting room for visitors hoping to get access to the *chambre*. Sometimes a great person
would come out into it, so that people not considered important enough to be admitted into
his *chambre* could pay their respect or present petitions. The room had little of the private
nature of a seventeenth-century withdrawing room.

The public, or relatively public, nature of *antechambre* and *chambre* was reflected in the
status of the *cabinet*. An English bedchamber with a bed in it for a child or a servant, sometimes a closet for private study or prayer. Such rooms were useful but not essential. French
cabinets were essential, because they were *the* private rooms. To get into the *cabinet* of a
monarch or great man one had to be in the inner ring of power. *Cabinets* could vary a good
deal in size; usually they were small rooms but very richly decorated, and they often contained their owners' most precious pictures, coins, medals, bronzes and curiosities. They were
like little shrines at the end of a series of initiatory vestibules.

At the other end of the sequence, the *grande salle* or *grand salon* was used for the same
kind of functions as a great chamber but had a different lineage. It descended from the
medieval *salle*, rather than the *chambre*. The *salle* had developed in exactly the opposite
way to the English hall. Instead of the family and their guests moving out of it and the
servants staying, the family had stayed and the servants been removed. Accordingly a
French *salon* was either entered directly from outside, like an English hall, or was preceded by a vestibule (or, if it was on the first floor, by a staircase). Vestibules could be
richly decorated but they were never large; they were rooms to pass through, not to
linger in.

The *salon* was normally expressed on the exterior by some kind of frontispiece. At Vaux-
le-Vicomte this rises up through two storeys into a dome. Dome and frontispiece form the

dominant feature of the facade; to either side the two *antechambres*, as the rooms of least importance, are treated as a relatively plain interlude before the *chambre* and *cabinet* at the privileged end of each *appartement*. The position of these is shown on the outside by pilasters and separate roofs forming terminal pavilions. The combination of a state centre for the saloon and pavilions for the priviliged end of the apartments was to become one of the commonest ways of organising facades all over Europe.

[. . .]

A typical grand house of the period, influenced by Pratt, France, and English court prac-tice is Ragley Hall in Warwickshire. It was designed in about 1678 by Robert Hooke for Lord Conway, Charles II's Secretary of State. Hooke was a distinguished scientist and a member of the Royal Society, as well as an architect. Ragley as he left it (it has been much altered) was an example of the scientific method applied to the rational arrangement of a country house (Figure 4.9). There was a state centre, of two-storey hall leading into 'salon' or dining room. Round this were four symmetrical apartments, each with a drawing room or antechamber leading to a bedroom, and with two small rooms and a backstairs beyond the bedroom. Between the apartments were two front staircases and two extra rooms – a chapel and a library. The backstairs descended into a basement, which contained the kitchens, cel-lars and servants' hall. There was no great chamber on the first floor. Its function was filled by a 'salon' or dining room (it is called both on the plans) on the level of the hall. As at Vaux-le-Vicomte both the state centre and the bedroom ends of the apartments were given external expression.[1]

Two features of Ragley deserve closer examination – the arrangement and use of the big rooms in the centre, and of the small rooms and backstairs at the extremities. The English, for whom the saloon took the place of the great chamber rather than the hall, had to decide what to do with the hall. Should it be reduced to a vestibule, on the con-tinental model, or kept to something resembling its traditional English size? In the long run the vestibule-hall was to be the winner, but well into the eighteenth century the weight of tradition retained old-style halls in many country houses. In addition to being rooms of entry and waiting, these big halls were used for dining on special occasions. As late as 1756 Isaac Ware suggested that, while halls in town houses need only be vestibules, in the country they should be 'large and noble'. A country-house hall, he pointed out, was more than a waiting room for 'people of the second rank; it serves as a summer-room for dining . . . and it is a good apartment for the reception of large com-panies at public feasts.'[2]

During the long intervals between great occasions, halls tended to pick up other func-tions. By 1678 the Elizabethan hall at Longford Castle in Wiltshire, besides being used as a 'great Banquetting Roome' for 'Christmas or such a time of extraordinary festival' contained a shovelboard and a newly-installed music gallery. The latter was probably used for music at all times of the year, and not just to provide musical accompaniment to ban-quets. The walls and screen in the hall were decorated with 'very great heads of foreigne or English deere'.[3] Sets of antlers on the walls, and occasional use for games or music, were to be features of halls for many years to come. Some halls were still hung with arms and armour, at first for use and later for decoration. In 1723 the Duke of Chandos's ser-vants were hanging up their arms on circular boards in the hall of the duke's house at Cannons; by the 1760s Robert Adam was decorating the hall at Osterley with low-relief plaster panels of military trophies, in memory of a custom that no longer had a practical function.

[. . .]

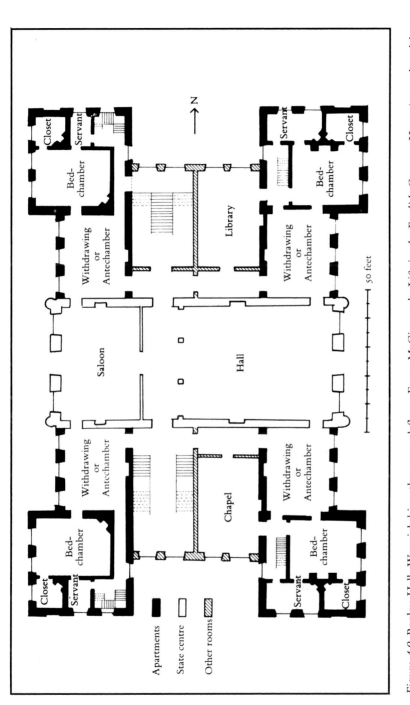

Figure 4.9 Ragley Hall, Warwickshire, the ground floor. From M Girouard, *Life in the English Country House* (reproduced by permission).

Before the introduction of saloons, the only large rooms at hall level had been the main parlour. To begin with, rooms filling the functions of saloons were quite often called parlours – usually great parlours or great dining parlours, to underline their new dignity – but the term saloon gradually ousted the traditional one. The upgrading of the parlour meant that another room was needed to fill its traditional informal function as a family sitting and eating room. The second parlour was normally called a common parlour – common being used in the sense of everyday. Common parlours were often on the ground floor, but were sometimes in the basement, if the house had one; the latter arrangement was recommended by Roger North, who wrote a treatise on house planning at the end of the seventeenth century.[4]

The ejection of servants from the hall revolutionized one aspect of the country house. Another was transformed by the equally revolutionary invention of backstairs – and of closets and servants' rooms attached to them. Roger North thought this the biggest improvement in planning that had taken place during his lifetime.[5] The gentry walking up the stairs no longer met their last night's faeces coming down them. Servants no longer bedded down in the drawing room, or outside their master's door or in a truckle bed at his feet. They became, if not invisible, very much less visible.

Some form of backstairs had existed in France since the sixteenth century. In England they appeared in embryo in the first half of the seventeenth century, but their systemization seems to have been the work of the great innovator Roger Pratt. He wrote down the principles in 1660, when he had already carried them out at Coleshill. Bedchambers must 'each of them have a closet, and a servant's lodging with chimney, both of which will easily be made by dividing the breadth of one end of the room into two such parts as shall be convenient'. The servant's room should have backstairs adjoining. In general, a house should be 'so contrived . . . that the ordinary servants may never publicly appear in passing to and from for their occasions there.'[6]

By the time Hooke designed Ragley, with its four backstairs, the system had reached the height of sophistication. A closet for prayer, study and private meetings, a little room for a servant, possibly a wardrobe, and a backstairs adjoining became the essentials of luxurious living. Sometimes one or more of these little rooms were put in a mezzanine; such mezzanines survive at Kinross in Scotland and Easton Neston in Northamptonshire, and give the latter its distinctive north facade.[7] The servant often shared his room with a close-stool; it was not till the eighteenth century that luxury advanced to the stage of putting these two useful aids into separate rooms. The servant, the contents of the close-stool, and anything that was undesirable or private could move or be moved up and down the backstairs, preferably to offices in the basement.

The servants thus neatly tidied away were a somewhat different body from the servants in an equivalent household a hundred years earlier. There were fewer of them, their social status was lower, and there were more women (though fewer gentlewomen) among them. The Earl of Derby at Knowsley in 1585, and the Earl of Dorset at Knole in about 1620, had households of 115 and 111 people.[8] Both were living in great state. The Duke of Chandos, living in equivalent state at Cannons in 1722, had a household of ninety; this included a private orchestra of sixteen musicians, which was an unusual feature for that period, even for a duke.[9] Reduction in numbers was accompanied by reduction in ceremony. Some remnants survived. On Sundays at Cannons, and when the duke had guests, the usher of the hall 'with his gown on and staff in his hand' preceded each course into the dining room, with the clerk of the kitchen walking behind him. But all the panoply of bowing, kissing and kneeling, of sewers, carvers and cupbearers, had disappeared.[10]

[. . .]

The gentlemen servants no longer included elder, or even younger, sons of good county families. They were recruited from, at best, a respectable middle-class background – the sons of merchants, clergymen and army officers. The duchess's gentlewoman was the daughter of a Liverpool knight, not a country squire. In 1724 a Mr Drummond, related to the Earl of Perth and the banking Drummonds, put in for the job of steward, but was rejected as too good for the job.[11] The steward at Cannons was a shadow of the stewards in great households of earlier days. His office had lost its social prestige, and lacked the value deriving from professional qualifications; in all large establishments estate business was now conducted by a separate land steward who usually did not live in the house. At £50 a year the house steward at Cannons was paid less than the master of music and head gardener (£100) or the secretary, chaplains and librarian (£75). On this salary-scale he was clearly no longer the chief household officer. Accordingly a new officer of master of the household had been created and given to an ex-army officer, Colonel Watkins.

All these gentlemen ate at their private table in the chaplains' room, except for the chaplain-in-waiting and Colonel Watkin, who ate with the duke.[12] There was a gap in prestige and possibly social background between the upper servants at the chaplains' table and the lesser gentlemen and gentlewomen, who ate in the gentleman-of-the-horse's room. These included the gentleman of the horse, who ran the stables, the gentleman usher, who looked after the main rooms, the duke's two gentlemen, descendants of the earlier gentlemen of the chamber, who were his personal attendants, the duchess's two gentlewomen, and the pages.

The decline or departure of gentlemen servants produced a corresponding increase in status of the former yeomen officers – now just known as the officers. They were promoted to the dignity of 'Mr', and ate in the gentleman-of-the-horse's room, although at a separate table. They included the clerk of the kitchen, the clerk of the check (roughly equivalent to the clerk-comptroller of earlier days), the head cook, the butler, and the groom of the chambers. The butler had absorbed the jobs of the yeomen of buttery, ewery and pantry, and was beginning the rise that was to lead to his nineteenth-century eminence. In 1726 the Cannons officers were amalgamated with the lesser gentlemen and sat at the same table with them. By then the latter were probably gentle only by courtesy, and the duke's gentlemen not so very different from the 'gentleman's gentleman' of later days.

All other servants ate in the kitchen or the servants' hall. Kitchen staff, other than the head cook and clerk of the kitchen, ate in the kitchen. Footmen, under-butler, porters, coachman, grooms, stable-boys, gardeners, odd men and maids other than kitchen-maids ate in the servants' hall.

Footmen had had a curious history. In the later Middle Ages and the sixteenth century a footman was an attendant who walked or ran on foot by the side of his master or mistress when they rode out on horseback or in a carriage.[13] He was mainly there for prestige, but could also be used to lead home a lame horse and to run messages, especially in London. A fast-running footman with plenty of staying power was much prized, and from at least the mid seventeenth century owners were racing their footmen against each other, and betting heavily on the result.

During the seventeenth century footmen began to come into the house to help wait at the less important tables.[14] By the end of the century both gentlemen and yeomen waiters had entirely disappeared, and footmen (at times supplemented by pages as personal attendants to important people) were waiting at the first table, under the butler and under-butler. At

Cannons the duke and duchess had seven footmen, one of whom was still employed as a running footman. Colonel Watkins had a footman of his own, and another waited at table in the chaplains' room.

Footmen supplanted waiters because, originally at any rate, they came from a lower social class and were cheaper. During the seventeenth century the same reasons of economy began to bring women into the non-ceremonial sections of the household. Women were invariably paid less than men for doing the same job. They had always been nurses, laundry-maids and personal attendants on the ladies of the house, but they now began to clean and cook. At Cannons all the cleaning and some of the cooking was done by women. There were two laundry-maids, a dairymaid, three housemaids and two cookmaids, as well as 'chairwomen' working in the laundry and kitchen. The female staff was under a housekeeper who had an assistant housekeeper to help her.

In the sixteenth century a housekeeper had been a person who looked after the house of a widower or a bachelor. As female staff increased during the seventeenth century, she became a regular feature of large households of all sorts. At Cannons she supervised the linen and the housework, controlled the supplies of tea, coffee, sugar, preserves, soap and candles, and showed the house to visitors. She still ranked low in the household hierarchy; she sat at the officers table but, at £10 a year, was paid less than any of them.[15]

Cannons is an example from the later days of the formal house. In the intervening period different houses had changed in different ways and at different rates. The Duke of Beaufort at Badminton in the 1680s had a household and style of living not so very different from that kept by his grandfather at Raglan Castle in the 1640s.[16] But the general drift was inexorable. By the end of the seventeenth century the ancient ceremonies had almost entirely disappeared. Large households were recruited from lower social grades. Servants were kept out of sight except when actually about their business, and even then kept as invisible as possible if their business was at all insalubrious. The departure of the servants from the front part of the house was accompanied by the departure of all the tenants, visitors on business and hangers-on who used to eat with them in the hall. Everyday hospitality at this level still went on, but it was kept out of sight of the grander visitors. It was a very different system from the communal and public hierarchy of great mediaeval or even great Elizabethan houses.

The changes were partly due to a growing feeling for privacy and a growing fastidiousness. But they also reflected the changing nature of society and the power structure. Great houses were no longer settings for the display of a united following of all social ranks, tied to their lord by service and hereditary loyalty, bound together by shared ceremony and ritual, and prepared if needs be to fight for him. The power of the central government and the institution of a standing army had destroyed the point and possibility of such followings. The protection offered by a great lord to his servants no longer attracted gentlemen of any standing, once the state maintained reasonable law and order, and numerous other routes of advancement were available to them. Grammar schools and universities offered a better education than could be picked up by the page of a great man. Younger sons went into commerce, the law, the armed forces or the government rather than household service. Moreover the Civil War, and the parliamentary battles which preceded it, had given many of the gentry a taste for independence. Some form of gentry service lingered on in a few houses. As late as 1700 Lord Paget, at Beaudesert in Staffordshire, still had the right to summon certain of the local gentry to wait on him 'on some solemn feast days' and occasionally exercised it. But, as Celia Fiennes commented, 'these things are better waived than sought'.[17] It had become demeaning for a gentleman to be a servant.

The growing independence of the gentry from the aristocracy presented both classes with a dilemma. Should the gentry act as loyal servants of the king or fight for greater political power at his expense? Should the aristocracy try to maintain their status by becoming powerful at court, or by leading the gentry in their aspirations for political independence through parliament? From the 1630s to the end of the century the dilemma split both gentry and aristocracy and divided family from family, brother from brother, and father from son. The division into what came to be called court and country parties ultimately ended in victory for the country party and for parliament. But as far as the architecture of country houses were concerned, the pace was set by the court party.

The court party maintained the sixteenth-century belief that a hierarchy under a single head was the only right order for society, because it was ordained by God and followed his model of the universe. But it placed much greater emphasis on the supreme power of the king, and on the central authority of the state, which derived from the king. This authority was absolute, because it came from God not man.[18] Outside their own households the members of the aristocracy had authority only because the king gave it to them. Because they were his chief servants and filled the top rank of the hierarchy below him they had to be treated with honour and respect. They still received visitors, or ate in state, under a canopy. They sat in their chapels framed in flamboyant pomp of curtains, coats of arms and coronets. Their wives walked with a train and a page to carry it, even through their own gardens. But they were not what they had been.

The formal house flourished because it reflected absolute monarchy and the society that went with it. In the late seventeenth and early eighteenth century, when absolute monarchy was at its most powerful, saloons between matching apartments were springing up from Russia to America,[19] and from Sweden to Sicily. The immense prestige of Louis XIV and his court set the fashion, but it was imitated by the opponents of France as well as its allies – by Prince Eugene at the Belvedere and the Duke of Marlborough at Blenheim. In England it flourished especially among adherents of the court, but even the leaders of the country party were unable to ignore it.

[. . .]

As far as country houses were concerned, the functions of the lower ranks within the hierarchy were now only those of respectful service to their superiors. They lived in the basement, or in subordinate wings to either side of the house. The main rooms were designed as the orderly setting for meetings between gentlemen, lords, and princes, who seldom forgot their rank. But behind the rigid etiquette which regulated their intercourse, continual jockeying for power, position and favours went on. The central government was a rich source of jobs and perquisites, which were distributed either by the king himself, or by his ministers and favourites. The main power of the court aristocracy now lay in its power of patronage; it was constantly being solicited for favours.

The formal house was beautifully calculated as an instrument both to express etiquette and to back up negotiation. Since each room in the sequence of an apartment was more exclusive than the last, compliments to or from a visitor could be nicely gauged not only by how far he penetrated along the sequence, but also by how far the occupant of the apartment came along it – and even beyond it – to welcome him (Figure 4.10). The situation changed radically depending on whether the visitor was grander or less grand than the person he or she was visiting. The less grand visitor hoped to penetrate as far as possible along the line, but did not always succeed. The grander visitor was pressed to penetrate to the inner sanctuary, but could not always be tempted.[20]

The system can be watched in action in a contemporary account of a visit paid by the King of Spain to Petworth in 1703.[21] The front half of Petworth had been built by the Duke of Somerset in 1680s. His new building was a very grand example of formal planning, possibly

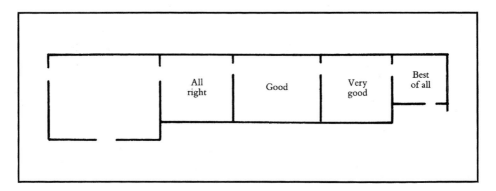

Figure 4.10 The axis of honour in the formal house. From M Girouard, *Life in the English Country House* (reproduced by permission).

designed by a Frenchman. It consisted of four apartments, stretched out to either side of the centre in two sets of two, one above the other. The lower two were probably for the duke and duchess, the upper two for important guests. In the centre was an entrance hall, and above it, under statues and a dome, there must originally have been a two-storey saloon.

The reception party for the King of Spain consisted of the Duke of Somerset, and Queen Anne's husband, Prince George of Denmark. The first point of etiquette was that the prince, being the queen's husband, acted as though Petworth were his own house. It was he who welcomed the king, and he who showed him round the house; the principal function of the duke seems to have been to pay the bills.

As the king arrived he was welcomed at the door by the prince and escorted to the entrance of his apartment on the first floor. After a decent interval to allow the king to settle in, a series of state visits were paid between the various great people. First, the prince sent a message to the king to ask if he could call on him. Permission being given, the prince emerged from his apartment, and proceeded through the ante-room and withdrawing room of the king's apartment to the door of his bedchamber. The king, who was sitting in an arm-chair in his bedchamber, came to the door – but no further – to welcome him, and sat him in an armchair opposite him – an armchair being a rank above a chair without arms, and two ranks above a stool (if it had been the case of one reigning monarch entertaining another, or if the business had been one of policy rather than courtesy, they might have gone into the cabinet). After they had passed the time of day for a few minutes, the prince returned to his apartment. Shortly afterwards the king sent a message to ask if he could call on the prince. Permission being given, the king emerged from his apartment and was met by the prince who, being of an inferior grade of royalty, came out of his own apartment to the top of the stairs to greet him. He was then conveyed to the prince's bedchamber, where *he* passed the time of day for a few minutes. At some stage the duke had appeared, and the king now asked him if he could pay a call on the duchess. King, prince and duke then proceeded down to the duchess's apartment on the ground floor. The duchess 'came forward several rooms, even to the bottom of the stairs, to meet the King, and making a very low obeisance she received a kiss from him, as also the two young ladies her daughters, whom she presented to him.' The king, however, advanced no further into the duchess's apartment than a 'little drawing room', where he passed three or four minutes in polite conversation. He was then shown round the rest of the house – by the prince of course, not the duke. Everyone now having called on everyone else, and the honours having been done, king, prince, duke and duchess finally emerged from their various apartments to have supper together in the saloon.

The supper was described as 'served up with so much splendour and profusion, yet with so much decency and order that I must needs say I never saw the like.' But the description gives no details. However, a detailed account survives of a combined dinner, ball and supper, 'the finest that ever was seen', given by the Earl of Portland for Prince Eugene of Savoy in 1711.[22] The entertainment lasted from six in the evening till five in the morning. It was held at the earl's house in St James's Square, mostly in a new room which Lord Portland had built on. It was referred to variously as a hall, 'sale', or great room, and filled the function of a saloon.

The evening started with dinner at the late hour of six o'clock to fit in with a sitting of the House of Lords; the normal time was now one or two o'clock. It was attended by the prince, seventeen noblemen, and no ladies. The waiting was all done by volunteer gentlemen 'that offered themselves to have an occasion to see the feast'. There was a buffet loaded with gilt and silver plate, and during the whole meal 'trumpets and kettle drum play'd in a room adjoining'. After dinner the company removed to Lady Portland's apartment on the first floor. Here 'several persons of both sexes had been invited to cards' and to hear a symphony performed by twenty singers and musicians from the opera. While this was going on, the saloon was cleared of tables and buffet for a ball. The company returned there at ten, and the ball lasted till three. The company then moved downstairs to Lord Portland's apartment, where supper was served. There were two separate tables, for gentlemen and ladies; Prince Eugene insisted on serving the ladies in person before he ate himself, and the other men followed his example. Supper concluded with much drinking of toasts. Everyone left at about five in the morning.

The separation of men from women at the dinner was still in the mediaeval tradition. Another interesting feature of the evening is the relatively small number of people involved. Eighteen sat down to dinner, fifteen couples danced at the ball. The entertaining was 'the finest that ever was seen' because of the style and richness of the accompaniments, not because of its size. This was typical of the period. Feasts for several hundred people were still being given in the country, to prepare for an election or celebrate Christmas, births, weddings, and comings of age. They usually centred round dinner in the hall, and could involve all the neighbouring gentry and near-gentry, and even the tenants and local freeholders. But the entertainments which enjoyed the most prestige were small but elaborate ones for relatively few people – just as the prestigious part of the house was devoted to a few large apartments for great people coming on what amounted to a state visit. A hard line was still drawn between the inner ring of the great and smaller fry.

The smaller fry were most likely to penetrate into a great house on the occasions of its owner's levy or levée. Although a big landowner often held a levée when he returned to the country, levées were, on the whole, London events. Great men (and the king) held them every morning. A man's levée was attended by men only.[23] It started while the giver of the levée was being powdered and curled in his bedroom – or, in some cases, in a separate dressing room or ante-room leading up to his bedchamber. The select few might be invited to talk to him in his bedroom or dressing room, but most waited patiently outside until he appeared in the ante-room, sometimes pursued by his barber putting the final touches to his toilet. The giver of the levée could gauge his rating by the number of people attending it; Lord Hervey describes how Sir Robert Walpole's levée suddenly emptied on the death of George I, when everyone expected him to be turned out of office. In the same way, those attending the levée could gauge how they stood with the great man by his affability – or lack of it – towards them.

Levées were especially used to present petitions, or to ask for jobs or favours. Of course, nothing in the least bit private could be discussed in the crowd in the outer room. That was reserved for the bedroom or better still, the closet or cabinet. And here the backstairs revealed yet another asset. While the crowd was hopefully approaching the great man by the official path – through the saloon and along the axis of honour – the person or persons to whom he really wanted to talk could bypass them entirely, and be quietly introduced at the inner end of the sequence by being brought up the backstairs.

In the time of Charles II and his successors, the backstairs acquired a recognized function in the king's political and private life. William Chiffinch, Charles's senior page of the backstairs and keeper of his cabinet-closet, was an extremely useful person to know, and an invaluable servant to the king. Under his supervision, priests, whores, opposition politicians and anyone else whom the king wished to see in secret, came discreetly up the backstairs.[24] Well into the eighteenth century the backstairs played a similar useful role in all palaces and large houses; hence the phrase 'backstairs intrigue'.[25]

The levée of a woman was of a more intimate and less official nature than that of a man. It was held entirely in her bedroom or dressing room and was angled towards flirtation and amusement rather than politics. As Goldsmith put it:

> Fair to be seen, she kept a bevy
> Of powdered Coxcombs at her levy[26]

He was writing at the end of the reign of the levée. A hundred years or so earlier, in 1683, John Evelyn had been fascinated but also shocked when he was brought to the levée of the Duchess of Portsmouth, Charles II's mistress, and found her 'in her morning loose garment, her maids combing her, newly out of her bed, his majesty and the gallants standing about her'.[27]

The Duchess of Portsmouth's levée took place in her dressing room, within her bedroom. Dressing rooms seem to have been an English refinement. They were the result of English couples, even very grand ones, tending to share the same bedchamber, rather than visiting each other from separate bedchambers, as in France. As early as the beginning of the sixteenth century, 'My Lord's chamber where he maketh him ready' at Wressel Castle was clearly a dressing room in fact if not in name. The term 'dressing room' seems first to have appeared in the second half of the seventeenth century. In grand houses of this period there could be two separate dressing rooms, for husband and wife, 'so that at rising each may retire apart and have several accommodation complete', as Roger North put it.[28] But at the end of the seventeenth century it became fashionable for women to dress in their bedchambers, probably as a result of French influence. Although the use of dressing rooms came back in strength in the eighteenth century, as late as 1743 Hogarth's *Marriage à la Mode* series shows a fashionable countess holding a levée in her bedchamber. The bed is in a recess in the French manner, and among her visitors and little court is a barber, a beau, and an antique dealer. It was probably French influence, too, which made separate apartments for husband and wife more common in the late seventeenth and early eighteenth century, especially in grand houses. At a period when marriages were still almost invariably arranged it was, after all, a sensible arrangement.

Although the basic idea of the formal house was a simple one, it admitted of endless variations. Formal houses were not necessarily large. Hooke's Ragley should be compared with the more modest, but exquisitely formal, house which he designed in about 1680 for Sir William Jones, the Attorney-General at Ramsbury in Wiltshire. Even a house as small as

Nether Lypiatt in Gloucestershire, where there was no room for a central hall and saloon, was arranged in the form of matching sets of apartments laid parallel to each other, with front and back stairs in between. Externally it was completely formal, from the disposition of the chimney-stacks to the arrangement of the subordinate pavilions each echoing the shape of the central house.

One of these pavilions may originally have contained the kitchen. The 1680s saw the beginning of the practise of moving the kitchen out of the main block and putting it in a separate pavilion.[29] The move had the practical advantage of taking kitchen smells out of the house, a convenience which seems at the time to have been thought to make up for the distance between kitchen and eating rooms. But it also suggested an aesthetic of house between pavilions which suited the contemporary feeling for hierarchy – as long as at least two pavilions or wings were provided. The problem then arose of what to put into the second pavilion. Should it be the stables – the most common solution? Or laundries and breweries? Or a chapel? Numerous different variations were adopted. The only one never found in England (as opposed to Ireland or America) was Palladio's arrangement of putting the farm in the wings. Although Palladio's villa plans had a strong influence on similar plans in England, a close connection between house and farm was entirely at variance with the English tradition.

Many decisions of this sort had to be made by the designers of formal houses. Should the saloon be put on the first floor, or on the level of the hall? Should there be two state apartments, or only one, balanced by a family apartment? Should there be one family apartment, or two, for husband wife? What floor should they be on? How should the state centre be expressed externally? How could a grand staircase, chapel or gallery be fitted into a plan without disrupting its symmetry? How many concessions should be made to convenience or tradition, at the expense of symmetry? Endless variations can be found, from houses which are exquisitely and ingeniously symmetrical, to houses based on traditional sixteenth-century planning, but brought modestly up-to-date by the provision of backstairs, closets and a formal exterior.

Formal planning could be applied to the alteration of remodelling of old houses as well as the building of new ones. Roger North was especially delighted with the remodelling of Ham House, as carried out by the Duke and Duchess of Lauderdale in the 1670s.[30] The main feature of this was the provision of a new range between the arms of the H-shaped Elizabethan house, in order to provide matching apartments for the duke and duchess. These were on the ground floor, to either side of a private dining room. As the scale of the rooms is small, but the decoration extremely luxurious, the result is both intimate and formal. Above these two apartments the new range was filled by a single state apartment known as the Queen's Apartment because Catherine of Braganza occupied it. The queen's bedchamber has been somewhat changed,[31] but her closet survives unaltered, and gives a vivid idea of the nature of these minute but important rooms.

Formalizing an old house could lead to problems of design, as happened at Chatsworth. Its main block appears to be a new building of the late seventeenth century, but is in fact an Elizabethan house sumptuously remodelled. The layout of the rooms was conditioned by this. There was no space to fit a saloon and matching apartments of appropriately grand scale into the main front. Instead a great dining chamber – in effect a saloon – at one end of the front led into a single apartment containing antechamber, withdrawing chamber, bedchamber and cabinet, filling the rest of the front. The arrangement is very grand, but lopsided. That it was felt to be so at the time is shown by the fact that at one end of the great dining chamber, where the missing apartment should have been, a mirror is set into the wall to reflect the enfilade of doors through the existing apartment. As long as one stands in the right place, the complete arrangement appears to be in existence. The lopsidedness is reflected in the exterior: the great dining chamber at one end of the front and the state bedroom and cabinet at the other are expressed by pilasters, but in the centre, where one would expect a portico or some external feature, there is nothing – quite logically, for there is nothing to express.

There was no such problem on the entrance front which was remodelled some years later. Here the first and second floors were each given over to a central room between two family apartments. As these were considerably smaller than the state apartment on the south front, there was no problem about fitting the rooms behind the facade although the need to incorporate a staircase prevented perfect symmetry. A pediment and columns suitably expressed the ground level entrance into the courtyard and the dignity of the central rooms above. The upper one of these survives relatively unaltered. It is magnificently frescoed by Thornhill, but originally had no fireplace. It was designed as what Roger North called an ante-room.[32] He considered such an arrangement 'the perfection which one would desire, and if understood easily obtained because it fits the humour of a front, whereof the middle windows may serve the ante-room, and on either side the chambers.' The central room 'need not have a chimney, because it is for passage, short attendance or diversion. Music is very proper in it. And it is scarce known what a life is given to the upper part of a house, when it is conveniently layed out and adorned.'[33]

At the end of the seventeenth century an architect of genius took the formal plan and used it to produce results that were both closely adapted to the needs and values of his clients and expressive works of art. The architect was Vanbrugh. Vanbrugh started with the two main elements of formal planning, axial vistas and symmetrical hierarchies, and dramatized them. His axial vistas are exquisitely interlocked, interminably extended, and vibrant with incident. Every part of his houses, from the smallest out-building by way of kitchens and stables to the apartments and saloon, is made to play its part in an extended hierarchy that gradually builds up to the central crescendo.

Vanbrugh is often thought of as an impractical architect. Most people consider Blenheim the acme of waste and ostentation. But by the standards of its times (and apart from the extravagances of its skyline) Blenheim was functional. It was, of course, on an enormous scale, because it was a palace for a national hero. But every element in the plan had its purpose.

Blenheim is based on the standard formal plan. A hall in the north front leads into a saloon between matching state apartments on the south front. This provides the major theme. It is echoed on a smaller scale by the minor theme of twin apartments for the duke and duchess, placed to either side of a central vestibule (which soon became a private dining room) on the east front. An inner zone, behind the main ranges of the apartments, contained corridors, backstairs, dressing rooms, wardrobes and closets.[34]

On the west front the space corresponding to the private apartments is filled by an enormous gallery. This provided display space for Marlborough's great collection of pictures, and a state route to the chapel in the west wing. The chapel corresponds in position to the kitchen in the east wing; the balance between spiritual and physical nourishment may have amused Vanbrugh. Beyond the kitchen is the kitchen court, and beyond the chapel the stable court; a cross axis across the main courtyard connects the two through a vista of archways, and is also the axis of the approach from Woodstock.

The main axis runs through saloon, hall and great court and continues across Vanbrugh's epic Roman bridge to a column on the hilltop a mile from the house. The duke, dining in state in the saloon, would (had he survived to see it all completed) have been enthroned on the line of a continuous celebration of his greatness. The column is surmounted by his statue, and a roll call of his victories is carved on its base. The ceilings of both hall and saloon are painted with his apotheosis. Externally they are crowned with trophies of victory, in the form of statues of prisoners and the bust of Louis XIV; the position now occupied by the bust was originally intended for a statue of Marlborough on horseback, trampling on his enemies. A triumphal arch, surmounted by the royal arms and cherubs blowing trumpets, leads from the hall to the inner glories of the saloon.

The hall was a room for great dinners, the saloon for grand ones. Both rise through two storeys. On a balcony under the arch between them musicians could transpose the fanfares of the cherubs into real life while dinner took place; the balcony originally opened into both rooms.[35] It also gave access to lesser apartments, on the first floor above the family and state apartments. As these upper apartments were of minor importance the staircases leading up to them are relatively inconspicuous; there is no grand staircase. In the nineteenth century the bedrooms from the lower apartments were moved upstairs, and the ground floor rooms run together as an interminable and largely meaningless sequence of twelve state rooms. The point of the plan had been destroyed.

At the beginning of the eighteenth century Vanbrugh and the Baroque went out of fashion and Palladianism came in. To begin with Palladianism did not mean a change of plan in the country-house world, it only meant a change of uniform. The reign of the saloon between apartments went on – but now the ceremonial centre could be neatly expressed in terms of a temple, with a portico at one or both ends. As in earlier models, the result did not necessarily have to be grand, and there was scope for a variety of arrangements. The apartments could vary in size from two rooms to four. The hall and saloon in the centre, could be large or small. In some scaled-down versions hall and saloon were elided into a single hall-saloon. The apartments could be arranged to produce houses with wings extended – that is to say with apartments strung out at length alone one axis – or with wings folded, with apartments turned back along either side of the hall and saloon to produce a compact, approximately square plan. The type with wings extended was much used for houses at the centre of great estates, where show was considered essential. The results were the immensely extended facades of houses like Stowe, Wanstead or Wentworth Woodhouse. The wings-folded arrangement worked very well for houses built for people of moderate fortunes but sophisticated tastes, or for the subsidiary and more private residences of the great. Such houses were known in the eighteenth century as villas, and were built in especially large numbers in areas within comfortable reach of London.[36]

Externally, English Palladian houses almost invariably followed the same formula, even if with many variations. Their lower storey was rusticated, and acted as a basement podium for one or more smooth-faced upper storeys, the proportions of which were dictated by a central frontispiece or portico. The basement storey was known in the eighteenth century as 'the rustic'. The arrangement derived ultimately from Roman temples, by way of Palladio and Inigo Jones. The main entrance was sometimes into the rustic, but was usually into the hall behind the portico, by way of an external flight of steps built in front of the rustic; in the latter case there was normally a subsidiary entrance into the rustic, under the main one.

The arrangement adapted well enough to English practice. In some houses the rustic was entirely filled by kitchen, cellars and service rooms. More usually it was divided between service rooms and informal living rooms. There were many variations. At Wanstead, in 1722, there were three complete apartments in the rustic: one of five rooms, for the owner, Lord Castlemain, one of four rooms, for his wife, and one 'designed for the entertainment of their friends'. The floor above was 'for the rooms of state' and contained four more apartments, in addition to the hall and saloon.[37] At Wolterton (a considerably smaller house) there were only four gentry rooms in the rustic; these may originally have been designed as one complete apartment, but by 1750 were being used as a family dining parlour, drawing room, study and breakfast room.[38] Houghton seems never to have had bedrooms in its rustic. Instead it was liberally supplied with informal living rooms, in the form of a breakfast room, supping parlour, hunting hall and coffee room, all grouped round a central vaulted hall, known as 'the arcade', and used for 'walking and *quid-nuncing*'.[39]

Twice yearly at Houghton Walpole gave what became famous as his Norfolk 'congresses'. A mixed party made up of his colleagues in the government and of local gentry assembled in large numbers to drink, hunt, eat and indulge in bawdy, gossip, sight-seeing and politics. The social life of the congresses went on entirely in the rustic. Here, as Lord Hervey, one of the guests, described it, they lived 'up to the chin in beef, venison, geese, turkeys etc. and generally over the chin in claret, strong beer and punch.'[40]

The floor above was described by Hervey as 'the floor of taste, expense, state and parade'. Its rooms were grouped in four matching apartments to either side of a hall and saloon, both two storeys high and decorated with extraordinary grandeur. The two eastern apartments were occupied by Walpole and his wife, but the rest of the floor only came to life on great occasions, such as the visit of the Duke of Lorraine, husband of the Empress Maria Theresa, in 1731. On this occasion 'the consumption both from the larder and the cellar was prodigious. They dined in the hall which was lighted by fifty wax candles, and the saloon with fifty.'[41]

On a first view the symmetrical arrangement of the main floor and the grandeur of the hall and saloon make Houghton the epitome of a formal house. But in fact it is one of the first great houses where the formal system began to crumble. It was not only that the bias of its social life was shifting to the informality of the rustic. In the year of the Duke of Lorraine's visit the main room in the north-west apartment was being fitted out as a dining room – not just an everyday dining room or a dining room for upper servants, but a state dining room richly furnished, lined with marble and designed to take over the dining function of the saloon.

Once the saloon had ceased to be used for formal meals its position as the ceremonial pivot of the house had gone – and the reasons for putting it in the centre of the house with a great portico in front of it had gone also. The balance of the system had dissolved and the days of the formal plan were numbered.

The social house 1720–1770

But a change [in architectural design] would inevitably have come sooner or later because it reflected a change in society. Its middle strata, shading from the lesser gentry to the professional classes and richer merchants, were increasing in numbers, wealth and independence. They were comfortably off, well educated, and socially presentable. The great could no longer win the support of such people by taking them into their households as upper servants, or inviting them to dinner once a year and putting them at a separate table or even in a separate room to themselves. But their support was important. It meant votes, and control of enough votes meant one or more seats in the House of Commons. By the early eighteenth century Parliament had won its battle with the Crown. Influence in the House of Commons was not the basis of power. It had become more important than having the ear of ministers or the king; it was, in any case, the best means of getting their ear.

The core of a man's voting strength was his own tenantry; as voting was still open, tenants normally voted as their landlord directed them. But he extended this core by forming what was known as his 'interest'. An interest was built up by constant entertaining, by giving favours small and large and by getting jobs for individuals and their dependants. All landowners inherited a certain amount of patronage, in the form, for instance, of jobs on their own estates and presentations to livings. They used their interest to get government jobs which gave them additional patronage; and they used the additional patronage to extent their interest. A political operator like the Duke of Newcastle could have an interest which extended over the whole country and included a string of parliamentary seats; a country squire had his little local interest, which people like the duke would bid for by dispensing favours and by entertaining him in a dignified but affable way.[42]

At the beginning of the eighteenth century only about five per cent of the population had a vote. The lower strata of the voting body consisted of the smaller freeholders. Some of these were tenants, politically tied to their landlord, but by no means all of them were. In contested elections much wooing of the smaller freeholders went on, and lavish dinners were given for them by local landlords. But in the course of the eighteenth century the larger property owners, assisted by the professional classes who also normally had a stake in property, succeeded in eliminating most of the friction from the political system. There were fewer and fewer contests at elections, which were usually fixed beforehand, by mutual agreement among local interests. The small freeholder became less important. In 1762 Samuel Egerton, M.P. for Cheshire, refused to entertain his freeholders, and when asked why said that 'he did not value them'.[43]

The combined results of the growing independence, culture and prosperity of the lesser gentry and professional classes, the sewing up of the parliamentary system, and the resulting decline in importance of the smaller freeholder was a growing gap between the polite world of the gentry and the impolite world of servants, farmers and smallholders. In terms of the country house this meant an increasing split between gentry upstairs and non-gentry downstairs. Gentlemen could now only enter household service as librarians, tutors or chaplains; in which case they did not consider themselves servants and ate with the family or on their own. The tenants and freeholders, on the other hand, had sunk in status with the upper servants. Up till the early eighteenth century they were still being entertained on occasions in the hall and even in the parlour; in the course of the century they were exiled to the steward's room, or to a separate tenants' hall or audit hall in the servants' part of the house.

[. . .]

To outsiders, the polite world could seem both exclusive and corrupt. But like all ruling classes, it worked out an ethical justification for itself. Between 1650 and 1714 there had been two revolutions, a republic and a change of dynasty. Most of the landowning classes had been involved in at least one, and sometimes all, of these events. Only a small minority continued to support the concept of a monarch as the source of all power, with authority derived from God, presiding over a complex of lesser hierarchies, all miniatures of the divine model. Instead, property became the basis and justification of government.[44]

The polite world saw themselves as an élite, whose claim to run the country was based on having a stake in it as property owners, and was reinforced by the culture, education and *savoir-faire* of which its country houses were an advertisement. The monarch was the head of the government, but his powers were defined and restricted, and derived from consent not right. The nobility were given the respect due to major and long-established property owners, but not the reverence due to gods in miniature. The members of the property-owning élite moved among themselves with relative equality. They no longer found the rigid hierarchies of the formal house a sympathetic setting.

[. . .]

One result of the nobility and gentry becoming more mobile and mixing more together was new kinds of parties. From the sixteenth to the early eighteenth century, whenever people decided to entertain, they did so in much the same way. They gave either a dinner on its own, or a dinner combined with dancing. The latter combination started with a meal, sometimes enlivened by music. After dinner the company retired to a withdrawing room, and passed an hour or so by taking tea or dessert, or playing cards, or listening to more music. They then returned to the room where they had dined, for dancing or as it tended to be called, a ball; in the early eighteenth century as few as seven couples dancing together could be described as a ball.[45] After dancing there was normally some kind of light refreshment, and then everybody went home. The refreshments at the end might, according to the century, be described as a banquet or a supper, the room for dinner and dancing a great chamber or a saloon; the dances danced, the music played and the food eaten changed, but the pattern remained much the same. The guests did one thing at a time, and they all did it together.

The eighteenth century introduced more variety. Balls developed and grew larger and more elaborate. The assembly, the masquerade, the rout, the drum, the *ridotto*, the *ridotto al fresco* and the musical party were all new forms of entertainment which only got under way in the eighteenth century, even if some of them had their origins in the seventeenth.

The most important of these was the assembly. Assemblies varied in their details, but basically conformed to the definition made in 1751: 'a stated and general meeting of the polite persons of both sexes, for the sake of conversation, gallantry, news and play'.[46] They took place in the evening. The guests either played cards, or drank tea, or just walked around talking and flirting. Some assemblies, but by no means all, ended with supper.

[. . .]

As a result, the formal house ceased to work. Instead of a hall and saloon, between apartments which were the private territories of the people occupying them, what was now needed was a series of communal rooms for entertaining, exclusive of the hall and all running into each other.

The first step in this direction was to open up the state apartment on occasions to general company. There had been occasions in the past when the best lodgings or state apartment had been the scene of general gatherings – at christenings or funerals, for instance, when the mother or the corpse, in suitably festive or funereal splendour, was on display in or adjoining the state bed. But this was when the bedchamber had an occupant with a functional part to play. The next stage was to throw the whole apartment open for assemblies, with card-tables in the withdrawing room and the guests parading through the unoccupied bedchamber and closet to admire their fittings and decorations. The stage after that was to increase the number of rooms in the state apartment, so that it could accommodate a big assembly or assembly-ball. The final stage was to hive the state bedchamber off from the apartment, leaving just a sequence of reception rooms.

In the formal house the state apartment had normally been strung out along the straight line of the axis of honour. The eighteenth century discovered that, for its changed needs, the most attractive and convenient way to arrange it was in a circle, around a top-lit central staircase. Top-lit staircases had first appeared in England in the late seventeenth century; but it was not until well into the eighteenth century that their convenience began to be appreciated.

[. . .]

In formal houses of the early eighteenth century where hall, saloon and main apartments had all been on the same floor, staircases had tended to become relatively utilitarian. In town houses, or smaller country houses like Harleyford, where even the main bedrooms and dressing rooms were on the upper floors, and at ground-floor level the staircase hall was in constant use as a circulation space, they needed to make more of a show. But there was no reason, and usually no space, for them to be as grand as the staircases leading up to the first-floor state rooms in sixteenth and seventeenth-century houses. Taylor and others evolved the solution; a top-lit circular or oval cantilevered staircase, often made of stone and fitted with a wrought-iron balustrade. Such staircases were spacious without being over large, and could be supremely elegant.

[. . .]

Saloons, although often used for dancing, were now seldom used for meals. A separate dining room had become an essential element of all houses of any pretensions; the grander ones often had a common parlour, for everyday use by the family as an eating and sitting room, and a dining room (or 'eating room') for entertaining company. The dining room was always one of the best and biggest rooms in the house. Plate on the sideboard or central table and large numbers of footmen waiting in splendid liveries could make a big dinner an impressive sight, but mediaeval ceremony had by now entirely vanished.[47] Each course was carried in by footmen and laid out on the central table; the more lavish the dinner, the greater the variety of dishes. The main meat dish was usually put in front of the host to carve. Footmen attended to the individual wants of guests by taking their plates to the dishes, rather than carrying the dishes round the table. The butler stayed at the sideboard with the wine; the footmen brought glasses to the sideboard to be filled or refilled. If the glasses had been used already the butler rinsed them in a cistern of water under the sideboard (or, as Swift complained, merely filled the dirty glasses).[48] The one element of ceremony was provided by the company not the servants, in the form of toasts. These were either drunk by the whole company, or when one individual asked another to drink with him; in both cases the relevant glasses were taken to the sideboard by footmen to be refilled. On occasions an orchestra in, or more usually next door to, the dining room played music throughout the meal.

The meal normally ended with dessert, after which the ladies removed to the drawing room. At Hagley the drawing room is separated from the dining room by the gallery. In 1752, when the plan was still being worked out, Lyttelton wrote to the architect that 'Lady Lyttelton wishes for a room of separation between the eating room and the drawing room, to hinder the ladies from the noise and talk of the men when left to their bottle, which must sometimes happen, even at Hagley.'[49] By then the English custom of the women leaving the men to drink, smoke and talk in the dining room was well established. Its origins are somewhat mysterious. It never obtained on the continent, where it was, and still is, regarded as the height of barbarism. There is no trace of it in the many dinners, of all kinds of social grades, described by Pepys in the 1660s. Yet in Congreve's *The Double Dealer* of 1694 the women are described as 'at the end of the gallery, retired to their tea and scandal, according to their ancient custom, after dinner.[50]

Congreve's reference to tea may provide an explanation. Drinking tea and coffee became fashionable in the 1670s and '80s. Both drinks were normally served after dinner and supper, and brewed by the hostess herself; by about 1680 the Duchess of Lauderdale had an 'Indian furnace for tea garnished with silver' in her closet at Ham.[51] It may be that what was to become one of the institutions of English upper-class life started as a short practical interval in which the ladies retired to brew tea or coffee, after which the gentlemen joined them to drink it. If so the interval grew longer and longer, until it could last several hours; by 1778 Robert Adam was celebrating it as the period in which the men of the ruling class discussed politics together.[52] They still, however, normally joined the ladies for tea or coffee in the end, unless they were incapable.

The long periods spent by gentlemen and ladies on their own in this way meant that the dining room began to be thought of as a mainly masculine, and the drawing room as a mainly feminine, room. Drawing rooms had now ceased almost entirely to be attached to individual bedrooms and people, or to be rooms used for comparatively short periods of time while dinner was being cleared. They were important rooms. In the seventeenth century they had invariably been smaller than the main eating room; in the eighteenth century they tended to be of more or less the same size.

The fact that so much more space was now being taken up by rooms of general resort by no means implies that the apartment system had been given up altogether. What had happened was that the balance had changed. People in country houses spent more time in the common rooms and less in their own apartments, and the importance and therefore the size of apartments shrank as a result. At the same time the relatively more democratic nature of general society meant that, instead of having a few very grand apartments designed for the entertainment of great people – from the king downwards – and relatively few other bedrooms, the tendency was to have a larger number of smaller apartments. The average apartment consisted of a bedroom and dressing room. Sometimes it also included a closet. A grand apartment for visitors, or the apartments of the owners, could have two dressing rooms, one for the man and one for the woman. Dressing rooms were invariably also used as private sitting rooms; they were often very handsomely furnished, and bigger than the bedroom. The owner's dressing room was sometimes on the ground floor, even when his bedroom was on the floor above. Such dressing rooms were not so different from studies – except that the owner came down from his bedroom in the morning, and saw people on business while his toilet was being finished off by his valet.[53]

Access for servants to the apartments was now usually by a combination of a single backstairs and corridors; there was a reaction against a plurality of backstairs, probably because of the space they took up. The top floor tended to be given over to a miscellaneous collection of smaller apartments, nurseries and maids' rooms. Bachelor guests were sometimes put in a communal dormitory, known as a 'barracks'; a barracks could also be provided for visiting men-servants.[54] Little effort was made to segregate the sexes. Dorothea Herbert describes how, at Castle Blunden in Ireland in 1780, the girls in the upstairs chamber were serenaded and teased by the 'bold boys' in the barracks; on one occasion they were caught 'en chemise' and 'in our confusion overturned the pot-de-chambre and the two doors being opposite the whole contents meandered across the lobby into their barrack – immediately the house rang with their laughter.[55] Such an incident would scarcely have been possible in Victorian houses.

The early-eighteenth-century practice of having some family rooms in the rustic continued through the century, especially in houses planned round a single circuit. The arrangements varied greatly from house to house. Sometimes the main entry was into a lower hall in the rustic, and so by an internal staircase up to the main floor. Sometimes the common parlour was in the rustic, or a complete apartment for the owner of the house, or just a billiard room or smoking parlour. A common arrangement was for the owner to have a study or business room in the rustic, with a room or rooms for the land-steward adjacent. In 1786 Lord Pembroke complained that at Wilton's steward's office *in the house* would be the very devil. One should never be free an instant from meeting people full of words and wants.' However, after a few months' reflection he became 'convinced of the absolute indispensable necessity of a land-steward, doing nobody's business but mine, living and boarding in the house, and transacting everything in my office.'[56]

Apart from family rooms, and a lower hall if there was one, the rustic normally contained the cellars, the steward's room (in big houses), the servants' hall, and the rooms belonging to the butler and housekeeper. Sometimes it also contained the kitchen and its appendages, but these were often in a separate pavilion, as in earlier houses. Sleeping quarters for servants could be up on the top floor, or in the kitchen or sometimes, in the case of menservants, over the stables. The tendency for the size of households to decrease continued, as was only to be expected in a society which preferred elegance to grandeur. The household of a peer was likely to vary from twenty-five to fifty people, depending on his wealth and rank. The proportion of women had increased to a third or even a half. The increase was partly due to a decrease in the showier parts of the male establishment, partly to an increase in the number of house-maids required to clean houses of growing elegance.[57]

The housekeeper accordingly became more important. As few ladies now had gentlewomen to wait on them she was in charge of all the women servants. She was recognized as the female counterpart to the steward (if there was one) or the butler, even if as a woman she was paid little more than half as much as they were. She lived in some comfort in her housekeeper's room, with a store-room and sometimes a still-room next door to it.

Still-rooms first appeared in country houses in the sixteenth century, but only became common in the seventeenth.[58] They were originally so called because they were fitted with stills, to distil the cordial waters used for banquets (in the Elizabethan sense), medicine or scent. At first distilling was one of the skills or hobbies thought proper for the mistress of the house and her gentlewomen, so that the still-room tended to be close to her lodgings. As ladies also concerned themselves with the preparation of delicate dishes for banquets the two functions were often accommodated in the still-room, which was accordingly also fitted with stoves and cupboards for storage.[59] The still-room at Hengrave was used in 1603 for 'preparing and keeping biskett cakes, marchpanes, herbs, spicebread, fruits, conserves, etc.'[60] In the course of the eighteenth century the housekeeper tended to take over the still-room from her mistress, and the increasing use of doctors and apothecaries made home-brewed medicine less important. Stills gradually disappeared, but preserves and cakes, and the stoves on which to make them, remained in the still-room.[61]

Housekeepers were usually permanently resident in one place. Where families owned more than one house, however, the majority of the household moved round with them, and went up to London for the season. Especially social or political families would be likely to spend more time in London or Bath, and especially sporting or farming families more time in the country. In the country the way of life varied comparatively little. The detailed account that survives of three weeks spent by a party of ten at Welford in Berkshire could have been parallelled in hundreds of other country houses.[62]

Notes

1   The house as built was rather simpler than the design reproduced [here] as Figure 4.9.
2   Isaac Ware, *Complete Body of Architecture* (London, 1756) p. 335.
3   Description by Henry Pelate, ed. H. C. Brentnall, 'A Longford Manuscript', *Wiltshire Archaeology and Natural History Magazine*, LII (1947) p. 39.
4   See North, *Of Building*, f. 40v. The treatise is full of shrewd comment and interesting examples, and deserves publication.
5   *Ibid.* f. 59v.

6 *Architecture of Roger Pratt*, p. 64.

7 The original arrangement at Kinross is shown in a plan of *c.* 1684 reproduced by J. G. Dunbar, 'Kinross House', *The Country Seat*, ed. H. Colvin and J. Harris (1970) p. 64.

8 *Stanley Papers*, II, pp. 123–7; Williamson, *Lady Anne Clifford*, p. 477.

9 Huntington, Stowe MS. ST 44/37–8.

10 *Chandos H.R.*, orders for usher of the hall.

11 C. H. and M. I. Collins Baker, *The Life and Circumstances of James Brydges, First Duke of Chandos* (Oxford, 1949) pp. 174–5.

12 Table seating and wages at Cannons are given in Huntington, Stowe MS. ST 44/27–30.

13 E.g. *Courtesy H.R.*, p. 320; Cavendish, *Thomas Wolsey*, Ch. V; Gage, *History of Hengrave*, p. 190.

14 At Raglan Castle in the 1630s footmen were waiting at the second table in the great chamber and the steward's table in the hall (*Northumberland H.R.*, p. 419). In the 1660s control of the Earl of Bedford's footmen was being disputed between the house steward and the gentleman of the horse (G. Scott-Thomson, *Life in a Noble Household* (London, 1937) p. 118).

15 Huntington, Stowe MS. ST 24, *passim*.

16 The household at Badminton is described in Roger North, *Lives of the Norths*, ed. A. Jessopp (1905) I, p. 172.

17 *The Journeys of Celia Fiennes*, ed. C. Morris (London, 1947) p. 334.

18 For contemporary theory, see *Patriarcha and other Political Works of Sir Robert Filmer*, ed. P. Laslett (Oxford, 1949) pp. 174–5.

19 Stratford Hall, Virginia (*Country Life*, CXLV, pp. 118–21) is a perfect example of a small formal house of *c.* 1730.

20 Obadiah Walker, mostly on the basis of an Italian book of etiquette *Il Maestro di Camera*, describes these and similar niceties in *Of Education*, 6th edn, pp. 224–6. *The Travels of Cosmo III through England*, are full of actual examples in an English context.

21 J. Dallaway, *West Sussex* (1832) II, p. 329 (quoting *Annals of Reign of Q. Anne* (1704) II, App. 3).

22 Nottingham University, Portland MS. PWB/79. B.M. Add. MS. 22226, f. 79.

23 A lively satirical poem describing the Duke of Argyll's levée in the early eighteenth century is in Nottingham University, Portland MS. PWV/718.

24 See 'The Political Function of Charles II's Chiffinch', *Huntington Library Quarterly*, XXXIX (1976) pp. 277–90.

25 For Dr Johnson's supposed indignation at being kept waiting by Lord Chesterfield while Colley Cibber was introduced by the back-stairs, see Boswell's *Life*, Everyman edn (London, 1906) I, p. 153.

26 Goldsmith, *Double Transformation* (1765), quoted in O.E.D.

27 Evelyn, *Diary*, 4 October 1683.

28 North, *Of Building*, f. 61.

29 E.g. at Easton Neston, *c.* 1685.

30 North, *Of Building*, ff. 26v–27.

31 The bed was originally on a raised dais, probably behind a balustrade. A reconstruction in model form is on show at Ham House.

32 In contemporary records it is described as the ante-room, painted room or upper saloon. F. Thompson, *A History of Chatsworth* (London, 1949).

33 North, *Of Building*, f. 57v.

34 The much reproduced plan of Blenheim in *Vitruvius Britannicus* can be usefully supplemented by that in Kip and Knyff, *Nouveau Théâtre de la Grande Brétague* (1714–16), I, which gives the arrangement of the basement.

35 Macky, *Journey through England* (London, 1724) II, p. 106.

36 For villas see John Summerson, 'The Idea of the Villa', *Journal of the Royal Society of Arts*, CXVII (1959) pp. 570–86.

37 Macky, *Journey through England*, I, pp. 20–1.

38 Joyce Godber, 'Marchioness Grey of Wrest Park', *Bedfordshire Historical Society*, XLVII (1968) p. 142, quoting diary of Philip Yorke.

39 *Lord Hervey and his Friends, 1726–38*, ed. Earl of Ilchester (1950) p. 71.

40 *Ibid.*

41 H.M.C., *Earl of Carlisle*, p. 85.

42 There is an admirable contemporary analysis of the connection between property and interest in a letter written by Lord Strafford to his wife in 1729, B.M. Add. MS. 22226, ff. 427–9.

43 *Diaries of a Duchess*, ed. J. Greig (1926) p. 35.

44 For contemporary theories of government, see especially P. Laslett's edn of J. Locke, *Two Treatises of Government* (Cambridge, 1960).

45 E.g. *Autobiography and Correspondence of Mrs. Delany* (London, 1861–2) 1st series, I, p. 224.

46 Quoted in O.E.D. under 'Assembly'.

47 Eighteenth-century household regulations are uninformative about the serving of meals. My account is mainly based on contemporary descriptions, pictures, and diagrams of the table lay out for courses, and Swift's satirical *Directions to Servants* (1745) new edn (Oxford, 1959).

48 *Ibid.* (1959) p. 17.

49 Hussey, *Country Houses: Early Georgian*, p. 196.

50 *The Double Dealer* (1694) I. 1.

51 An extra entry (described as 'added since') in the 1679 inventory.

52 *Works in Architecture of R. and J. Adam*, I (London, 1778) pp. 8–9.

53 E.g. Herbert Pugh's caricature of Lord Granard in his dressing room (*c.* 1771) reproduced in J. Cornforth and J. Fowler, *English Decoration in the Eighteenth Century* (London, 1974) Fig. 200.

54 E.g. John Macdonald, *Memoirs of an Eighteenth-Century Footman*, ed. J. Beresford (London, 1927) p. 46; William Adam, *Remarks on the Blair Adam Estate* (1834) p. 111.

55 *Reprospections of Dorothea Herbert*, ed. G. F. Mandeville (London, 1929–30) I, p. 68.

56 *Pembroke Papers*, ed. Earl of Pembroke (London, 1950) pp. 299, 304.

57 Lord Petre's household at Thorndon in 1742 contained 19 men and 14 women. Lord Salisbury's household at Hatfield in 1797 contained 18 men and 18 women (Essex Record Office, D/DP Z14/10; Hatfield MS. Family Papers XI, p. 177). Both totals inclusive of indoor and stable servants only.

58 At Holdenby there was a 'still-house' under the water cistern in the conduit house in the garden, probably dating from the 1570s (Parliamentary Survey, 1650 quoted Hartshorne, *History of Holdenby*).

59 For the skill of Queen Elizabeth's gentlewomen in 'devising delicate dishes' and 'distillation of waters' see Harrison, *Elizabethan England*, p. 219.

60 Gage, *History of Hengrave*, pp. 36–7.

61 Distilled waters still figure prominently in Samuel and Sarah Adams, *The Complete Servant* (London, 1825) pp. 176–90.

62 Alice Archer-Houblon, *The Houblon Family* (1907) II, pp. 118–52.

In search of cultural history
E H Gombrich

[. . .]

IV: Hegelianism without metaphysics

Not that Hegelian metaphysics were accepted in all their abstruse ramifications by any [of the cultural historians of the nineteenth century]. The point is rather that all of them felt, consciously or unconsciously, that if they let go of the magnet that created the pattern, the atoms of past cultures would again fall back into random dust-heaps.

In this respect the cultural historian was much worse off than any other historian. His colleagues working on political or economic history had at least a criterion of relevance in their restricted subject matter. They could trace the history of the reform of Parliament, of Anglo-Irish relations, without explicit reference to an all-embracing philosophy of history.

But the history of culture as such, the history of all the aspects of life as it was lived in the past, could never be undertaken without some ordering principle, some centre from which the panorama can be surveyed, some hub on which the wheel of Hegel's diagram can be pivoted. Thus the subsequent history of historiography of culture can perhaps best be interpreted as a succession of attempts to salvage the Hegelian assumption without accepting Hegelian metaphysics. This was precisely what Marxism claimed it was doing. The Hegelian diagram was more or less maintained, but the centre was occupied not by the spirit but by the changing conditions of production. What we see in the periphery of the diagram represents the superstructure in which the material conditions manifest themselves. Thus the task of the cultural historian remains very much the same. He must be able to show in every detail of the period how it reflects its essential economic character.[1]

Lamprecht, whom I mentioned before as one of Warburg's masters, took the opposite line. He looked for the essence not in the material conditions but in the mentality of an age.[2] He tried, in other words, to translate Hegel's *Geist* into psychological terms.

[. . .]

In my own field, the History of Art, it was Alois Riegl who, at the turn of the century, worked out his own translation of the Hegelian system into psychological terms.[3] Like Hegel he saw the evolution of the arts both as an autonomous dialectical process and as wheels revolving within the larger wheel of successive 'world-views'. In art the process went spiralling twice: from a tactile mode of apprehension of solid matter to an 'optic' mode, first in the case of isolated objects and then in that of their spatial setting. As in Hegel, also, this process with its inevitable stages puts the idea of 'decline' out of court. By classical standards of tactile clarity the sculpture of the Arch of Constantine may represent a decline, but without this process of dissolution neither Raphael nor Rembrandt could have come into being.

Moreover, this relentless development runs parallel with changes in the 'world views' of mankind. Like Hegel, Riegl thought that Egyptian art and Egyptian *Weltanschauung* were both on the opposite pole from 'spiritualism'. He postulates for Egypt a 'materialistic monism' which sees in the soul nothing but refined matter. Greek art and thought are both dualistic while late antiquity returns to monism, but at the opposite end of the scale, where (predictably) the body is conceived of as a cruder soul. 'Anyone who would see in the turn of late antiquity towards irrationalism and magic superstitions a decline, arrogates for himself the right to prescribe to the spirit of mankind the way it should have taken to effect the transition from ancient to modern conceptions.'[4] For Riegl was convinced that this late antique belief in spirits and in magic was a necessary stage without which the mind of man could never have understood electricity. And he proved to his own satisfaction (and to that of many others) that this momentous process was as clearly manifested in the ornamentation of late Roman fibulae as it was in the philosophy of Plotinus.

It was this claim to read the 'signs of the time' and to penetrate into the secrets of the historical process which certainly gave new impetus to art historical studies. Max Dvořák, in his later years, represented this trend so perfectly that the editors of his collected papers rightly chose as title *Kunstgeschichte als Geistesgeschichte*[5] ('Art History as a History of the Spirit'), a formulation which provoked Max J. Friedländer to the quip, 'We apparently are merely studying the History of the Flesh' ('Wir betreiben offenbar nur Körpergeschichte'). The great Erwin Panofsky, like Dilthey, presents a more critical and sophisticated development of this programme, but those who have studied his works know that he too never renounced the desire to demonstrate the organic unity of all aspects of a period.[6] His *Gothic Architecture and Scholasticism*[7] shows him grappling with the attempt to 'rescue' the traditional connection between these two aspects of medieval culture by postulating a 'mental habit' acquired in the schools of the scholastics and carried over into architectural practice. In his *Renaissance and Renascences in Western Art*[8] he explicitly defended the notion of cultures having an essence against the criticism of George Boas.

But perhaps the most original rescue attempt of this kind was made by the greatest cultural historian after Burckhardt, his admirer, critic and successor, Johan Huizinga.[9]

It will be remembered that Burckhardt had advised his friend to ask himself: 'How does the spirit of the fifteenth century express itself in painting?'

The average art historian who practised *Geistesgeschichte* would have started from the impression Van Eyck's paintings made on him and proceeded to select other testimonies of the time that appeared to tally with this impression. What is so fascinating in Huizinga is that he took the opposite line. He simply knew too many facts about the age of Van Eyck to find it easy to square his impression of his pictures with the voice of the documents. He felt he had rather to reinterpret the style of the painter to make it fit with what he knew of culture. He did this in his captivating book, *The Waning of the Middle Ages*,[10] literally the autumn of the Middle Ages, which is Hegelian even in the assumption of its title, that here medieval culture had come to its autumnal close, complex, sophisticated and ripe for the sickle. Thus Van Eyck's realism could no longer be seen as a harbinger of a new age; his jewel-like richness and his accumulation of detail were rather an expression of the same late-Gothic spirit that was also manifested, much less appealingly, in the prolix writings of the period which nobody but specialists read any more.

The wheel had come full circle. The interpretation of artistic realism as an expression of a new spirit, which is to be found in Hegel and which had become the starting point for Burckhardt's reading of the Renaissance, was effectively questioned by Huizinga, who subsequently devoted one of his most searching essays to this traditional equation of Renaissance and Realism.[11] But as far as I can see, he challenged this particular interpretation rather than the methodological assumption according to which the art of an age must be shown to express the same spirit as its literature and life.

Critical as he was of all attempts to establish laws of history, he still ended his wonderful paper on 'The Task of Cultural History'[12] with a demand for a 'morphology of culture' that implied, if I understand it correctly, a holistic approach in terms of changing cultural styles.

Now I would not deny for a moment that a great historian such as Huizinga can teach the student of artistic developments a lot about the conditions under which a particular style like that of Van Eyck took shape. For obviously there is something in the Hegelian intuition that nothing in life is ever isolated, that any event and any creation of a period is connected by a thousand threads with the culture in which it is embedded. Who would not therefore be curious to learn about the life of the patrons who commissioned Van Eyck's paintings, about the purpose these paintings served, about the symbolism of his religious paintings, or about the original context of his secular paintings which we only know through copies and reports?

Clearly neither the *Adoration of the Lamb* nor even the lost *Hunt of the Otter* can be understood in isolation without references to religious traditions in the first case and to courtly pastimes in the second.

But is the acknowledgement of this link tantamount to a concession that the Hegelian approach is right after all? I do not think so. It is one thing to see the interconnectedness of things, another to postulate that all aspects of a culture can be traced back to one key cause of which they are the manifestations.[13]

If Van Eyck's patrons had all been Buddhists he would neither have painted the *Adoration of the Lamb* nor, for that matter, the *Hunting of the Otter*, but though the fact that he did is therefore trivially connected with the civilization in which he worked, there is no need to place these works on the periphery of the Hegelian wheel and look for the governing cause that explains both otter hunting and piety in the particular form they took in the early decades of the fifteenth century, and which is also expressed in Van Eyck's new technique.

If there is one fact in the history of art I do not find very surprising it is the success and acclaim of this novel style. Surely this has less to do with the *Weltanschauung* of the period than with the beauty and sparkle of Van Eyck's paintings.

I believe it is one of the undesirable consequences of the Hegelian habit of exegetics that such a remark sounds naïve and even paradoxical. For the habit demands that everything must be treated not only as connected with everything else, but as a symptom of something else. Just as Hegel treated the invention of gunpowder as a necessary expression of the advancing spirit, so the sophisticated historian should treat the invention of oil painting (or what was described as such) as a portent of the times. Why should we not find a simpler explanation in the fact that those who had gunpowder could defeat those who fought with bows and arrows or that those who adopted the Van Eyck technique could render light and sparkle better than those who painted in tempera?[14] Of course no such answer is ever final. You are entitled to ask why people wanted to defeat their enemies, and though the question may once have sounded naive we now know that strong influences can oppose the adoption of a better weapon. We also know that the achievement of life-like illusion cannot always be taken for granted as an aim of painting. It was an aim rejected by Judaism, by Islam, by the Byzantine Church and by our own civilization, in each case for different reasons. I believe indeed that methodologically it is always fruitful to ask for the reasons which made a culture or a society reject a tool or invention which seemed to offer tangible advantages in one particular direction. It is in trying to answer this question that we will discover the reality of that closely knit fabric which we call a culture.[15]

But I see no reason why the study of these connections should lead us back to the Hegelian postulates of the *Zeitgeist* and *Volksgeist*. On the contrary, I have always believed that it is the exegetic habit of mind leading to these mental short-circuits which prevents the posing of the very problem Hegelianism set out to solve.[16]

V: Symptoms and syndromes

One may be interested in the manifold interactions between the various spheres of a culture and yet reject what I have called the 'exegetic method', the method, that is, that bases its interpretations on the detection of that kind of 'likeness' that leads the interpreter of the scriptures to link the passage of the Jews through the Red Sea with the Baptism of Christ. Hegel, it will be remembered, saw in the Egyptian sphinx an essential likeness with the position of Egyptian culture in which the Spirit began to emerge from animal nature, and carried the same metaphor through in his discussion of Egyptian religion and Egyptian hieroglyphics. The assumption is always that some essential structural similarity must be detected which permits the interpreter to subsume the various aspects of a culture under one formula.[17] The art of Van Eyck in Huizinga's persuasive morphology is not only to be connected with the theology and the literature of the time but it must be shown to share some of their fundamental characteristics. To criticize this assumption is not to deny the great ingenuity and learning expended by some cultural historians on the search for suggestive and memorable metaphorical descriptions. Nor is it to deny that such structural likenesses between various aspects of a period may be found to be interesting, as A.O. Lovejoy tried to demonstrate for eighteenth-century Deism and Classicism.[18] But here as always a priori assumptions of such similarity can only spoil the interest of the search. Not only is there no iron law of such isomorphism, I even doubt whether we improve matters by replacing this kind of determinism with a probablistic approach as has been proposed by W.T. Jones in his book on *The Romantic Movement*.[19] The subtitle of this interesting book demands attention by promising a 'New Method in Cultural Anthropology and History of Ideas'; it consists in drawing up such polarities as that between static and dynamic, or order and disorder, and examining certain periods for their bias towards one or the other end of these scales, a bias which would be expected to show up statistically at the periphery of the Hegelian wheel in art, science and political thought, though some of these spheres might be more recalcitrant to their expression than others. In the contrast between 'soft focus' and 'hard focus' the Romantic, he finds, will be likely to lean towards the first in metaphysics, in poetical imagery and in paintings, a bias that must be symptomatic of Romantic mentality.

Such expectations, no doubt, accord well with commonsense psychology; but in fact no statistics are needed to show in this case that what looks plausible in this new method of salvaging Hegel still comes into conflict with historical fact. It so happens that it was Romanticism which discovered the taste for the so-called 'primitives' in painting, which meant, at that time, the hard-edged, sharp-focused style of Van Eyck or of the early Italians. If the first Romantic painters of Germany had one pet aversion it was the soft-focused bravura of their Baroque predecessors. Whatever their bias in metaphysics may have been, they saw in the smudged outline a symptom of artistic dishonesty and moral corruption. Their bias in the syndrome – to retain this useful term – was based on very different alternatives, alternatives peculiar to the problems of painting. Paradoxically, perhaps, they identified the hard and naïve with the otherworldly and the chaste. It was soft-focused naturalism that was symptomatic of the fall from grace.

[. . .]

VI: Movements and periods

The distinction at which I am aiming here is that between movements and periods. Hegel saw all periods as movements since they were embodiments of the moving spirit. This spirit, as Hegel taught, manifested itself in a collective, the supra-individual entities of nations or periods. Since the individual, in his view, could only be thought of as part of such a collective it was quite consistent for Hegelians to assume that 'man' underwent profound changes in the course of history. Nobody went further in this belief than Oswald Spengler, who assigned different psyches to his different culture cycles. It was an illusion due to sentimentalizing humanitarians to believe that these different species of man could ever understand each other.

The same extremism was of course reflected in the claims of the totalitarian philosophies which stemmed from Hegel to create a new 'man', be it of a Soviet or of a National Socialist variety. Even art historians of a less uncompromising bent took to speaking of 'Gothic man' or 'Baroque psychology', assuming a radical change in the mental make-up to have happened when building firms discarded one pattern book in favour of another. In fact the study of styles so much fostered a belief in collective psychology that I remember a discussion shortly after the war with German students who appeared to believe that in the Gothic age Gothic cathedrals sprang up spontaneously all over Europe without any contact between the building sites.

It is this belief in the existence of an independent supra-individual collective spirit which seems to me to have blocked the emergence of a true cultural history. I am reminded of certain recent developments in natural history which may serve as illustrations. The behaviour of insect colonies appeared to be so much governed by the needs of the collective that the temptation was great to postulate a super-mind. How else, argued Marais in his book *The Soul of the White Ant*,[20] could the individuals of the hive immediately respond to the death of the queen? The message of this event must reach them through some kind of telepathic process. We now know that this is not so. The message is chemical; the queen's substance picked up from her body circulates in the hive through mutual licking rather than through a mysterious mental fluid.[21] Other discoveries about the communication of insects have increased our awareness of the relation between the individual and the hive. We have made progress.

I hope and believe cultural history will make progress if it also fixes its attention firmly on the individual human being. Movements, as distinct from periods, are started by people. Some of them are abortive, others catch on. Each movement in its turn has a core of dedicated souls, a crowd of hangers-on, not to forget a lunatic fringe. There is a whole spectrum of attitudes and degrees of conversion. Even within the individual there may be various levels of conviction, various conscious and unconscious fluctuations in loyalty. What seemed acceptable during the mass rally or revivalist meeting may look pretty crazy on the way home. But movements would not be movements if they did not have their badges, their outward signs, their style of behaviour, style of speech and of dress. Who can probe the motives which prompt individuals to adopt some of these, and who would venture in every case to pronounce on the completeness of the conversion this adoption may express? Knowing these limitations, the cultural historian will be a little wary of the claims of cultural psychology. He will not deny that the success of certain styles may be symptomatic of changing attitudes, but he will resist the temptation to use changing styles and changing fashions as indicators of profound psychological changes. The fact that we cannot assume such automatic connections makes it more interesting to find out if and when they may have existed.

The Renaissance, for instance, certainly had all the characteristics of a movement.[22] It gradually captured the most articulate sections of society and influenced their attitude in various but uneven ways. Late Gothic or Mannerism were not, as far as I can see, the badge of any movement, though of course there were movements in these periods which may or may not have been correlated with styles or fashions in other cultural areas. The great issues of the day, notably the religious movements, are not necessarily reflected in distinctive styles. Thus both Mannerism and the Baroque have been claimed to express the spirit of the Counter-Reformation but neither claim is easy to substantiate. Even the existence of a peculiar Jesuit style with propagandist intentions has been disproved by the more detailed analysis of Francis Haskell.[23]

We need more analyses of this kind, based on patient documentary research, but I venture to suggest that the cultural historian will want to supplement the analysis of stylistic origins by an analysis of stylistic associations and responses. Whatever certain Baroque devices may have meant to their creators, they evoked Popish associations in the minds of Protestant travellers. When and where did these associations become conscious? How far could fashion and the desire for French elegance override these considerations in a Protestant community? I know that it is not always easy to answer these questions, but I feel strongly that it is this type of detailed questioning that should replace the generalizations of *Geistesgeschichte*.

[. . .]

VII: Topics and techniques

Having criticized a Hegel, a Burckhardt, or a Lamprecht for their excess of self-confidence in trying to solve the riddles of past cultures, I am bound to admit in the end that without confidence our efforts must die of inanition. A scholar such as Warburg would not have founded his Library without a burning faith in the potentialities of *Kulturwissenschaft*. The evolutionist psychology that inspired his faith is no longer ours, but the questions it prompted him to ask still proved fruitful to cultural history. In proposing as the principal theme of his Institute 'das Nachleben der Antike' – literally the after-life of ancient civilization – he at least made sure that the historian of art, of literature or of science discovered the need for additional techniques to hack a fresh path into the forest in pursuit of that protean problem. Warburg's library was formed precisely to facilitate the acquisition of such tools. It was to encourage trespassing, not amateurishness.

Warburg's problem arose in a situation when the relevance of the classical tradition for the cultural life of the day was increasingly questioned by nationalists and by modernists. He was not out to defend it so much as to explain and assess the reasons for its long 'after-life'. The continued value of that question for the present generation lies in the need to learn more about a once vital tradition which is in danger of being forgotten. But I would not claim that it provides the one privileged entry into the tangled web of Western civilization.

Both the dilemmas and the advantages of cultural history stem from the fact that there can be no privileged entry. It seems to me quite natural that the present generation of students is particularly interested in the social foundations of culture; having myself been born in the reign of his Apostolic Majesty the Emperor Francis Joseph, who had come to the throne in 1848, I certainly can appreciate the rapidity of social change that prompts fresh questionings about the past. That all-pervasive idea of rank and hierarchy that coloured man's reaction to art, religion and even to nature, has become perplexing to the young. It will be the task of the cultural historian to trace and to explain it wherever it is needed for our understanding of the literature, the philosophy or the linguistic conventions of bygone cultures.

Perhaps this example also illustrates the difference between the social and the cultural historian. The first is interested in social change as such. He will use the tools of demography and statistics to map out the transformations in the organization of society. The latter will be grateful for all the information he can glean from such research, but the direction of his interest will still be in the way these changes interacted with other aspects of culture. He will be less interested, for example, in the economic and social causes of urban development than in the changing connotations of words such as 'urbane' or 'suburbia' or, conversely, in the significance of the 'rustic' order in architecture.

The study of such derivations, metaphors and symbols in language, literature and art provides no doubt convenient points of entry into the study of cultural interactions.[24] But I do not think more should be claimed for this approach than it is likely to yield. By itself it cannot offer an escape from the basic dilemma caused by the breakdown of the Hegelian tradition, which stems from the chastening insight that no culture can be mapped out in its entirety, while no element of this culture can be understood in isolation. It appears as if the cultural historian were thus still left without a viable programme, grubbing among the random curiosities of antiquarian lore.

I realize that this perplexity looks pretty formidable in the abstract, but I believe it is much less discouraging in practice. What Popper has stressed for the scientist also applies to the scholar.[25] No cultural historian ever starts from scratch. The traditions of his own culture, the bias of his teacher, the questions of the moment can all stimulate his curiosity and direct his questionings. He may want to continue some existing lines of research or to challenge their result; he may be captivated by Burckhardt's picture of the Renaissance, for instance, and fill in some of the gaps left in that immensely suggestive account, or he may have come to distrust its theoretical scaffolding and therefore feel prompted to ask how far and by whom certain Neo-Platonic tenets were accepted as an alternative to the Christian dogma.

Whether we know it or not, we always approach the past with some preconceived ideas, with a rudimentary theory we wish to test. In this as in many other respects the cultural historian does not differ all that much from his predecessor, the traveller to foreign lands. Not the professional traveller who is only interested in one particular errand, be it the exploration of a country's kinship system or its hydroelectric schemes, but the broad-minded traveller who wants to understand the culture of the country in which he finds himself.

In trying to widen his understanding the traveller will always be well advised to treat inherited clichés about national characters or social types with a healthy suspicion, just as the cultural historian will distrust the second-hand stereotypes of the 'spirit of the age'. But neither need we ever forget that our reactions and observations will always be dependent on the initial assumptions with which we approach a foreign civilization. The questions we may wish to ask are therefore in no way random; they are related to a whole body of beliefs we wish to reinforce or to challenge. But for the cultural historian no less than for the traveller the formulation of the question will usually be precipitated by an individual encounter, a striking instance, be it a work of art or a puzzling custom, a strange craft, or a conversation in a minicab.

[. . .]

Notes

1 See my review of Arnold Hauser in 'The Social History of Art' (1953), in *Meditations on a Hobby Horse* (1963), 4th edn, reprinted, London, 1994; and 'Style', *International Encyclopedia of the Social Sciences*, New York, 1968.

2 See Karl J. Weintraub, *Visions of Culture*, Chicago and London, 1966.

3 Alois Riegl, *Die Spätrömische Kunstindustrie* (1901), Vienna, 1927.

4 Ibid., p. 404.

5 Max Dvořák, *Kunstgeschichte als Geistesgeschichte*, Munich, 1924.

6 Erwin Panofsky, *Aufsätze zu Grundfragen der Kunstwissenschaft*, Berlin, 1964. See now my *The Sense of Order: a Study in the Psychology of Decorative Art* (1979), 2nd edn, reprinted, London, 1994, chapter 8.

7 Erwin Panofsky, *Gothic Architecture and Scholasticism*, Latrobe, PA, 1951.

8 Erwin Panofsky, *Renaissance and Renascences in Western Art*, Stockholm, 1960, p. 3.

9 R.L. Colie, 'Johan Huizinga and the Task of Cultural History', *American Historical Review*, LXIX, 1964, pp. 607–30; Karl J. Weintraub, op. cit. See now also my 'Huizinga's *Homo Ludens*', *Bijdragen en Mededelingen Betrefende de Geschiedenis der Nederlanden* 88/2, 1973, pp. 275–96; and in *Tributes: Interpreters of our Cultural Tradition*, Oxford, 1984, pp. 139–63.

10 Johan Huizinga, *The Waning of the Middle Ages* (1919), London, 1924. Huizinga later regretted the choice of title for this reason, as I mentioned in 'Huizinga's *Homo Ludens*', op. cit.

11 Johan Huizinga, 'Renaissance and Realism' (1926), *Men and Ideas*, New York, 1959.

12 Johan Huizinga, 'The Task of Cultural History' (1929), *Men and Ideas*, New York, 1959.

13 Morse Peckham, *Man's Rush for Chaos*, New York, 1966; Edgar Wind, 'Kritik der Geistes geschichte, Das Symbol als Genenstand kulturwissenschaftlicher Forschung', *Kultur-wissenschaftliche Bibliographie zum Nachleben der Antike*, Einleitung, ed. Bibliothek Warburg 1, Leipzig, Berlin, 1934.

14 See my *Art and Illusion: a Study in the Psychology of Pictorial Representation* (1960), 5th edn, reprinted, London, 1994; and 'From the Revival of Letters to the Reform of the Arts: Nicolò Niccoli and Filippo Brunelleschi', in *The Heritage of Apelles: Studies in the Art of the Renaissance* (1976), reprinted, London, 1993, pp. 93–111.

15 See my 'The Logic of Vanity Fair, Alternatives to Historicism in the Study of Fashions, Style and Taste', in *Ideals and Idols: Essays on Values in History and in Art* (1979), reprinted, London, 1994.

16 See my 'Art and Scholarship' (1957), in *Meditations on a Hobby Horse*, op. cit.; and *Art and Illusion*, op. cit.

17 See Morse Peckham, op. cit.

18 A.O. Lovejoy, 'The Parallel between Deism and Classicism', *Essays in the History of Ideas*, Baltimore, 1948.

19 W.T. Jones, *The Romantic Syndrome*, The Hague, 1961.

20 Eugene Marais, *The Soul of the White Ant* (1934), London, 1937.

21 Colin G. Butler, *The World of the Honey-bee*, London, 1954.

22 See now my 'The Renaissance – Period or Movement?', in *Background to the English Renaissance: Introductory Lectures*, J. B. Trapp, ed., London, 1974, pp. 9–30.

23 Francis Haskell, *Patrons and Painters*, London, 1963.

24 Edgar Wind, op. cit.

25 K.R. Popper, 'Truth, Rationality and the Growth of Scientific Knowledge (1960), *Conjectures and Refutations*, London, 1963.

5
The illusion of inclusion
The guidebook and historic architecture

I want to focus on how systems of viewing and methods of description influence our touristic experience of architecture. The practice of viewing architecture together with verbal and visual recordings of buildings is an important tradition throughout the period under review in this book. We can see how the formulation of distinct relationships between architecture and social and cultural identities have come about through the construction of canons of taste and value which are often calibrated against class. Tourism,[1] and here I mean the consumption of both public and private architecture and the built environment, can be described as

> the ceremonial ratification of authentic attractions as objects of ultimate value . . . The actual act of communion between the tourist and attraction is less important than the *image* or the *idea* [MacCannell's emphases] of society that the collective act generates.[2]

This helps us to interpret the act of visiting buildings and the reading and experience of its histories as a confirmation of an entire body of social, economic and aesthetic values that reinforce the dominant assumptions and the existing structure of society. Architecture has played an active role in perpetuating the cultural hegemony of the ruling élite through the practice of visiting, and I discuss this in the first half of this chapter. In this way we see how architecture remains a signifier of the social order and so a benchmark of class difference and how the appreciation of historic architecture relates to this.

The proliferation of published material and the development of a print culture has made architecture available to an ever-expanding range of publics and this runs parallel to the increasingly popular practices of visiting or home tourism. The bulk of this body of literature comprises guidebooks, commentaries and surveys, which despite the richness of the archive remain little studied.[3] The features of guidebooks and commentaries remain surprisingly constant throughout the period. Visual or written discussions of architecture could either replace a visit or accompany a visitor to a building or indeed a city. In this chapter I refer to a range of these publications as 'guidebooks' and use the term ahistorically to include commentaries and printed materials concerned with the analysis and (re)presentation of buildings. Visual sources might, for instance, include maps and surveys such as those made by Jean Rocque in the mid-eighteenth century (Figure 5.1), whereas verbal sources might list the contents of a building or offer instead the appreciation of the abstract qualities of architecture, which related to the concerns of moral and aesthetic theorists who saw their social and cultural ideals as intrinsic to the principles of design. Early manifestations of the role played by architecture in intellectual debate can be seen in poetry, particularly the work of Alexander Pope. Architecture is seen to embody much that Pope both admires and scorns about contemporary society. This is nowhere more apparent than in his *Epistle to Lord Burlington*, 1730–1, where Pope links architectural design to taste:

You show us Rome was glorious, not profuse
And pompous buildings once were things of use.
Yet shall (my lord) your just and noble rules
Fill half the land with imitating fools;
Who random drawings from your sheets shall make;
Load some vain church with old theatric state,
Turn arcs of triumph to a garden-gate;
Reverse your ornaments, and hang them all
On some patched dog-hole eked with ends of wall;
Then clap four slices of pilaster on't,
That, laced with bits of rustic, makes a front;
Or call the winds through long arcades to roar,
proud to catch cold at a Venetian door;
Conscious they act a true Palladian part,
And, if they starve, they starve by rules of art.

(23–38)

At this time the language and vocabulary of architectural criticism was undeveloped. Consequently the absence of correct and accurate terminology was a stumbling block to discussing architecture *per se* and so its symbolic meaning became the way of formulating ideas about it. Removing the discussion of the aesthetic and moral qualities of architecture to the realms of poetry helped to overcome these problems of taxonomy. This is important as early

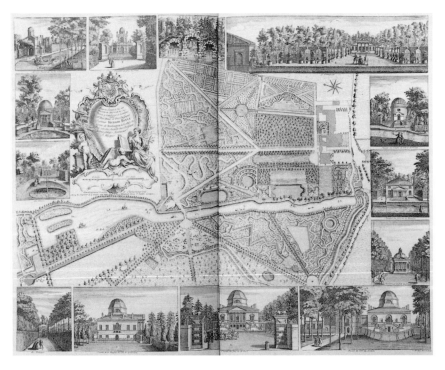

Figure 5.1 Plan and views of Chiswick House and gardens by Jean Rocque. Engraving 1736 (private collection).

in the eighteenth century architecture begins to be represented as an abstract entity embodying social and cultural values.

Perhaps more importantly for us, the openly subjective nature and tone of these early accounts underlines the role of the narrator/author of these texts as an interlocutor between reader and building. This is apparent in Horace Walpole's *Journals of Visits to Country Seats*, which cover his reactions to country houses during his regular tours from July 1751 to September 1784.[4] Some of his comments were of a distinctly personal nature – not least his remarks about Boughton, home to the Montagu family:

> . . . a vast house in the French Style of Architecture, stands in a hole . . . What is most striking, is the prodigious quantity of pedigrees heaped all over the House, along friezes of whole galleries, over chimnies, & even at the end of every step of the stairs, with no meaning that I can conceive, unless the late Duke, by whose order they were put up, & who was a humourist, intended it for the *Descent* [Walpole's emphasis] of the Montagus.[5]

This kind of subject/object relationship, where one inflects on the other, is not confined to verbal guidebooks, commentaries or poetry. In terms of the visual guides the work of Kyp and Knyff as published in *Britannia Illustrata* and their later two volume *Nouvel Théâtre de la Grande Bretagne* (1707 and 1715) show how visual images can also act as commentaries. These volumes were visual surveys of British architecture containing bird's eye views which contextualise subjects such as the country house within its geographical setting with figures in the illustrations providing a pictorial narrative (Figure 5.2). Indeed the method and

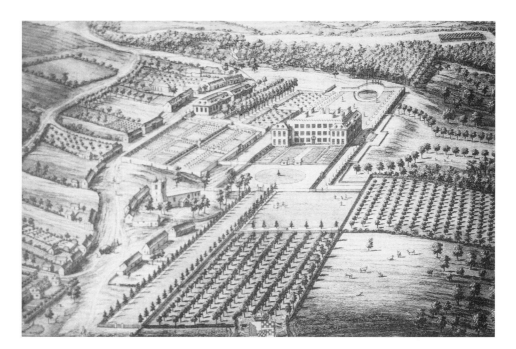

Figure 5.2 Londesborough, Yorkshire as illustrated in *Nouvel Théâtre de la Grande Bretagne*. Engraving, 1715 (private collection).

conventions of representation in these volumes subjugated the architecture of the country house in favour of the detailed representation of the gardens and the estate. Moreover, these images were embellished with features which had not yet been built, and sometimes never were, which were included at the behest of house owners. The recognition of the importance of the landscape to the social and cultural meaning of the house has resonance with Pope's discourse in the *Epistle* and shows how social and cultural concerns can influence verbal and visual representations.[6] The size and weight of these volumes confined them for use in the library, drawing room or cabinet of curiosities, which meant Kyp and Knyff offered a kind of virtual tour of real and imagined British architecture.

Kyp and Knyff operated firmly within the tradition of prints that provided some narrative elements – their images were pictorial and therefore, one might say, visually discursive. Yet it was Colen Campbell's method of representing the most notable British buildings that became the predominant mode of recording architecture in our period and helped establish a tighter visual taxonomic system for the representation of architecture. The first three volumes of Campbell's survey *Vitruvius Britannicus* appeared between 1715 and 1725. John Woolf and James Gandon published volumes four and five of *Vitruvius Britannicus* in 1767 and 1771 respectively, and republished Campbell's initial three volumes.[7] The series was later revivified by George Richardson as the *New Vitruvius Britannicus*, which appeared in two volumes in 1802–1808 and 1808–1810.[8] If we consider the tradition established by *Vitruvius Britannicus* its distinctiveness and significance becomes apparent. The techniques of making visual representations of architecture are relevant here as the plates in *Vitruvius Britannicus* divorce architecture from any background or setting (Figures 5.3 and 5.4). The anti-pictorial nature of the plates is further emphasised as elevations are drawn in orthogonal

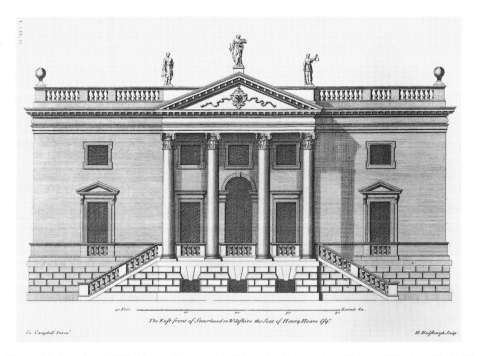

Figure 5.3 Stourhead, Wiltshire as illustrated in *Vitruvius Britannicus*, Volume III, plate 42, 1725 (private collection).

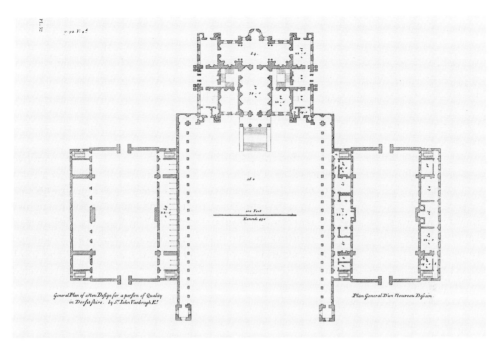

Figure 5.4 General Plan for a new Design for a person of Quality in Dorsetshire. Ground plan of Eastbury as illustrated in *Vitruvius Britannicus*, Volume II, plate 52, 1717 (private collection).

perspective.[9] Ground plans provide the only guide to the three-dimensional form of the building. The result is a more abstract representation and concept of architectural design. This meant that the reductive images of plans and elevations could be appreciated for their composition and rhythm and even their classical references.

The process of distancing architecture from its physical context and making it part of intellectual debate in both verbal and visual terms had important consequences in the opening years of the eighteenth century. First, architecture became the concern of the patrician élite and their aesthetic and moral values were expressed by such writers as Pope and codified into a visual language by the likes of Campbell. Second, the codification of architecture into a distinct, recognisable and readable system of verbal and visual signs ultimately placed architectural discourse in the wider public domain. Once the language which codified architecture was established the principles could be grasped by the literate classes. As the visual language of architecture became more widely understood so ideas were spread. Just as the number of literary accounts and pictorial guides to the architecture of Britain proliferated in the long eighteenth century, so did the abstract discussions of architectural design. It is in these texts that the beginnings of the democratising principles of the appreciation of architecture through inexpensive publications can be seen to be at work. But it was the appreciation of an architecture which was symbolic of a patrician élite. The veneration of the architecture of antiquity as representative of superior social values was enshrined in the architecture of the eighteenth century, together with verbal and visual representations of it. Guidebooks facilitated an appreciation of this by a diverse viewing public whereby appreciation of these aesthetic formulae was part of the cultural operation of buying into a certain social class.

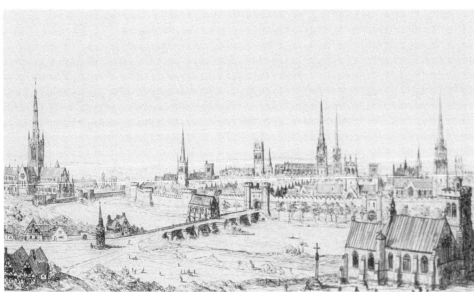

Figure 5.5 'Two English Towns 1441 and 1841' from A N W Pugin *Contrasts*, 1841.

This is not to say, however, that mediaeval architecture went unnoticed.[10] William Stukeley did much to help popularise gothic architecture and argued that it was based on an imitation of nature. His *Itinerarium Curiosum . . . an Account of the Antiquities and Remarkable Curiosities in Nature or Art observed in Travels through Great Britain*, published in 1725 was one of the first surveys to contain plans of mediaeval buildings. Stukeley was secretary to the Society of Antiquaries whose members maintained an active interest in the discovery and recording of ancient indigenous architecture.[11] By the early nineteenth century the verbal and visual mapping of mediaeval architecture came to the fore. The interest in the Gothic Revival as an architectural style and as a symbol of Christian virtues was a driving force in this cultural movement. Perhaps the best-known example of this is A N W Pugin's argument for the historic and moral value of gothic as set out in his *Contrasts* 1836 and *True Principles of Christian or Pointed Architecture* of 1841 (Figure 5.5). Whilst Pugin beat the drum for Christian moral certitude through an appropriate aesthetic, others were fighting a more familiar battle about stylistic influence. The Rev. G D Whittlington amongst others published histories[12] which argued that Gothic had originated in France and had then come to Britain. Perhaps more importantly Thomas Rickman in his *Attempt to Discriminate the Styles of English Architecture, from the Conquest to the Reformation* of 1817 for the first time successfully distinguished between the different styles of building from this period and this influenced his own work (Figure 5.6). This volume became extremely popular, running to seven editions and remaining in print until the 1880s. Although these publications are not strictly guidebooks, they functioned as important interlocutors between the viewing public and the architectural antiquities of Britain, providing both a visual record and a taxonomic system which enabled classification, description and criticism.

Figure 5.6 St John's College, Cambridge by Thomas Rickman, 1821–1827 (photo, author).

The opening decades of the nineteenth century witnessed a real boom in the production of a national culture and a passion for the past. Sir Walter Scott did much to fuel this early manifestation of the heritage industry with novels such as *Waverley*, 1814 and *Ivanhoe*, 1819. The common touch of the heroic princes and knights of Scott's writings ignited popular imagination and formed an important link between the mass of the literate population and the past through a romanticised representation of those cultural ideals and social values. This vision of the past spread through a wide range of media[13] and helped the Victorian veneration for the old pre-industrial world and within it the Gothic style of building as means of providing some kind of counterbalance to the modernity of the new industrialised, capitalistic society. Importantly, this kind of connection with the past focused more on popular culture than the élite sensibilities of antiquarianism. And Scott helped fuse the two, merging a popular interest and desire to know about the past with a renewed sense of connection with its chivalric values on the part of the ruling élite. This notion of the common heritage led to an interest in buildings from the remote past – not least the neglected Haddon Hall and Kirby Hall (Figures 5.7 and 5.8) as well as the recently popularised Warwick Castle and the well-preserved Knole. Commensurate with this growth in popular interest was the proliferation of memorabilia, guidebooks, and histories of country houses like these. The home tourist trade continued to grow in the opening decades of the twentieth century, fuelled by the founding of the National Trust by Octavia Hill and Robert Hunter in 1894, although the number of country houses available to the public remained small.[14] Moreover, cities and their architecture, with few notable exceptions, were not at this point seen as objects for the touristic gaze. In the post-Second World War era, however, many impoverished landowners encouraged by the government were enticed into the National Trust and the number of houses open to the public rose sharply from around 1950 with lists of houses open to the public published by *Country Life* and *Historic Houses, Castles and Gardens*.[15] The post-war years witnessed the emergence of a reasonably well-off literate mobile public hungry for knowledge of its past in order to feel a sense of belonging to its heritage. And there is no doubt that the country house as representative of these long-standing social and cultural traditions played an essential role in this process. The 'heritage industry', as it has been called by Robert Hewison, is tangential to the concerns of this chapter but some of the points Hewison makes reinforce the kind of readings of architectural history that heritage and historic architecture/literature invite, not least through the medium of the guidebook:

> The question is then not whether or not we should preserve the past, but what kind of past we have chosen to preserve, and what that has done to our present.
>   . . . the peculiarly strong hold that . . . [country houses] have on the British – though for once it seems more appropriate to say English – imagination. Because there has been no foreign invasion, civil war or revolution since the seventeenth century these houses both great and small represent a physical continuity which embodies the same adaptability and change with a respect for precedent and tradition . . . they enshrine the rural values that persist in a population that has been predominantly urban for more than a century.
>   . . . Such is the power and the cult of the country house. A building that can only be glimpsed becomes the object of desire of a lover locked out. Yet he seems unaware of his exclusion. By a mystical process of identification the country house becomes the nation, and love of one's country makes obligatory a love of the country house.[16]

Figure 5.7 Haddon Hall, Derbyshire (photo, author).

Figure 5.8 Kirby Hall, Northamptonshire (photo, author).

And this repackaging of historic architecture continues as part of an active 'heritage industry' in which the guidebook continues to play a very important part in perpetuating myths and the hegemony of the ruling élite. As Hewison remarks:

> At best, the heritage industry only draws a screen between ourselves and our true past. I criticise the heritage industry not simply because so many of its products are fantasies of a world that never was; not simply because at a deeper level it involves the preservation, indeed reassertion, of social values that the democratic progress of the twentieth century seemed to be doing away with, but because far from ameliorating the climate of decline, it is actually worsening it. If the only new thing we have to offer is an improved version of the past, then today can only be inferior to yesterday.[17]

My purpose here has been to establish the enduring links between architecture and social and aesthetic values through its consumption both verbally and visually by a range of publics. From this the role of the guidebook, in all its various manifestations, emerges as an essential interlocutor where the subject/object relationship creates and reinvents a series of readings of this kind of architectural history or architectural aesthetic. And it is at this intersection of architecture and history that we find the persona of the author/narrator at its most apparent. Moreover, the role of the reader/viewer of these kinds of histories also inflects on the subject/object relationship within a touristic context. I want now to revisit the post-Second World War years – the historical moment of the emergence of architectural history as an academic discipline in Britain to consider what role the guidebooks played in the perception and consumption of this newly mapped terrain. If we accept that even the presentday tourist undertakes travel for pleasure, as it allows escape into the unknown and imaginary, then travel is also then a metaphor for exploration and economic conquest which enables the amassing of information the possession of which can infer control or dominance. Guidebooks fit into this system as they facilitate the ordering of the touristic experience and hence a sense of mastery of the terrain being visited and/or experienced through linguistic conventions. Furthermore, guidebooks link places, names and buildings and set up relationships between objects, so giving directions. In this way the guidebook helps forge sets of social relationships which correspond the Guy Debord's ideas about society and spectacle. Debord argues that the production and consumption of commodities in modern society results in life being lived though a series of images. These images through which social relationships are expressed as Debord's 'spectacle' – a capitalistic gloss over social inequality:

> THE SPECTACLE APPEARS at once as society itself, as part of society and as a means of unification. As part of society, it is that sector where all attention, all consciousness converges. Being isolated – and precisely for that reason – this sector is the locus of the illusion and false consciousness; the unity it imposes is merely the official language of generalized separation.[18]

How then was the architecture of Britain packaged for this new viewing public? In the post-war era the spirit of the New Elizabethans and the celebration of things British were powerful cultural forces. Moreover, the concept of deep England and with it the invention of the 'heritage' and the 'countryside' enhanced the allure of country houses newly acquired by the state or the National Trust. The destruction wrought on many British towns and cities endowed these scarred urban landscapes with a symbolic meaning; they stood as emblems of what had so nearly been lost. At this moment even Sir John Summerson, a committed modernist, was driven to write *Georgian London*[19] in an effort to record what remained of this spectacular phase of London's development. This is a distinctive historical moment in which the past is reinvented to serve the social and cultural needs of the present.[20] Sir Roy Strong remarked on this writing on the late 1970s. Although Strong's purpose was to fight for the preservation of the 'heritage' and the country house in particular[21] he makes some pertinent observations about the relationship between past and present as expressed through architecture:

> It is in times of danger, either from without or within, that we become deeply conscious of our heritage . . . within this word there mingle varied and passionate streams of ancient pride and patriotism, of a heroism of times past, of a nostalgia too for what we think of as a happier world which we have lost. In the 1940s we felt all this deeply because of the danger from without. In the 1970s we sense it because of the dangers from within . . . [these are] changes within the structure of society, of the dissolution of old values and standards . . . The heritage represents some form of security . . . [and] is therefore a deeply stabilising and unifying element within our society.[22]

We have already seen how Sir Howard Colvin and Sir John Summerson responded to the wealth of archival material and increased interest in the built environment in the post-war years. Their work is complemented, not least in its initial Anglocentric rather than British focus, by a set of guidebooks known as the *Buildings of England*, of which Sir Nikolaus Pevsner was founder editor and author of many of the original volumes and whose name remains closely connected with the series. The *Buildings of England* emerged in the years directly after the end of the Second World War. It provided a comprehensive mapping of architectural sites of touristic interest to the viewing public and remains the best-known and most widely used set of serious architectural guidebooks in this country. The close relationship of the series to the self-conscious mapping, validation and preservation of British architecture and its histories is perhaps revealed in Pevsner's dedication of the volume on Hampshire: 'The Ministry of Housing and Local Government, whose lists of buildings of architectural or historic interest are one of the finest tools we have'.[23]

Each volume in the *Buildings of England* series is a meticulous survey of the architecture of a county within the British Isles beginning with an introductory essay followed by a discussion of the buildings of the towns or cities and those within the geographical area in alphabetical order followed by a series of suggested perambulations. Its success can be measured by the fact that its scope has broadened to include Wales, Scotland and Ireland and many of the original editions are being updated and enlarged.[24] The format and approach of the series is often seen as a collection of rather dry empirical lists minimally expanded into a thin kind of prose, but Pevsner was a historian with a distinct methodological approach to architectural history. Pevsner's enthusiasm for Hegelian dialectic and belief in zeitgeist may no longer be fashionable for historians but his work still has resonance today, as seen in the long shelf life of such texts as his *Pioneers of Modern Design*. The *Buildings of England* series stands next to the more far-reaching *Pelican History of Art* series as part of Pevsner's vast intellectual project that endures to the present day. But little attention has ever been paid to the methods used by Pevsner, and to which many still adhere, in the *Buildings of England* – perhaps his fullest contribution to the mapping of architectural history of this country. This is especially surprising as Pevsner's discussion of *The Englishness of English Art* caused a great deal of national upset.[25] Yet he remains the natural and unrivalled companion for the informed visitor, academic and conservationist on an architectural tour of the British Isles.

The mainstay of Pevsner's activities as an historian was his appetite for empirical information and the mapping of our knowledge of the visual world. Here Pevsner's German academic training can be seen to influence his approach, which was modelled on George Dehio's five-volume *Handbucher der deutschen Kunstdenkmaler* published between 1905 and 1912, which was an inventory of buildings. The economy of discussion and the lack of illustrations in Dehio's work were influential on Pevsner's early guides but the difference here is that the brevity of Pevsner's guides was so that they could be used on site rather than from the armchair – they encouraged people to go and look. Indeed, Pevsner expected the reader to do just this and to think for him/herself. In a reply to Alec Clifton-Taylor's observation that in his description of churches he did not state if they were good, Pevsner commented 'You must go and look at them and make up your own mind. I have given you the facts.' His economical comments make us look and appreciate the aesthetic. Imagine, for instance, the church at Mereval: 'The church is approached through a gatehouse so intensely medieval that it is at once recognised as Victorian.' And even Pevsner could not resist a value judgement on the Albert Memorial: 'The epitome on many ways of High Victorian ideals and high Victorian Style, rich, solid, pompous, a little vulgar, but full of faith and self confidence.'

Partly because of this Pevsner has been accredited with opening the eyes of the British to their own architecture, and legitimate claims have been made that Pevsner was the most widespread and formative influence on the visual sensibilities of Englishmen since John Ruskin. Arguably this is still the case as the *Buildings of England* series remains a dominant force in the mapping of British architecture. But here perhaps more than anywhere else the resentment at a foreigner schooled in the tradition of European intellectual debate telling the British what to see and how to think about it came to the fore. Sir John Betjeman, author of the rival *Shell Guides*, which were discursive rather than analytical, referred to Pevsner as 'Herr Professor Doctor'. This rather coarse remark exemplifies the resentment of the input of scholars from the European intellectual school of thought to the writing of architectural histories of Britain. But Pevsner's effect on the study of architectural history and our view of it goes much deeper than the sometimes resented meticulous empiricism of his guides. This absence of questioning of how guidebooks make us read historic architecture and how we might read the kind of architectural histories they present may result from the way in which the guides are often used. Entries on all kinds of buildings are consulted independently of their context. But the guides are not conceived solely as lists of buildings made in alphabetical order or in order of importance. They are homogeneous surveys of the architecture of specific geographical areas, many of which are cities. If the writing of architectural history is complicated, formulating that of a city can only be more so and it is on this aspect of the Buildings of England that I wish to focus.

The 'perambulations' are a dominant feature of the guides and they underpin Pevsner's way of narrating the architecture of cities. The city is subdivided into areas which can be covered on foot, and each perambulation presents a prescribed route through an area that does not just focus on the key buildings. This method of travelling through the city is significant as it influences the viewpoint from which buildings are seen. The popularity of motorised travel and the tour bus are ignored in favour of the pedestrian visitor, as Pevsner exhorts the historian to encounter the building at ground level from specific, stationary positions. Indeed the guides contain very few illustrations of any kind. This may mean they are less attractive as armchair reading but they do encourage the user to confront the building and use their own eyes. Many historians represent cities and buildings through means that are not visible from the ground, such as aerial shots and/or abstract discussions of plans but these are ignored by Pevsner as they are not part of the pedestrian's experience. The building stock of a city is not classified according to its perceived level of architectural importance; seeing 'Rome in a day' is not possible using these guides, as no judgement is made of what are the most important 'must-see' offerings of a city. Instead buildings are rooted firmly in their physical context and the visitor encounters them as they appear next to each other in no order of merit or chronological sequence but simply as part of a linear exploration of the cityscape. This absence of hierarchy helps to underline the significance of ordinariness, especially in this context as the importance of buildings can be based on factors other than style or the status of the architect. For Pevsner, or indeed any historian, the absence of any kind of chronological survey must have significance. The guides focus on what is visible today and do not try to recreate the architectural development of an area. The perambulatory exploration of the city complements this as glimpses of previous street patterns emerge in the discussion, so showing how past and present are constantly interacting in a kind of Foucauldian 'archaeology' of the temporal discontinuities of our knowledge of the past.[26] The chronological historical analysis this denies is more than compensated for by that fact that it allows the full exploration of the juxtapositions of form, function and period which makes the urban fabric of Britain so rich. These pathways through architecture can be likened to Foucault's structures of power which transformed 'a human multiplicity' into a 'disciplinary' society and of managed, differentiated and classified space which secretly enable the structuring of the determining conditions of social life.

These methodological issues do not detract from challenging question posed by the *Buildings of England*: What makes a city? Does it have a shape or definable form and if so how can that be translated into a textual analysis? Furthermore, if this analysis is to correlate to our actual experience of a city it should correspond to the way in which we encounter it. A visitor to a city experiences it through exploration of directed routes or street patterns which provide vignettes of the whole. The juxtapositions of buildings from different historical periods on the street also gives glimpses of previous points in history.

Michel de Certeau remarks on this kind of experience of architecture:

> Their story begins on ground level, with footsteps. They are myriad, but do not compose a series. They cannot be counted because each unit has a qualitative character: a style of tactile apprehension and kinesthetic appropriation. Their swarming mass is an innumerable collection of singularities. Their intertwined paths give their shape to spaces. They weave places together. In that respect, pedestrian movements from one of these 'real systems whose existence in fact makes up the city.' They are not localized; it is rather what they spatialize.
>
> . . .
>
> It is true that the operations of walking on can be traced on city maps in such a way as to transcribe their paths (here well-trodden, there very faint) and their trajectories (going this way and not that). But these thick or thin curves only refer, like words, to the absence of what has passed by. Surveys of routes miss what was: the act itself of passing by. The operation of walking, wandering or 'window shopping,' that is, the activity of passers-by, is transformed into points that draw a totalising and reversible line on the map. They allow us to grasp only a relic set in the nowhen of surface projection. Itself visible, it has the effect of making invisible the operation that made it possible. These

Figure 5.9 Visitors admiring Wanstead, Essex. Eighteenth-century engraving (private collection).

Figure 5.10 A View of Whitehall looking north east (showing the Banqueting House amidst buildings of different dates) by William Marlow, late eighteenth century. The image shows the range of street life and social interraction in London (courtesy of the Paul Mellon Centre for Studies in British Art).

fixations constitute procedures for forgetting. The trace left behind is substituted for the practice. It exhibits the (voracious) property that the geographical system has of being able to transform action into legibility, but in doing so it causes a way of being in the world to be forgotten.[27]

The *Buildings of England* series covers architecture in both urban and rural environments. We have seen how, as inheritor of a literary and visual tradition of guidebooks, its perpetuation of the idea of historic architecture and the attached social and cultural values of heritage contributes to our continuing fascination with the country house (Figure 5.9). This apparent kind of empowerment of the viewing public continues in a more complex fashion on the representation of urban environments (Figure 5.10). Here the guides respond to the complex nature of cities and the telling of its histories with their apparent simplicity which engenders a sense of 'ownership' of a more complex architectural manifestation of social power structures. I have juxtaposed extracts from the *Buildings of England* with Roland Barthes' *Blue Guide*, an essay in *Mythologies*, as means of showing how we might read the architectural histories presented in guidebooks and what this might tell us about ourselves. The selection of passages from the *Buildings of England* includes Pevsner's discussion of the methodological issues which affect the writing of guides to cities with specific reference to London in the immediate post World War II period. In addition, I have selected examples of entries on individual buildings and perambulations. The extracts also contain references to the work of Sir John Summerson and Sir Howard Colvin, so demonstrating the connectivity between the different narratives of architectural history.

Notes

1 Domestic tourism and its social and political significance is discussed by L Colley in, amongst other writings, *Britons: Forging the nation 1707–1837*, New Haven, CT and London, Yale University Press, 1992.

2 D MacCannell, *The Tourist : A new theory of the leisure class*, New York, Schocken, 1976 p. 14.

3 On this point see A Tinniswood, *A History of Country House Visiting: Five centuries of tourism and taste*, Oxford and London, Blackwell and the National Trust, 1st edn 1989 and E Moir, *The Discovery of Britain: the English tourists 1540–1840*, London, Routledge 1964.

4 H Walpole, Journals of visits to country seats &c, in P Toynbee (ed.), *Walpole Society*, vol. XVI, 1928.

5 H Walpole, op. cit., p. 54. Boughton was owned by the Dukes of Montagu.

6 An overview of the evolution of portraits of country houses including views of their landscape is given in J Harris, *The Artists and the Country House*, London, Sotheby's, 1986. The significance of the representation of the landscapes is discussed in D Solkin, *Richard Wilson and the Landscape of Reaction*, London, Tate Gallery, 1986.

7 See E Harris and N Savage, *Architectural Books and Writers 1556–1795*, Cambridge University Press, Cambridge, 1990, pp. 496–498 esp.

8 See E Harris and N Savage, op. cit., pp. 387–390 esp.

9 Volume III does contain some views with a landscape setting.

10 On this point see D Watkin, *The Rise of Architectural History*, London, Architectural Press, 1980, pp. 49–69 esp.

11 See J Evans, *A History of the Society of Antiquaries*, Oxford, Oxford University Press, 1956 and more recently S Smiles *Eye Witness: Artists and visual documentation in Britain 1770–1830*, Aldershot, Ashgate 2000.

12 Rev. G D Whittlington, *An Historical Survey of the Ecclesiastical Antiquities of France with a View to Illustrate the Rise and Progress of Gothic Architecture in Europe*, London, 1809.

13 On this point see S Bann, *The Clothing of Clio: A study of the representation of history in nineteenth-century Britain and France*, Cambridge, Cambridge University Press, 1984.

14 The resurgence of the country house 'industry' is discussed in Peter Mandler, *The Fall and Rise the Stately Home*, New Haven, CT and London, Yale University Press, 1997.

15 This originally appeared as *ABC Coach Guides*.

16 R Hewison, *The Heritage Industry: Britain in a Climate of Decline*, London, Methuen, 1987 p. 10.

17 R Hewison, op. cit., pp. 9–10.

18 G Debord, *The Society of the Spectacle*, trans. Donald Nicholson-Smith, New York, Zone Books, 1994 p. 12.

19 Sir John Summerson, *Georgian London*, Penguin, Harmondsworth, 1st edn, 1945.

20 Only a decade later the new spirit of Britain prompted the destruction of the historic cores of many towns and cities. The Euston Arch in London and the redevelopment of the centres of Bath and Bristol are poignant examples of this new enthusiasm for modernism.

21 See also Sir Roy Strong, *The Destruction of the Country House 1875–1974*, London, Thames and Hudson, 1975.

22 Sir Roy Strong, Introduction to P Cormack, *Heritage in Danger*, 2nd edn, London, Quartet, 1978, p. 10.

23 N Pevsner and D Lloyd, *The Buildings of England: Hampshire and the Isle of Wight*, Harmondsworth, Penguin, 1st edn 1967.

24 Indeed, the volumes are of international significance as the ongoing *Buildings of the United States* series, edited by Damie Stillman, which examines America's architecture state by state is based on Pevsner's model.

25 This book was based on the series of Reith Lectures broadcast by Pevsner in October and November 1955.

26 M Foucault, *The Archaeology of Knowledge*, trans. A M Sheridan Smith, London, Tavistock, 1972.

28 M de Certeau, *The Practice of Everyday Life*, trans. Stephen F Rendall, Berkeley, University of California Press, 1984, p. 97.

The buildings of England

Sir Nikolaus Pevsner

THE CITIES OF LONDON AND WESTMINSTER

Foreword to the first edition (1957)

The volume of *The Buildings of England* called 'London, except the Cities of London and Westminster' came out in 1952. It is referred to in these pages as 'Volume Two'. This is its companion volume, and deals with the rest of London, that is, the Cities of London and Westminster with that part of the borough of Holborn left out of the other volume.

[...]

The usual arrangement in *The Buildings of England* is: Introduction, Churches, Public Buildings, Perambulations. In Volume Two it was easy to follow this system, for the County of London has twenty-seven boroughs; so the arrangement could be repeated twenty-seven times. But the material to go into the present volume [...] falls in fact into no more than three natural divisions, and I have retained them:

   I. The City of London. [...]
  II. South Holborn and the Strand and Fleet Street area. [...]
 III. The City of Westminster. [...]

The advantage of these divisions seems to me to be that they correspond to visitors' needs.

[...]

The next problem was the treatment of data. [...] There is only one for the whole volume, and this should at some stage be read side by side with that of Volume Two. For neither by itself can give the whole story of the architectural growth of London. Each of the three parts then has its churches and public buildings listed and discussed in the usual manner. It was with the Perambulations that I found myself in an unprecedented position.

The system of Perambulations has found favour with the users of *The Buildings of England*; there can be no doubt about that. In the present volume it worked easily in such cases as Pimlico or Belgravia, more easily indeed than, say, for St Marylebone in Volume Two. It was clear to me, and correspondents have confirmed it, that St Marylebone went to the limit, if not beyond the limit, of what can be done in the form of Perambulations. If you do not go out for a consistent walk but want to know what may be of interest in Queen Anne Street, it will take you some time to find it, perhaps owing to insufficient cross-referencing (to be improved in the next edition).

I have therefore in this volume adopted another system which, I admit, is a compromise and lacks logic. The City of London is such a small area and yet contains so many facts which I had to put in that streets are listed in alphabetical order. Any other arrangement, I am convinced, would have resulted in confusion. As for South Holborn etc., and Westminster, most streets are dealt with in the same way, but some are grouped together, because they belong to one square or lead off one street. This is done for the benefit of the visitor to the area. For reference purposes every street, etc., is in addition indexed individually.

Another problem was posed (and always is posed) by Public Buildings. What are they? The Bank of England has strictly speaking been a public building only since 1946. The BBC is in one way a public building, but in another not. Westminster School is not so at all; most hospitals were not until they were nationalized. It is obviously quite impossible to be consistent here. What I decided to include are: Barracks, Bridges, Colleges, Government Offices, Hospitals, Inns of Court, Law Courts, Libraries, Markets and Exchanges, Museums and Galleries, Palaces, Police Stations, Post Offices, Railway Stations, Schools, Telephone Exchanges, and Town Halls and other local government offices. But Theatres, Livery Companies' Halls, and Clubs are treated under their streets, but indexed under their own names. In many other cases minor public buildings appear in their street context, and are also indexed under their own names.

It was perhaps a bad moment to undertake an architectural guide to the City of London. There are, at the time of writing, still whole areas lying waste after bombing in the Second World War. A number of the City churches, also, are not yet repaired or restored. Yet the publication of this volume was much asked for; so I decided to undertake it in spite of these disadvantages.

[. . .]

During the last stages of the preparation of this volume Mr Howard Colvin's *Dictionary of English Architects, 1660–1840*, appeared, a memorable achievement of patient scholarship. It was my good fortune to be able to make use of his London results, as a check on my own, and also as a source of additional information.

WILTSHIRE

Wilbury House, 1 m. N of Newton Toney

The great importance of Wilbury House lies less in its appearance now than in its appearance as it was first built and illustrated in *Vitruvius Britannicus*. It was designed by and built for *William Benson* in 1710. He is notorious for having been made Wren's successor in 1718, when George I dismissed Wren as a Tory and an old man, and for having failed so completely that he himself was replaced only one year later. But he is memorable as the designer of the first, not Neo-Palladian, but neo-Inigo-Jones house in England. For this is what Wilbury was, as Sir John Summerson was the first to point out. The house then had a four-column Corinthian portico of tall columns set well away from the wall.

[. . .]

Wilton House

The first earl of Pembroke was granted the nunnery estate in 1544. Of his house, which was built round a courtyard, the general shape remains, and certainly the so-called HOLBEIN PORCH, now a garden ornament to the W of the S front, but originally the porch from the courtyard to the Great Hall, which lay in the N range (cf. e.g. Dingley and Deene Park, both Northants), is a typical piece of *c.* 1560–70, open on three sides and with three façades. Pairs of fluted Ionic columns below, pairs of fluted Corinthian columns above. The latter frame a field with a coat of arms and two frontal portrait busts in round recesses. Top with two shell-gables. Inside a transverse depressed tunnel-vault.

As for the first earl's house itself, a good deal of the masonry must belong to it,[1] and also at least the outline on the most imposing side, that facing E. We have a drawing dated 1566 which shows this side as it then (i.e. at the time of the Holbein Porch – *see* above) was, and this has the same tall central frontispiece with archway and tall oriel window and lantern as it has today, the same lower connecting links, and the same higher corner pavilions. Only every detail is changed. The archway – it was the main entrance up to the C19 – looks medieval in the drawing, the details of the three-storeyed oriel differ, the top is a prominent pediment – early for 1566, though preceded about 1550 at Somerset House, the Lord Protector's London house. The present frontispiece has a different archway and different fenestration, adjustments made by *James Wyatt* when he worked at Wilton.[2] The connecting links, now with two bays of classical windows in two and a half storeys,[3] had just one five-light transomed window surprisingly high up and again top pediments; and the corner pavilions, now of the C17 on the l. and repeated thus on the r., had straight gables with big chimneys and also five-light windows lower down. The windows had no arched lights and were in that respect again remarkably advanced.

Wyatt was called in by the eleventh earl in 1801. He did much to the house. He rebuilt the W range recessed by two steps in the centre and then only one-storeyed and provided with a large bay window. Inside this range a Gothic Library was contrived. It was ungothicized in 1913 by *Edmund Warre* and is now a drawing room (not shown to the public).[4] Wyatt also rebuilt the N front, which originally contained the Great Hall, and made it the main entrance. To do so he raised the level of the forecourt and gave it its embattled walls. The details of the N front are a mixture of the Wyatt Elizabethan and the C20 Classical. The arms of Henry VIII, however, may well be original work of *c.*1544.[5] The forecourt is closed to the town by a splendid ARCHWAY with coupled Corinthian pilasters framing a tunnel-vaulted arch on Tuscan columns to the N and S. On the entrance side there are columns instead of pilasters. In the spandrels paterae with garlands hanging oddly, as if they were going to slide down any moment. On top on a stepped base the equestrian statue of Marcus Aurelius. This arch was designed by *Sir William Chambers* just before 1759 and erected on top of the hill to the S of the house. Wyatt brought it down to close the forecourt and create a worthy overture to the house. He added the two cubic LODGES l. and r. The GATES are of the C18, from Mount Merrion near Dublin. They were bought in Italy *c.*1840. Wyatt also converted the former main entrane on the E side into a GARDEN HALL and made various internal alterations (*see* below).

The only front of the house not interfered with by Wyatt is the SOUTH FRONT. This range has traditionally been ascribed to *Inigo Jones*, but the date and architect of its present form are problematic. The S front was built for Philip, the fourth Earl, who had succeeded his brother in 1630. To the two brothers the First Folio is dedicated. According to Aubrey, it was Charles I, who visited Wilton every summer, who 'did put Philipp Earl of Pembroke upon making this magnificent garden and grotto, and to new build that side of the house that fronts the garden, with two stately pavilions at each end, all *al Italiano*'. Work was in progress on the gardens in 1632–3, and it has recently been discovered that the rebuilding of the house began in 1636. The man responsible for both was *Isaac de Caus*, but Aubrey mentions that he had the 'advice and approbation' of *Inigo Jones*. But the S range was burnt in 1647–8 and rebuilt, according to Aubrey, again with the advice of Jones (who was then very old), by *John Webb*. So the problems are: is the present S range a work of 1648 by *Webb*, or one of 1636 by *de Caus*, and to what extent was *Jones* involved? There is a further complication. A drawing now at Worcester College Oxford, first published by Mr Colvin, shows the de Caus garden laid out in front of a S range twice the length of the present one, with a centre motif of six giant Corinthian columns with a wider interval in the middle, and a pediment. It can be assumed that the drawing is an echo of pediment. It can be assumed that the drawing is an echo of Jones's ideas. The scheme was certainly taken seriously, as the gardens were actually constructed on this scale. The reduced version of the s front that exists today has no portico, and includes raised end pavilions, a feature entirely missing in the Oxford drawing. But the similarities between other details of the drawing and the present building, and the fact that Aubrey mentions the end pavilions, suggests that the present exterior is substantially the one built by de Caus in 1636, as a reduced version of the grand design, and that only the interiors were reconstructed after the fire. The s front is nine bays wide, of Chilmark stone, the bays very generously spaced, and has a semi-basement with segment-headed windows with heavy keystones, a principal floor with the State Rooms, and an attic floor above crowned by a balustrade. The centre window is of the Venetian type with a coat of arms over, flanked by very French-looking figures in shallow relief. Main windows otherwise have just straight entablatures, and the angle bays are raised by one storey into pedimented pavilions, one bay wide and two bays deep. In these angle bays the main window has a pediment and the top window a segmental pediment. That is all. It is an extremely restrained front which does not prepare for the luxuriance inside. The originally projected centre motif would of course have given it additional grandeur. The windows in the c17 can, needless to say, not have been sashed, and one must assume stone crosses of mullion and transom. The motif of the raised angle pavilions appears in Scamozzi's *Idea dell'Architettura* of 1615 and can be traced back to Serlio (VII, 21), the principal Italian Cinquecento source book of the years before Palladio. But they also recall, and perhaps incorporate some of the structure of, the corner towers of the Tudor mansion.

[. . .]

HAMPSHIRE

Inner Southampton, perambulation

The Bargate of *c.*1200 was a single arch between earthen banks with outside ditches. The NORTH WALL replaced the banks in the late c13. It survived largely intact, although much hidden by houses, until 1932–7, when the parts adjoining the Bargate were demolished to make way for a traffic roundabout, leaving the gate to look like a piece of huge stage scenery, a sort of medieval Arc de Triomphe in an insipid c20 setting. Only the stumps of the walls flanking the gate remain, with the parapet neatly stepped down from the level of the roof of the gateway to that of the walls. To pick up the wall again to the E, one has to go down a passageway between the shops, behind which an impressive stretch begins, and, although the Perambulation proper goes w from the Bargate, it is worth-while to make a short detour in the opposite direction to see this stretch of wall. There are two half-round towers, neither rising to its original height, then a gap at YORK BUILDINGS, where the walls were breached in the c18 and an attractive brick archway built on their line.[6] At the NE corner of the walled town is the round POLYMOND TOWER, coeval with the wall, but enlarged in the later c14. Only two storeys remain, the third having been demolished in 1828. A small tree grows, apparently quite harmlessly, at the top of the tower, giving this corner of the walls something of the romantic, ruinous, vegetation-covered appearance which they have in early c19 prints.

w of the Bargate the North Wall survives only intermittently; a wide breach was made as recently as 1960 to accommodate a ring road. At the NW corner of the walled town is the ARUNDEL TOWER, a round tower built in the early to mid c13, with another stage added in the later c14 (probably in 1377–9, when Sir John Arundel was governor of the castle). It stands against what was originally a natural cliff, with the Test estuary to the w; only the uppermost two stages, ruinous at the top and roofless, rise above the level of the ground on the landward side, their shell entered through a tall round arch. Inside, the lower of these two storeys has the shape of a heptagon, with the space of two of the sides occupied by the entrance arch, and tall arrow slits opening to NW, N, and NE, each with wide inward splays like those of lancet windows. To the w a doorway leads to a small (probably late c14) salient which projects from the line of the town wall like a large buttress, but with a polygonal embattled parapet. A small PUB of 1899, with neo-Tudor gables and prominent brick castellated turret, clings to the N side of the tower; it will soon be demolished, when the tower is restored.

[. . .]

BUCKINGHAMSHIRE

Chesham, perambulation

The perambulation starts from the churchyard. At its E entrance, the vicarage (now called the RECTORY), built for his incumbent by the Duke of Bedford *c.*1767, red brick, of three bays with a one-bay pediment, the ground-floor windows under blank arches and a Doric porch. Then through contemporary gates down into CHURCH STREET. It starts with the sort of c18 and early c19 cottage façades that give the street its unassuming but almost continuously attractive character. Nos. 57 and 63, with red and blue chequer fronts and doorhoods on simple carved brackets, are typical. Many such fronts, including No. 57, hide c17 timber-frames. Two uncharacteristic buildings break in almost at once: the former NATIONAL SCHOOL of 1845 by *Street*, with its plain red brick gables and spired cupola, and, opposite (E side) at No. 44, a jolly brick and terracotta shopfront of *c.*1880. This also screens a c17 timber-framed building. Then on the same side, exposed timber-framing. Nos. 54–6 is a c14 house with hall and cross wing, enlarged and altered in the c17. On the cross wing (No. 54) some curved bracing and the original traceried head of a timber window. There is another blocked one at the back and inside one crown-post roof truss. Next to this No. 58 (LINDLEY HOUSE), c17 with a mid-c18 front of smooth orange brick with two giant pilasters framing three of the five bays, a parapet and a skimpy Doric doorcase. Opposite Lindley House, timber-framed cottages at Nos. 63, 65–71 (s side).

They face the two lodges to THE BURY, a fine preparation for the only grand c18 house in Chesham. They are one-storeyed with rusticated brick quoins and parapets. The later Doric porches are grand additions to the original small boxes. The house is dated 1712(16?) on the rainwater heads. It was built for William Lowndes, Secretary to the Treasury, but nothing about its façades resembles Lowndes' more famous house, Winslow Hall (q.v.). It has its main façade to the s. This s FRONT was originally narrower than it is now. It had no more than five bays. The wide bays to the l. and r. with their low Venetian windows on the upper floor are a late c18 addition; the Doric porch and two bay windows on the ground floor look early c19 but may be much later, like the shutters. The original windows are segment-headed. No decoration other than the rusticated brick quoins and the panelled parapet, repeated on the later wings. Hipped roof. To the w a long wing in the same style (of 1853–4?) with a brick loggia linking it to a summerhouse, and a much extended service court behind. Carriage entrance by the N front in English Early Renaissance style.

The U-shaped N FRONT has been much altered. The E wing extends from the garden façade but the slightly larger w wing was added later, with a Doric loggia leading to the entrance door. The interior has been massacred in a conversion to offices. The entrance hall looks Edwardian but the staircase which leads out of it in a narrow well is original with turned balusters and a plaster ceiling with an oval wreath. Some much rearranged original panelling and door surrounds. In its grounds (now LOWNDES PARK) to the N, an c18 prospect MOUND.

[. . .]

Here the pleasant backwaters of Chesham are easily forgotten. The main traffic route forges through the Market Square and on to the w along St Mary's Way, a barrier between the High Street and the open space of Lowndes Park. So the High Street is hemmed in unpleasantly by a major road on one side and the railway on the other. The MARKET SQUARE once looked much like Amersham's, but in 1965 it forfeited its c18 Market Hall, a less prepossessing version of Amersham's, partly rebuilt in 1856, and then, in the 1980s, lost its sense of enclosure in the road widening. A classical CLOCK TOWER (1990–2 by *Chiltern District Council*) is now the chief landmark.

In the HIGH STREET very little of interest. Though the narrow street winds promisingly and opens out into a broad space in the middle, almost all the buildings of whatever period are particularly mean.

[. . .]

Notes

1 See a recent opening in the sw corner of the upper cloister, i.e. outside the Single Cube Room.

2 The present cupola, inspired by that shown in the drawing of 1566, was designed by the sixteenth *Earl of Pembroke* and *Barber, Bundy & Greenfield*, 1962. It replaced one by *Wyatt*.

3 The balustrades were added in the c20. They replaced Wyatt's battlements.

4 It has a Jonesian marble fireplace and two extraordinary Baroque doorways brought from elsewhere. Each has a broken pediment supported by terms.

5 In the N entrance hall a STATUE of Shakespeare leaning on an urn. It is by *Scheemakers*, 1743.

6 This has recently been demolished.

The Blue Guide

Roland Barthes

The *Blue Guide*[1] hardly knows the existence of scenery except under the guise of the picturesque. The picturesque is found any time the ground is uneven. We find again here this
bourgeois promoting of the mountains, this old Alpine myth (since it dates back to the nineteenth century) which Gide rightly associated with Helvetico-Protestant morality and which
has always functioned as a hybrid compound of the cult of nature and of puritanism (regeneration through clean air, moral ideas at the sight of mountain-tops, summit-climbing as civic
virtue, etc.). Among the views elevated by the *Blue Guide* to aesthetic existence, we rarely
find plains (redeemed only when they can be described as fertile), never plateaux. Only
mountains, gorges, defiles and torrents can have access to the pantheon of travel, inasmuch, probably, as they seem to encourage a morality of effort and solitude. Travel according
to the *Blue Guide* to aesthetic existence, we rarely find plains (redeemed only when they can
be described as fertile), never plateaux. Only mountains, gorges, defiles and torrents can have
access to the pantheon of travel, inasmuch, probably, as they seem to encourage a morality
of effort and solitude. Travel according to the *Blue Guide* is thus revealed as a labour-saving
adjustment, the easy substitute for the morally uplifting walk. This in itself means that the
mythology of the *Blue Guide* dates back to the last century, to that phase in history when the
bourgeoisie was enjoying a kind of new-born euphoria in *buying* effort, in keeping its image
and essence without feeling any of its ill-effects. It is therefore in the last analysis, quite logically and quite stupidly, the gracelessness of a landscape, its lack of spaciousness or human
appeal, its verticality, so contrary to the bliss of travel, which account for its interest.
Ultimately, the *Guide* will coolly write: '*The road becomes very picturesque (tunnels)*': it matters little that one no longer sees anything, since the tunnel here has become the sufficient
sign of the mountain; it is a financial security stable enough for one to have no further worry
about its value over the counter.

Just as hilliness is overstressed to such an extent as to eliminate all other types of scenery,
the human life of a country disappears to the exclusive benefit of its monuments. For the *Blue
Guide*, men exist only as 'types'. In Spain, for instance, the Basque is an adventurous sailor,
the Levantine a light-hearted gardener, the Catalan a clever tradesman and the Cantabrian a
sentimental highlander. We find again here this disease of thinking in essences, which is at the
bottom of every bourgeois mythology of man (which is why we come across it so often). The
ethnic reality of Spain is thus reduced to a vast classical ballet, a nice neat commedia dell'arte,
whose improbable typology serves to mask the real spectacle of conditions, classes and professions. For the *Blue Guide*, men exist as social entities only in trains, where they fill a 'very
mixed' Third Class. Apart from that, they are a mere introduction, they constitute a charming and fanciful decor, meant to surround the essential part of the country: its collection of
monuments.

If one excepts its wild defiles, fit for moral ejaculations. Spain according to the *Blue
Guide* knows only one type of space, that which weaves, across a few nondescript lacunae, a
close web of churches, vestries, reredoses, crosses, altar-curtains, spires (always octagonal),

sculpted groups (Family and Labour), Romanesque porches, naves and life-size crucifixes. It can be seen that all these monuments are religious, for from a bourgeois point of view it is almost impossible to conceive a History of Art which is not Christian and Roman Catholic. Christianity is the chief purveyor of tourism, and one travels only to visit churches. In the case of Spain, this imperialism is ludicrous, for Catholicism often appears there as a barbaric force which has stupidly defaced the earlier achievements of Muslim civilization: the mosque at Cordoba, whose wonderful forest of columns is at every turn obstructed by massive blocks of altars, or a colossal Virgin (set up by Franco) – denaturing the site which it aggressively dominates – all this should help the French bourgeois to glimpse at least once in his life that historically there is also a reverse side to Christianity.

Generally speaking, the *Blue Guide* testifies to the futility of all analytical descriptions, those which reject both explanations and phenomenology: it answers in fact none of the questions which a modern traveller can ask himself while crossing a countryside which is real *and which exists in time*. To select only monuments suppresses at one stroke the reality of the land and that of its people, it accounts for nothing of the present, that is, nothing historical, and as a consequence, the monuments themselves become undecipherable, therefore senseless. What is to be seen is thus constantly in the process of vanishing, and the *Guide* becomes, through an operation common to all mystifications, the very opposite of what it advertises, an agent of blindness. By reducing geography to the description of an uninhabited world of monuments, the *Blue Guide* expresses a mythology which is obsolete for a part of the bourgeoisie itself. It is unquestionable that travel has become (or become again) a method of approach based on human realities rather than 'culture': once again (as in the eighteenth century, perhaps) it is everyday life which is the main object of travel, and it is social geography, town-planning, sociology, economics which outline the framework of the actual questions asked today even by the merest layman. But as for the *Blue Guide*, it still abides by a partly superseded bourgeois mythology, that which postulated (religious) Art as the fundamental value of culture, but saw its 'riches' and 'treasures' only as a reassuring accumulation of goods (cf. the creation of museums). This behaviour expressed a double urge: to have at one's disposal a cultural alibi as ethereal as possible, and to maintain this alibi in the toils of a computable and acquisitive system, so that one could at any moment do the accounts of the ineffable. It goes without saying that this myth of travel is becoming quite anachronistic, even among the bourgeoisie, and I suppose that if one entrusted the preparation of a new guide-book to, say, the lady-editors at *L'Express* or the editors of *Match*, we would see appearing, questionable as they would still probably be, quite different countries: after the Spain of Anquetil or Larousse, would follow the Spain of Siegfried, then that of Fourastié. Notice how already, in the *Michelin Guide*, the number of bathrooms and forks indicating good restaurants is vying with that of 'artistic curiosities': even bourgeois myths have their differential geology.

It is true that in the case of Spain, the blinkered and old-fashioned character of the description is what is best suited to the latent support given by the *Guide* to Franco. Beside the historical accounts proper (which are rare and meagre, incidentally, for it is well known that History is not a good bourgeois), those accounts in which the Republicans are always '*extremists*' looting churches – but nothing on Guernica – while the good 'Nationalists', on the contrary, spend their time '*liberating*', solely by '*skilful strategic manoeuvres*' and '*heroic feats of resistance*', let me mention the flowering of a splendid myth-alibi: that of the *prosperity* of the country. Needless to say, this prosperity is 'statistical' and 'global', or to be more accurate: 'commercial'. The *Guide* does not tell us, of course, how this fine prosperity is shared out: *hierarchically*, probably, since they think it fit to tell us that '*the serious and patient effort of this people has also included the reform of its political system, in order to achieve regeneration through the loyal application of sound principles of order and hierarchy.'*

Note

1 Hachette World Guides, dubbed 'Guide Bleu'
   in French.

6

Reading architectural herstories

The discourses of gender

When I say 'gender' you think 'women'. And it is true that most gender history is written from a woman-centred perspective, but much research covers both men and women and importantly the relationships between the two. Recently, masculinity has been recognised as a topic in its own right and the emergence of Queer Studies encourages the necessary wider exploration of gender.[1] Gender has proved to be a central concept to historians, sociologists and cultural geographers as its meaning goes beyond the biological differences between male and female. Instead it connotes the cultural definitions of behaviour which are considered appropriate for male and female members of a society at any given point in time. For the purposes of this book I do want to focus on gender as regards women and explore how it becomes an important element in the social relationships which are based on the differences between the sexes. In this way gender becomes a signifier of power.[2] If gender is then a social construction it must, therefore, have a history. It is this history of gender that interfaces with our understanding of gender and architecture.

My method so far in this book has been to problematise the topic under review in each chapter and then to proceed to give examples of canonical histories and more theoretically driven writings to offer possible rereadings of these issues. This becomes more difficult when considering the relationship between gender and architectural history. First, there is the question of my gender and how the subject/object relationship, here more than anywhere in this book, overlaps through my role as author, historian and woman. Moreover, gender requires a rereading of almost the entire canon of British architectural history in the period covered in this volume. As a result I do not, as in previous chapters, present a general discussion of the issues followed by a consideration of a specific example. Instead, I want the discourses around gender to be projected back onto the other chapters in the volume in an attempt to examine the absence of 'other' voices from the histories of architecture. I have chosen two texts which offer different ways of reading the relationship between gender and architecture serve as exemplars of the range of possibilities this line of enquiry enables: one concerns the appropriation of the function of space; the other is to do with aesthetics and architecture.

Herstories

The invisibility of women in canonical histories might lead us to believe that women have no history. Surely then a female history is an essential tool in the emancipation of women? This is partly because if we have no history we are 'trapped' in the present where oppressive social relations can continue unchallenged. Furthermore, history can be seen as evidence that things can and do change.[3] But this revision of the narratives of history has its own internal problems. Assumptions that the category of 'women' can represent all women from the past and present regardless of their age, ethnicity, sexual orientation and so on merely replaces one hegemony with another. The white western male can thus be replaced by the white western feminist female – an historical construction of 'woman', but the burgeoning body of literature has ensured the diversity of the female subject.[4] It is now over a generation ago that the first feminist writings began to appear mapping out a different way of seeing and understanding cultural production and the social relationships expressed therein. Griselda Pollock and Rozsika Parker identify the crucial paradox about attitudes to women in the writing of histories, specifically here those concerned with creativity:

> Women are represented negatively, as lacking in creativity, with nothing significant to contribute, and a having no influence on the course of art. Paradoxically, to negate them women have to be acknowledged; they are mentioned in order to be categorised, set apart and marginalised. [This is] one of the major elements in the construction of the hegemony of men in cultural practices in art.'[5]

There is no doubt of the tendency to accept whatever *is* as natural, whether in regard to academic enquiry or our social systems. This is aided by our linguistic acknowledgement of woman as 'different': we use 'she' instead of the presumably neutral 'one' – in reality the white male position accepted as natural, or the hidden 'he' as the subject of all scholarly predicates – is a decided advantage, rather than merely a hindrance or subjective distortion.[6] This impacts on architectural history as well as other modes of cultural production where the white western male viewpoint is unconsciously and unquestioningly accepted as *the* viewpoint of the historian. It is, of course, élitist and therefore morally unacceptable. But it is also intellectually dishonest as it reveals the failure of history to take account of this implicit value system where we find an overlap between subject and object of historical investigation. At a moment when all disciplines are becoming more self-conscious, and aware of their presuppositions as seen in the very languages and structures of the various fields of scholarship, acceptance of 'what is' as 'natural' may be intellectually fatal, and it is certainly fatally flawed. Even in the nineteenth century John Stuart Mill saw male domination as one of a long series of social injustices that had to be overcome if a truly just social order were to be created. Following on from this, the continuing domination of white male subjectivity in the assumptions and writing of histories is part of a series of intellectual distortions which must be corrected in order to achieve a more adequate and accurate view of historical situations. Yet, there is tension in feminist methodology between representing women's lives as they experience them and the description and challenging women's oppression. Projecting our views back onto the women of Britain *c.* 1600–1840 and their relationship to architecture raises the issue of whether these women considered themselves as experiencing oppression because of their gender. We may discover if these women saw themselves as objects of gender-based oppression through diaries and other personal accounts. But, history is as much about the present as the past, so should we offer a gendered reading of their life story, regardless of the circumstances of their lives? This can lead to an uncomfortable choice whereby the historian either privileges her/his own interpretation of another's life – a hallmark of masculinist methodology – or compromises her/his commitment to challenging oppression which the historical subject may fail to identify.

I do not want here to try to assert the role of women in histories of architecture in order to begin to right this historical bias. The focus of this volume is rather on exploring the resonance between histories and theories and the effect this has on our readings of both. So I want instead to show that it is not so much the material we have that shapes our understanding of architecture, it is rather the questions we choose to ask of the archive. In this way the perceived absence of certain voices from the archive may then reveal as much as if they were present. Questions are culturally determined and it is the determinants that I want to explore. But first, why, in the early twenty-first century is this even necessary? Judy Chicago gives us some idea in her discussion of *The Dinner Party* – an installation piece that celebrates famous women from the past.

> My idea for *The Dinner Party* grew out of research into women's history that I had begun at the end of the 1960s . . . the prevailing attitude towards women's history can be best summed up by the following story. While an undergraduate at UCLA, I took a course titled the Intellectual History of Europe. The professor, a respected historian, promised that at the last class he would discuss women's contributions to Western thought. I waited eagerly all semester, and at the final meeting, the instructor strode in and announced: Women's contributions to European intellectual history/ They made none.
>
> I was devastated by his judgment, and when later my studies demonstrated that my professor's assessment did not stand up to intellectual scrutiny, I became convinced that the idea that women had no history – and the companion belief that there had never been any great women artists – was simply a prejudice elevated to intellectual dogma. I suspected that many people accepted these notions primarily because they had never been exposed to a different perspective.
>
> As I began to uncover what turned out to be a treasure trove of information about women's history, I became both empowered and inspired. My intense interest in sharing these discoveries through my art led me to wonder whether visual images might play a role in changing the prevailing views regarding women and women's history.[7]

There is no doubt that the archive concerned with women and architecture is out there, it is perhaps then more a question of how we should interrogate it, and then revise and reconfigure our histories. And we still find those who question whether this is necessary at all, as seen in this extract which appeared in a book published the same year as Chicago's:

> Poststructuralists have attempted to reformulate Enlightenment ideals about liberty, equality and fraternity in terms of a theory of the radical relativity of all thought as related to a model of oppression and victimization . . . a pernicious 'canon' . . . (now deemed an instrument of oppression) and this has been accompanied by a belittling of moral and intellectual values that for millennia constituted the core of the Western tradition. The popular phrase 'dead White male,' used to reject a work of art . . . on the basis of the gender and race of the artist, as well as the time in which *he* [my emphasis] worked – that is, before the 'canon' was assaulted by poststructuralism, – reflects this attitude.
>
> It is ironic that this orientation arises at a time in which opportunity is extended to entire categories of people who to a greater or lesser extent have been excluded from power within Western democracies. In politics more women and minorities are acquiring positions of leadership . . . In culture the art of non-Western traditions is receiving not simply more acclaim but also is being given its own prestigious institutions within the pantheon of high art . . . If Voltaire were to return among us and see these aspects of progress, all conceived in the spirit of the eighteenth-century Enlightenment that saw the birth of modern Western democracies, he undoubtedly would be extremely gratified.
>
> Yet, having reached this level of achievement . . . it is as if intellectuals have taken for granted the assumptions on which social progress has been grounded and have felt the need to proceed one step further. The problem basically resides in knowing when a

proper balance has been achieved if not in the arena of actual realization then at least in the domain of ideals and expectations.[8]

Perhaps then, on the basis of these two texts, we should all be grateful for what we are about to receive when the Western [not my capitalization] white male hegemony is ready to give it – on their terms, of course.

Gendered spaces

Mindful of the issues raised in Chapter 4 on the importance of gender performance, we can see how our expectations of gender can influence our readings of space and its role in the construction of social identities through architecture. Doreen Massey encapsulates the appropriation of space by a specific male social group in this anecdote

> I remember very clearly a sight which often used to strike me when I was nine or ten years old. I lived on the outskirts of Manchester, and 'Going into Town' was a relatively big occasion; it took over half an hour and we went on the top deck of a bus. On the way into town we would cross the wide, shallow valley of the River Mersey, and my memory is of dank, muddy fields spreading away into a cold, misty distance. And all of it – all of these acres of Manchester – was divided up into football pitches and rugby pitches. And on Saturdays, which was when we went into Town, the whole vast area would be covered with hundreds of little people, all running around after balls, as far as they eye could see . . .
>
> I remember all of this very sharply. And I remember, too, it striking me very clearly – even then as a puzzled, slightly thoughtful little girl – that all this huge stretch of the Mersey flood plain had been entirely given over to boys . . .
>
> I did not go to those playing fields – they seemed barred, another world . . . But there were other places to which I did go, and yet where I still felt that they were not mine, or at least they were designed to, or had the effect of, firmly letting me know my conventional subordination.[9]

Griselda Pollock shows us the 'other' side of the coin, as it were, the spaces of femininity

> The spaces of femininity operated not only at the level of what is represented, the drawing-room or sewing-room. The spaces of femininity are those from which femininity is lived as a positionality in discourse and social practice. They are the product of a lived sense of social locatedness, mobility and visibility, in the social relations of seeing and being seen. Shaped within the sexual politics of looking they demarcate a particular social organization of the gaze which itself works back to secure a particular social ordering of sexual difference. Femininity is both the condition and the effect . . .
>
> Woman was defined by this other, non-social [interior] space of sentiment and duty from which money and power were banished. Men, however, moved freely between spheres while women were supposed to occupy domestic space alone. Men came home to be themselves but in equally constraining roles as husbands and fathers, to engage in affective relationship . . .[10]

It is not then difficult to see how the perceptions of space can influence our readings of architecture as regards gender especially in terms of its function.[11]

Different canons

Jennifer Bloomer sums up the other way of reading the relationship between gender and architecture. Here she focuses on the classical style, which as we have seen is privileged over all others in histories of the period under review in this book. I have already argued that classicism is representative of a hegemony of the ruling élite through its associative values with the culture and society of antiquity. Bloomer takes this argument further by exploring the notion of sexual difference:

> Western architecture, is by its very nature, a phallocentric discourse: containing, ordering, and respecting through firmness commodity and beauty; consisting of orders, entablature, and architrave; base, shaft, and capital and nave, choir, and apse; father, son and spirit, world without end. Amen
>
> In the Garden of Eden there was no architecture. The necessity for architecture arose with the ordination of sin and shame, with dirty bodies. The fig leaf was a natural first impulse towards architecture, accustomed as it was to shading its vulvate fruit, its trunk and roots a complex woven construction of undulating forms. Was it the fig tree that was hacked to build the primitive hut (that precursor of classical architecture)?
>
> The primitive hut and all its begettings constitute a house of many mansions, a firm commodious, and beautiful erection. The primitive hut is the house of my fathers.[12]

Bloomer rightly detects a note of anxiety in the construction of this male canon. The opposites of the stylistic terminology reveal this anxiety through language for instance firmness/limpness, beauty/ugliness, erection/demolition. The order of the classical (male) canon is polarised by the disorder of the non-classical (female canon). We need then to reconsider our value judgements and resist the privileging of order, proportion and rule of the classical over other styles and reconfigure the canon to encompass creative practice by women. In this way the antimony identified through a psychoanalytic analysis of gender relationship can be averted.

> The problem of dealing with difference without constituting an opposition may just be what feminism is all about (might be what psycho-analysis is all about). Difference produces great anxiety. Polarisation, which is the theatrical representation of difference, tames and binds that anxiety. The classic example is sexual difference, which is represented as polar opposition (active-passive, energy-matter, and all the other polar oppositions that share the trait of taming the anxiety that specific differences provoke).[13]

There are two main strands to come out of this brief survey. Although it is now clear that women have been involved in and around architecture in ways beyond our socially predetermined notions of gender roles or performance, there is little point in trying to look for great female architects, as the criteria for greatness or genius was laid down by men and still has resonance today. That said, our constructions of genius are being challenged and reconfigured together with the value system attached to it.[14] Moreover, we have also seen how our culturally determined expectations of gender can influence histories of architecture. If, however, we remove architecture from the aesthetic realm where it is separate from any social context and see architecture as production we can accept the Marxist view that architecture is the result of social relations which have formed the conditions of production. So it is not so much the consumers of architecture but the social production which is important as it is then located within the whole of society rather than select groups based on such categories as gender, class or race. In this way architecture encodes various conventions which help set out a series of social processes or ideologies. In order to understand our role in all of this as subjects and objects we need to be aware of the cultural practices in and around architecture. This can be achieved through a system of signs and psychoanalysis. Marxist theory might enable us to explore the historical and economic situation but we need psychoanalytic models through which to begin to understand the relationship between these ideologies and sexuality where the visual becomes important as a means of expressing sexual difference. It is important that we remember that this kind of historical approach makes gender an essential tool in historical analysis rather than just a way of narrating 'herstory', and we can then change the present by rethinking the ways is which we construct the past and *read* its histories. Gender *does* have a history, and it isn't all about women.

This volume concludes with two articles which address different aspects of reading gender and architectural history. They are intended to complement rather than critique each other and, I hope, provide an extra layer of analysis and debate to the other chapters and extracts in this volume. In *Room at the Top* Denise Scott Brown discusses her career as a female architect and the different perceptions of her and her husband, who is also a practising architect. Alice Friedman discusses a sixteenth-century architectural patron and head of household Bess of Hardwick, offering a rereading of her house Hardwick Hall through a consideration of gender relations expressed through architectural space and style. These texts combine with the issues outlined in this chapter to show how gender can redirect the narrative structures and help our reading of architectural history in terms of biography, style, social rituals and cultural practices.

Notes

1 See for instance *inter alia* H Brod (ed.), *The Making Of Masculinities: The new men's Studies*, Boston, MA and Allen and Unwin, London: M Roper and J Tosh, *Manful Assertions: Masculinities in Britain since 1800*, London, Routledge, 1991; J Butler, *Gender Trouble: Feminism and the subversion of identity*, New York and London, Routledge, 1990; H L Moore, *A Passion for Difference: Essays in anthropology and gender*, Cambridge, Polity, 1994.

2 On this point see J M Bennett 'Feminism and History' *Gender and History*, 1, 1989, pp. 251–272.

3 On this point see G Jordan and C Weedon, *Cultural Politics: Class, gender, race in the postmodern world*, Oxford, Blackwell, 1995.

4 See for instance bell hooks, *Feminist Theory: From margin to centre*, Boston, South End, 1984; C Hall, *White Male and Middle Class: Explorations in feminism and history*, Cambridge, Polity 1992; V Ware, *Beyond the Pale: White women, racism and history*, London, Verso, 1992.

5 G Pollock and R Parker, *Old Mistresses: Women, art and ideology*, London, Routledge and Kegan Paul, 1981.

6 On this point see K Canning, 'Feminist History after the Linguistic Turn: Historicising discourse and experience', *Signs*, 19, 1994, pp. 368–404.

7 J Chicago, *The Dinner Party*, Harmondsworth, Penguin, 1996, pp. 3–4.

8 R Etlin, *In Defense of Humanism*, Cambridge, Cambridge University Press, 1996, p. 74.

9 D Massey, *Space, Place and Gender*, Cambridge, Polity, 1994.

10 G Pollock, 'Modernity and the Spaces of Femininity' in *Vision and Difference: Femininity, feminism and histories of art*, London, Routledge, 1992.

11 This is explored in B Colomina (ed.), *Sexuality and Space*, Princeton, Princeton University Press, 1992.

12 J Bloomer 'Big Jugs' in A Kroker and M Kroker (eds), *The Hysterical Male: New feminist theory*, London, Macmillan, 1991.

13 J Gallop, *Feminism and Psychoanalysis: The daughter's seduction*, London, Macmillan, 1982.

14 See for instance my essay 'Defining Femininity: Women and the country house' in D Arnold, *The Georgian Country House: Architecture, landscape and society*, Stroud and New York, Sutton, 1998.

Sexism and the star system in architecture

Denise Scott Brown

Most professional women can recount 'horror stories' about discrimination they have suffered during their careers. My stories include social trivia as well as grand trauma. But some less common forms of discrimination came my way when, in mid-career, I married a colleague and we joined our professional lives just as fame (though not fortune) hit him. I watched as he was manufactured into an architectural guru before my eyes and, to some extent, on the basis of our joint work and the work of our firm.

When Bob and I married, in 1967, I was an associate professor. I had taught at the Universities of Pennsylvania and Berkeley, and had initiated the first program in the new school of architecture at UCLA. I had tenure. My publication record was respectable; my students, enthusiastic. My colleagues, mostly older than I, accorded me the same respect they showed each other, and I had walked the same corridors of power they had (or thought I had).

The first indication of my new status came when an architect whose work I had reviewed said, 'We at the office think it was Bob writing, using your name.' By the time we wrote *Learning from Las Vegas,* our growing experience with incorrect attributions prompted Bob to include a note at the beginning of the book asking that the work and ideas not be attributed to him alone and describing the nature of our collaboration and the roles played by individuals in our firm. His request was almost totally ignored. A body of theory and design in architecture apparently must be associated by architecture critics with an individual; the more emotional their criticism, the stronger is its focus on one person.

To avoid misattributions, our office provides an information sheet describing our preferred forms of attribution – the work to our firm, the writing to the person who signed the article or book. The result is that some critics now make a pro forma attribution in an inconspicuous place; then, in the body of the text, the *design* of the work and the *ideas* in the writing are attributed to Robert Venturi.

In the Japanese journal *Architecture and Urbanism,* for example, Hideki Shimizu wrote:

> A review of his plan for the Crosstown Community that Venturi is not so much affording his theory new development as giving the source of his architectural approach clear form in a fundamental attitude toward city planning. . . . Venturi's position in relation to city planning is the thing that enables him to develop his basic posture in relation to architecture. The Crosstown Community reveals a profound mood of affectionate emotion.[1]

This would be fine except that the Crosstown Community was my work and was attributed as such in our book; I doubt whether, over a period of three years, Bob spent two afternoons on it.

When Praeger published a series of interviews with architects,[2] my name was omitted from the dust jacket. We complained and Praeger added my name, although objecting that this would spoil the cover design. On the inside flap, however, 'eight architects' and 'the men behind' modern architecture were mentioned. As nine were listed on the front, I gather I am still left out.[3]

There have been exceptions. Ada Louise Huxtable has never put a foot wrong with me. She works hard at reporting our ideas correctly too. A few critics have changed their methods of attribution in response to our requests, but at least one, in 1971, was on the warpath in the opposite direction, out to prove that Great Art can only be made by one Man, and that Robert Venturi (read Howard Roark) is led astray when 'he joins his wife Denise Scott Brown in praising certain suburban practices.' And the consort and collaborator of a famous architect wrote to me that, although she sees herself in his work, the work owes its quality to his individual talents and not to her collaboration. When real artists collaborate, she claimed, their separate identities remain; she gave as an example the *lieder* of Schubert and Goethe. We countered with the Beatles.

The social trivia (what Africans call *petty apartheid*) continue too: 'wives' dinners' ('We'll just let the architects meet together, my dear'); job interviews where the presence of 'the architect's wife' distressed the board; dinners I must not attend because an influential member of the client group wants 'the architect' as her date; Italian journalists who ignore Bob's request that they address me because I understand more Italian than he does; the tunnel vision of students toward Bob; the 'so you're the architect!' to Bob, and the well-meant 'so you're an architect too?' to me.[4]

These experiences have caused me to fight, suffer doubt and confusion, and expend too much energy. 'I would be *pleased* if my work were attributed to my husband,' says the designer wife of an architect. And a colleague asks, 'Why do you worry about these things? We know you're good. You know your real role in the office and in teaching. Isn't that enough?' I doubt whether it would be enough for my male colleagues. What would Peter Eisenman do if his latest article were attributed to his co-editor, Kenneth Frampton? Or Vincent Scully, if the book on Newport houses were attributed to his co-author, Antoinette Downing – with perhaps a parenthesis to the effect that this was not intended to slight the contribution of others?

So I complain to the editor who refers to 'Venturi's ducks,' informing him that I invented the 'duck.' (He prints my letter under the title 'Less is a Bore,' a quotation from my husband.) But my complaints makes critics angry, and some have formed lasting hostilities against both of us on this score. Architects cannot afford hostile critics. And anyway I begin to dislike my own hostile persona.

That is when self-doubt and confusion arise. 'My husband is a better designer than I am. And I'm a pretty dull thinker.' The first is true, the second probably not. I try to counter with further questions: 'How come, then, we work so well together, capping each other's ideas? If my ideas are no good, why are they quoted by the critics (even though attributed to Bob)?'

We ourselves cannot tease our contributions apart. Since 1960 we have collaborated in the development of ideas and since 1967 we have collaborated in architectural practice. As chief designer, Bob takes final design responsibility. On some projects, I am closely involved and see many of my ideas in the final design; on others, hardly at all. In a few, the basic idea (what Lou Kahn called the What) was mine. All of our firm's urban planning work, and the urban design related to it, is my responsibility; Bob is virtually not involved with it, although other architects in the firm are.[5]

As in all firms, our ideas are translated and added to by our co-workers, particularly our associates of long standing. Principals and assistants may alternate in the roles of creator and critic. The star system, which sees the firm as a pyramid with a Designer on top, has little to do with today's complex relations in architecture and construction. But as sexism defines me as a scribe, typist, and photographer to my husband, so the star system defines our associates as 'second bananas' and our staff as pencils.

Short of sitting under the drawing board while we are around it, there is no way for the critics to separate us out. Those who do, hurt me in particular but others in the firm, too, and by ignoring as unimportant those aspects of our work where Bob has interfaced with others, they narrow his span to meet the limits of their perception.

Although I had been concerned with my role as a woman years before the rebirth of the movement, I was not pushed to action until my experience as an architect's wife. In 1973 I gave a talk on sexism and the star system to the Alliance of Women in Architecture, in New York City. I requested that the meeting be open to women only, probably incorrectly, but for the same emotional reasons (including hurt pride) that make national movements initially stress separatism. Nevertheless, about six men came. They hid in the back and sides of the audience. The hundred or so women identified strongly with my experience; 'Me too!' 'My God, you too?' echoed everywhere. We were soon high on our shared woe and on the support we felt for and from each other. Later, it struck me that the males had grown glummer as we grew more enthusiastic. They seemed unable to understand what was exercising us.

Since then I have spoken at several conferences on women in architecture. I now receive inquiries of interest for deanships and departmental chairs several times a year. I find myself on committees where I am the only woman and there is one black man. We two tokens greet each other wryly. I am frequently invited to lecture at architecture schools, 'to be a role model for our girls.' I am happy to do this for their young women but I would rather be asked purely because my work is interesting.

Finally, I essayed my own interpretation of sexism and the star system in architecture. Budd Schulberg defines 'Star Quality' as a 'mysterious amalgam of self-love, vivacity, style and sexual promise.'[6] Though his definition catches the spirit of architectural stardom, it omits the fact that stardom is something done to a star by others. Stars cannot create themselves. Why do architects need to create stars? Because, I think, architecture deals with unmeasurables. Although architecture is both science and art, architects stand or fall in their own estimation and in that of their peers by whether they are 'good designers,' and the criteria for this are ill-defined and undefinable.

Faced with unmeasurables, people steer their way by magic. Before the invention of navigational instruments, a lady was carved on the prow of the boat to help sailors cross the ocean; and architects, grappling with the intangibles of design, select a guru whose work gives them personal help in areas where there are few rules to follow. The guru, as architectural father figure, is subject to intense hate and love; either way, the relationship is personal, it can only be a one-to-one affair. This accounts for the intensely *ad hominem* stance of some of 'Venturi's' critics. If the attribution were correct the tone would be more even, as one cannot easily wax emotional over several people. I suspect, too, that for male architects the guru must be male. There can be no Mom and Pop gurus in architecture. The architectural prima donnas are all male.

Next, a colleague having her own difficulties in an American Studies department brought the work of Lionel Tiger to my attention. In *Men in Groups*, he writes that men run in male packs and ambitious women must understand this.[7] I recalled, as well, the exclamation of the French architect Ionel Schein, writing in *Le Carré Bleu* in the 1950s: 'The so-called studio spirit is merely the spirit of a caste.' This brings to mind the upper-class origins of the American architecture profession, the differences between upper-class and middle-class attitudes to women, and the strong similarities that still exist today between the architecture profession and a men's club.

American architectural education was modeled on the turn-of-the-century, French Ecole des Beaux-Arts. It was a rip-roaring place and loads of fun, but its organization was strongly authoritarian, especially in its system for judging student work. The authoritarian personalities and the we-happy-few culture engendered by the Beaux-Arts stayed on in Modern architecture long after the Beaux-Arts architectural philosophy had been abandoned; the architecture club still excludes women.

The heroically original, Modern architectural revolutionary with his avant-garde technology, out to save the masses through mass production, is a macho image if ever there was one. It sits strangely on the middle-aged reactionaries who bear its mantle today. A more conserving and nurturing (female?) outlook is being recommended to the profession by urban planners and ecologists, in the name of social justice and to save the planet. Women may yet ride in on this trend.

The critic in architecture is often the scribe, historian, and kingmaker for a particular group. These activities entitle him to join the 'few', even though he pokes them a little. His other satisfaction comes from making history in his and their image. The kingmaker-critic is, of course, male; though he may write of the group as a group, he would be a poor fool in his eyes and theirs if he tried to crown the whole group king. There is even less psychic reward in crowning a female king.

In these deductions, my thinking parallels that of Cynthia F. Epstein, who writes that elevation within the professions is denied women for reasons that include 'the colleague system,' which she describes as a men's club, and 'the sponsor-protégé relationship, which determines access to the highest levels of most professions.' Epstein suggests that the high-level sponsor would, like the kingmaker-critic, look foolish if he sponsored a female and, in any case, his wife would object.[8]

You would think that the last element of Schulberg's definition of a star, 'sexual promise,' would have nothing to do with architecture. But I wondered why there was a familiar ring to the tone – hostile, lugubriously self-righteous, yet somehow envious – of letters to the editor that follow anything our firm publishes, until I recognized it as the tone middle America employs in letters to the editor in pornography. Architects who write angry letters about our work apparently feel we are architectural panderers, or at least we permit ourselves liberties they would not take, but possibly envy. Here is one, by an English architecture instructor: 'Venturi has a niche, all right, but it's down there with the flagellant, the rubber-fetishist and the Blagdon Nude Amateur Rapist.' These are written by men, and they are written to or of Bob alone.

I have suggested that the star system, which is unfair to many architects, is doubly hard on women in a sexist environment, and that, at the upper levels of the profession, the female architect who works with her husband will be submerged in his reputation. My interpretations are speculative. We have no sociology of architecture. Architects are unaccustomed to social analysis and mistrust it; sociologists have fatter fish to fry. But I do get support for my thesis from some social scientists, from ironists in architecture, from many women architects, from some members of my firm, and from my husband.

Should there be a star system? It is unavoidable, I think, owing to the prestige we give design in architecture. But the schools can and should reduce the importance of the star system by broadening the student's view of the profession to show value in its other aspects. Heaven knows, skills other than design are important to the survival of architecture firms. The schools should also combat the student's sense of inadequacy about design, rather than, as now, augmenting it through wrongly authoritarian and judgmental educational techniques.

With these changes, architects would feel less need for gurus, and those they would need would be different – more responsible and humane than gurus are asked to be today.

To the extent that gurus are unavoidable and sexism is rampant in the architecture profession, my personal problem of submersion through the star system is insoluble. I could improve my chances for recognition as an individual if I returned to teaching or if I abandoned collaboration with my husband. The latter has happened to some extent as our office has grown and our individual responsibilities within it take more of our time. We certainly spend less time at the drawing board together and, in general, less time writing. But this is a pity, as our joint work feeds us both.

On the larger scene, all is not lost. Not all architects belong to the men's club; more architects than before are women; some critics are learning; the AIA actively wants to help; and most architects, in theory at least, would rather not practice discrimination if someone will prove to them that they have been and will show them how to stop.

The foregoing is an abridgment of an article I wrote in 1975. I decided not to publish it at the time, because I judged that strong sentiments on feminism in the world of architecture would ensure my ideas a hostile reception, which could hurt my career and the prospects of my firm. However, I did share the manuscript with friends and, in *samizdat*, it achieved a following of sorts. Over the years I have received letters asking for copies.

In 1975, I recounted my first experience of the new surge of women in architecture. The ratio of men to women is now 1 : 1 in many schools. The talent and enthusiasm of these young women has burst creatively into the profession. At conferences today I find many women participants; some have ten years or more in the field.

Architecture, too, has changed since I wrote. My hope that architects would heed the social planners' dicta did not pan out, and women did not ride in on that trend. Postmodernism did change the views of architects but not in the way I had hoped. Architects lost their social concern; the architect as macho revolutionary was succeeded by the architect as *dernier cri* of the art world; the cult of personality increased. This made things worse for women because, in architecture, the *dernier cri* is as male as the prima donna.

The rise in female admissions and the move to the right in architecture appear to be trends in opposite directions, but they are, in fact, unrelated because they occur at either end of the seniority spectrum. The women entrants are young; the cult of personality occurs at the top. The two trends have yet to meet. When they do, it will be fascinating to see what happens. Meanwhile, affirmative action programs have helped small female-owned firms get started but may have hindered the absorption of women into the mainstream of the profession, because women who integrate large existing practices gain no affirmative action standing unless they own 51 per cent of the firm.

During the eighties there has been a gradual increase of women architects in academe. (I suspect that the growth has been slower than in other professions.)

I now receive fewer offers of deanships, probably because there are more female candidates than before and because word is out that I am too busy to accept. I have little time to lecture. As our office has grown, Bob and I have found more, rather than less, opportunity to work together, since some of our responsibilities have been delegated to the senior associates and project directors who form the core of our firm.

During this period, we have ceased to be regarded as young turks and have seen a greater acceptance of our ideas than we would have dreamed possible. Ironically, a citation honoring Bob for his 'discovery of the everyday American environment' was written in 1979 by the same critic who, in 1971, judged Bob lacking for sharing my interest in everyday landscape.

For me, things are much the same at the top as they were. The discrimination continues at the rate of about one incident a day. Journalists who approach our firm seem to feel that they will not be worth their salt if they do not 'deliver Venturi.' The battle for turf and the race for status among critics still require the beating-off of women. In the last twenty years, I cannot recall one major article by a high-priest critic about a woman architect. Young women critics, as they enter the fray, become as macho as the men and for the same reasons – to survive and win in the competitive world of critics.

For a few years, writers on architecture were interested in sexism and the feminist movement and wanted to discuss them with me. In a joint interview, they would ask Bob about work and question me about my 'woman's problem.' 'Write about my work!' I would plead, but they seldom did.

Some young women in architecture question the need for the feminist movement, claiming to have experienced no discrimination. My concern is that, although school is not a nondiscriminatory environment, it is probably the least discriminatory one they will encounter in their careers. By the same token, the early years in practice bring little differentiation between men and women. It is as they advance that difficulties arise, when firms and clients shy away from entrusting high-level responsibility to women. On seeing their male colleagues draw out in front of them, women who lack a feminist awareness are likely to feel that their failure to achieve is their own fault.

Over the years, it has slowly dawned on me that the people who cause my painful experiences are ignorant and crude. They are the critics who have not read enough and the clients who do not know why they have come to us. I have been helped to realise this by noticing that the scholars whose work we most respect, the clients whose projects intrigue us, and the patrons whose friendship inspires us, have no problem understanding my role. They are the sophisticates. Partly through them I gain heart and realise that, over the last twenty years, I have managed to do my work and, despite some sliding, to achieve my own self-respect.

Notes

1 Hideki Shimizu, 'Criticism,' *A + U (Architecture and Urbanism)* 47 (November 1974): 3.
2 John W. Cook and Heinrich Klotz, *Conversations with Architects* (New York; Praeger Publishers, Inc., 1973).
3 The architects originally listed were Philip Johnson, Kevin Roche, Paul Rudolph, Bertrand Goldberg, Morris Lapidus, Louis Kahn, Charles Moore, and Robert Venturi. Also omitted from the dust jacket was the architect Alan Lapidus, interviewed with his father, Morris. Alan did not complain; at least he's up there with those men behind the architecture.
4 The head of a New York architecture school reached me on the phone because Bob was unavailable: 'Denise, I'm embarrassed to be speaking to you because we're giving a party for QP [a well-known local architect] and we're asking Bob but not you. You see, you *are* a friend of QP and you *are* an architect, but you're also a wife, and we're not asking wives.'

5 Bob's intellectual focus comes mainly from the arts and from the history of architecture. He is more of a specialist than I am. My artistic and intellectual concerns were formed before I met Bob (and indeed before I came to America), but they were the base of our friendship as academic colleagues. As a planner, my professional span includes the social sciences and other planning-related disciplines that I have tried to meld into our critique and theory of architecture. As an architect, my interests range widely but I am probably most useful at the initial stages of a design as we work to develop the *parti*.
6 Budd Schulberg, 'What Price Glory?,' *New Republic* 168 (6 and 13 January 1973): 27–31.
7 Lionel Tiger, *Men in Groups* (New York: Random House, 1969).
8 Cynthia F. Epstein, 'Encountering the Male Establishment: Sex-Status Limits on Women's Careers in the Profession,' *American Journal of Sociology* 75 (May 1970): 965–82.

Planning and representation in the early modern country house

Alice T Friedman

In the history of English architecture, the period from 1590 to 1620 is characterized by the gradual ascendance of Palladian planning over the conventions of medieval English tradition. This shift in approach, which occurred in the plan of the English country house more than two decades before it appeared in elevation, focused on the handling of the great hall and its subsidiary spaces. In a number of prominent new houses of the period, the traditional access of this double-height space along a narrow screens passage and through a tripartite screen at one end – an arrangement still found, for example, at Longleat in the 1560s – gave way to an entrance door on axis that opened directly into the great hall. While such historians as Sir John Summerson and Mark Girouard have paid a great deal of attention to these changes as stylistic and even socioeconomic developments, no significant analysis has yet been proposed of the roles either of the patrons or of their programs (broadly defined to include both conscious and unconscious goals) in the making of these pivotal buildings.[1] This lack of attention is especially surprising given that Hardwick Hall (1590–97), the earliest of them, was built for a woman whose status as the head of her own household marked both her and it as unconventional and whose very role as an architectural patron transgressed the values and gender categories of her time. In this paper, I propose to reexamine these stylistic shifts through the lens of convention and unconventionality in planning techniques, gender relations, and household structure. Using household orders (written descriptions of the tasks of all household members including family and servants), letters, diaries, and handbooks of advice, I will trace the ideological context in which domestic planning ordinarily took place and reconstruct the attitudes toward the family, sexuality, and the female body – with particular attention to sight, spectatorship, and display – that structured these conventions. This approach suggests that gender played a subtle yet pronounced role in monumental domestic architecture that surpassed the interests and tastes of the individual architect or builder. Because design typology depends on conventional social relations, it is evident from the cases presented here that the destabilizing of conventional patterns that resulted from the presence of a female patron opened the way for the unexpected, including experiments in design that might not have been proposed in a more typical and thus more highly predetermined cultural and visual environment.[2]

Discussions of female spectatorship among feminist film critics over the last fifteen years have relentlessly pursued the elusive problem of gender and visual representation through various intriguing, but ultimately unsatisfactory, models in linguistic, psychoanalytic, and narrational convention. Early enthusiasm for a feminist critical method derived from Lacan and centred around his description of the role of the gaze in structuring both representation and identity – as outlined most notably in Laura Mulvey's 'Visual Pleasure and Narrative Cinema' of 1975 – inevitably reached an impasse due to the theory's inability to account satisfactorily for female spectatorship. Mulvey's reply to those critics who raised the problem of the female spectator fell back on an interpretive model drawn from post-structuralist literary criticism, the notion of oscillating identifications between the various roles offered by conventional narrative structure, thus diluting her original contention. Similarly, E. Ann Kaplan's 'Is the Gaze Male?' seemed to ask the right question but equivocated on the issue of female subjectivity; she tentatively proposed a model of maternal power drawn from work on object relations to theorize a parallel (yet, in the end, secondary and almost apologetic) role for the female spectator.[3] By adhering closely to psychoanalytic paradigms, these critical interventions failed to comprehend female agency, identity, and pleasure. Still more frustrating, particularly for the cultural historian, has been the apparent inadequacy of psychoanalytic and linguistic theory to account for the power of institutional and cultural systems in the past, despite the example (albeit not a feminist one) offered by Foucault.[4]

Nevertheless, some recent critical writing in feminist film theory does suggest certain points of departure for cultural, in particular architectural, analysis. Kaja Silverman's 'Fassbinder and Lacan: A Reconsideration of Gaze, Look and Image' takes the Lacanian model in a different direction.[5] Silverman shifts attention from the identity of the spectator to the constitution of the image, focusing on the processes through which identities are constructed and represented within visual culture. Her analysis, based on a close reading of Lacan's *Four Fundamental Concepts of Psychoanalysis*, rests on a key distinction between *look*, 'seeing' from the myriad viewpoints of individual subjects, and gaze, a more sustained, all-encompassing, and thus more menacing operation of vision that implies disembodied and transcendent authority, surveillance, and, ultimately, the creation of categories that distinguish between conformity and transgression.[6] Through Lacan, Silverman points to the role of convention in the formation of images and to the highly contested operations of vision and visuality that confer authority (and powerlessness). Her analysis calls attention to the role of the object in forming both its own image and that of the spectator. Moreover, by stressing the notion that seeing and being seen are reciprocal positions in the same operation, she returns us to the dual nature of representation: at once inscribing the image of the thing represented and revealing its own culturally constituted structure.[7]

Such a strategy has a number of potential applications for feminist architectural theory. The persistence of a naturalized social history of architecture, which proposes that typical forms are an inevitable, logical response to natural conditions and preexisting structures, has obscured the role that architecture – as representation and as convention – plays in the cultural system. Within a naturalized architectural history and criticism, moreover, the representation (or, more accurately, the marginalization) of women in the established order has come to appear inevitable. Images of women as essentially recessive, nurturing, and domestic or as complicit, masquerading objects of narcissism and desire persist unchallenged. Here feminist film theory's emphasis on vision has a significant bearing on architectural experience. Not only can architecture control, and limit, physical movement (and inevitably, of course, control the faculty of sight as part of this physical experience), it can also create an arena and a frame for those who inhabit its spaces. Through screening, sight lines, contrasts of scale, lighting, and other devices, architecture literally stages the value system of a culture, foregrounding certain activities and persons and obscuring others. These attributes of built form were briefly suggested by Griselda Pollock in 'Modernity and the Spaces of Femininity,' a first step toward examining the role of the nineteenth-century city in representing and controlling the status of women as spectators and as objects of sight in the public arena.[8] My attempt here is to establish the outlines of an interpretive method in the area of domestic architecture, one that would account for the persistence of convention in visual culture while also pointing to the destabilizing effects of cultural change, particularly in gender relations. Furthermore, by emphasizing the constructed nature of spectatorship and spectacle in early modern England, I hope to make a more general point about architecture as representation, that is, as a medium in which function and imagery are viewed not as separate but as overlaid aspects of a system through which meaning is constituted.

[. . .]

Hardwick Hall must be read in this context.[9] Bess had begun restoring and enlarging her ancestral manor house at Hardwick in the late 1580s (during a time when she was officially separated from the earl); however, in 1590, after Shrewsbury's death, she turned her attention to another project, commissioning an enormous new house from the fashionable architect Robert Smythson, builder of Longleat and Wollaton. Hardwick Hall represents a watershed in English architecture, not only because its patron was a woman, but because it radically altered the typology of the English country house through its most distinctive feature, the form and placement of the great hall. By situating the great hall at the center of a symmetrical plan and providing a means of direct visual and physical access to it, Smythson and his client openly defied tradition, constituting both a new form and a new meaning for the country house.

Castles and fortified manor houses, distinguished by their imposing size and defensibility, had existed in England since the Norman Conquest, and the roots of their characteristic formal elements – the great hall and the tower – can be traced to Roman precedents.[10] The form of the great hall had evolved over centuries to serve the functional, ceremonial, and symbolic needs of the medieval household. The porch, passage, and screen limited access by establishing a series of barriers and checkpoints for visitors entering the household. Security was maintained less by surveillance over the house as a whole than by the disorienting effects of a mazelike path from one room or area of the estate to another. Visitors and residents alike moved through an environment in which they could never step back to survey the overall arrangement of space except in specific places devoted to spectacle: the courtyard, the great hall, and, later, the gallery and great chamber. In the hall, the ample light from the large windows, the raised dais, the unbroken sight lines, and the high vaulted ceiling created the ideal stage for the performance of rituals of service and hospitality, leaving the onlookers with a forceful impression of power and authority.

Although the need for active military defense of land and property subsided during the Tudor regime, the dominant military model and the disproportionate number of male servants in the great households continued well into the seventeenth century.[11] Yet with the gradual disappearance of the old feudal order, the large aristocratic household became obsolete and the focus of its activities had to be broadened to include a new range of social and economic pursuits. This necessitated changes in both the outward appearance of the great houses and in the size and variety of interior living spaces. Still more erosive of tradition, a new order of clients was commissioning large houses and for different reasons than had motivated the nobility or members of the court: the upper gentry and London-based professionals began to build country houses as places for leisure and as a form of display.[12] Yet despite their smaller households and their emphasis on entertainment and family privacy, these builders often replicated older ceremonial and symbolic forms such as the great hall and tower. The persistence of these emblems of authority is also noticeable in renovated family seats, such as Haddon Hall and Penshurst Castle, where great halls, turrets, and armories were preserved and valued well into the seventeenth century.

Tending an apparently antithetical direction, contemporary interest in Italian Renaissance architecture, especially northern Italian and specifically Palladian examples, ran high among architects, craftsmen, and educated patrons in court circles. Numerous sketches for country houses with distinctly un-English plans, derived from the works of Palladio and Serlio, appear in the portfolios of Smythson and other architects during this period.[13] Architectural treatises and handbooks on the topic fill the libraries of patrons and amateurs.[14] Yet while many builders had, since mid-century, incorporated isolated ornamental elements of Italianate classicism into their houses, none had gone so far as to replace the highly special-ized form of the hall with the ordered symmetries and open spaces of the axial or central plan.[15] Loss of the aura of tradition associated with these conventional forms – an indis-pensable ingredient in the representation of power in this period – was apparently too great a risk. Wollaton Hall (1580–88), built by Smythson for Sir Francis Willoughby, is an impor-tant transitional example of this phenomenon. The house combines many aspects of the traditional ground-floor plan, including the screens passage, screen, and great hall, with a new compactness and axial planning in an upper-floor plan derived from Palladian models. Wollaton's exterior also integrates the two traditions, creating a characteristically late-Elizabethan mixture of superimposed medieval and classicizing images.

Turning from Wollaton back to Hardwick Hall – both the work of the same architect – we must ask whether it can be simple coincidence that the first break with traditional planning in England occurs in a country house built for a woman. To understand the design of Hardwick fully, we have to remember that in the spatial hierarchy of the country house only the master had access to all spaces; here the master was the mistress. Bess, as head of the household, oversaw the activities of her servants within her home and throughout her vast estates. She had learned the lessons of gender and power firsthand. In her earlier married life she had lived quite conventionally and, like others of her class, often felt the strain of con-flicting expectations about money and power in her husbands' households. Caught more than once in a web of household intrigue – one former servant described her home as a 'hell' in which 'her ladyship had not one about her which faithfully love and honour in deed' – Bess resolved to keep a firm grip on the reins of power in her own home at Hardwick.[16] Like the queen (whose methods she knew well as a frequent petitioner at court and former lady-in-waiting), she understood that she could not rely solely on the traditional system of allegiances or on the inherited rituals of dominance to maintain control. Instead, she capi-talized on her ability to see and be seen, flaunting her power and undermining the challenges of others. Moreover, Bess invented her own new imagery, employing a strategy similar to that of the queen, making subtle but fundamental shifts in design and household organization that altered the meaning of traditional forms.

At Hardwick, the hall – whose patriarchal significance Bess surely viewed in a different light than did her male counterparts – became an open room entered directly from the front door, with a waist-high screen and a vestigial, strictly symbolic, screens passage. Only the lower servants ate their meals here; the upper servants, whose number included more women than in other households, retired to dining rooms on the second floor, one for men and one for women, adjacent to Bess's own.[17] Thus, while the hall and its occupants remained at the center of the house, status shifted to the spaces above. The actual change in architectural effect, though visually striking, was functionally minor – indeed, in daily use its effects could be virtually ignored – but it nonetheless represented a radical break with the demands of both planning convention and representation.

This is a crucial point. I am not arguing here that Bess of Hardwick consciously saw her status as a female patron as an opportunity to alter the form of the hall nor that her house-hold's use of the hall differed significantly from that of her contemporaries. No evidence exists for either assertion. On the contrary, Bess was much too cautious about her own status to cast off ritual and much too protective of the future of her children and descendants (notably, her son William Cavendish and her granddaughter Arabella Stuart) to propose a radical departure from convention. Bess built Hardwick with these descendants in mind and she no doubt anticipated its use by a more conventional household than her own. Nevertheless, it was Bess who was the client and Bess whose image (albeit an image strongly tied to both the past and the future) it represented. As such, the image of patriarchal and military power adhering to the hall could only have provided a very general outline into which Bess and her architect slipped the far more flexible and less gendered image of the powerful, perhaps androgynous courtly patron represented by the axial Palladian plan. In so doing, she undermined the conventional reading of the hall, suppressing gendered imagery while taking care to preserve all the traditional elements, both functional and symbolic, intact.[18]

Among Elizabethan and Jacobean country houses, Hardwick is distinguished by the rationality of its design.[19] As is clear even to the casual visitor, the three stories of the house were each designed to accommodate a different sort of activity: the ground floor was primarily devoted to service, the middle floor to the everyday needs of the mistress and her upper servants, and the top floor to formal entertainment, estate business, and state occasions. Unlike Wollaton, Hardwick has no basement; instead, the kitchen, buttery, and scullery occupy the north side of the ground floor adjacent to the hall. The so-called Low Great Chamber, dining chamber for the household, was reached by way of a back staircase on this side; the main stairs led from the nursery and small bed chambers on the south side of the ground floor to Bess's own chamber and withdrawing chamber above, whence it led to the High Great Chamber, the largest and most formal chamber of state, on the top floor. Here the Palladian plan structures the functional organization, imposing a discipline that forced Smythson to observe the axis and thus to make the house more compact and higher than his previous buildings.

Like others with ties to the court, Bess had a taste for Renaissance classicism and she knew which designers and craftsmen to hire for her jobs. Though hardly an intellectual, her long-standing interest in architecture had matured over decades. At Chatsworth, her nearby country house built some forty years earlier, she had used the best London-based craftsmen; at Hardwick she assembled a team of skilled artists and gave them an enormous budget and an imposing site to work on. She allowed her architect to try out new ideas while retaining the elements essential to the buildings practical and symbolic operation. Bess welcomed the fusion of tradition and innovation that made her new house a fashionable showplace. At Hardwick, accordingly, ceremonial spaces are stacked up and elaborated in an unprecedented manner: the hall, the staircase, the great chambers, the gallery, and the roof terraces all present long vistas that far exceed the grandeur and spaciousness previously achieved by Smythson at Longleat or Wollaton. Moving through these spaces or sitting in her chair of state, Bess of Hardwick became part of the spectacle: each space was designed to present an image through which she assumed the central role in an orchestrated representation of power, a totalizing image composed of intricately patterned and highly colored architecture, painting, furnishings, and textiles. In this way, physical presence and architectural presence are uniquely elided at Hardwick, an elision that capitalizes on the notions of woman as spectacle and of window as matriarch. It is, of course, through operations of vision that this chain of representational processes is put into motion.

Like other Elizabethan builders, Bess was careful to celebrate the sovereign under whose reign she prospered: the chimney-piece in the hall displays the Hardwick coat of arms, but the queen's arms dominate the High Great Chamber.[20] Yet clearly, the subject rather than the sovereign is the focus of attention in this house. Bess's own initials, ES, decorate the high parapets, in unambiguous terms marking the house as its builder's property and personal creation. Thus Hardwick is more than a stage; it is also an emblem that piles up and displays its imagery in a complex and rather disordered series of overlapping texts. Large rectangular windows, each signifying enormous expense, light up the opulent fabrics and furnishings in the expansive rooms; these windows foreground the gaze, calling attention to both display and surveillance. Similarly, the high towers provide not only a vantage point from which Bess could survey her property, but also a symbolic image of dominance. Instead of playing the shamefast wife, Bess created a new female role at Hardwick, becoming the master of her house and borrowing some of the attributes of the good housewife to augment her power. From her high towers she oversaw the running of her estate, in her great chamber and gallery she received visitors of every rank. The country house took on a new and unique meaning at Hardwick because the gaze of authority it embodied was female.

[. . .]

Notes

Earlier versions of this paper were presented at a conference on Women in Early Modern England at the University of Maryland (October 1990), at Northwestern University (November 1990), and at the Renaissance Studies Colloquium at Brown University (March 1991). I am grateful to Margaret Carroll, Ann Rosalind Jones, Katherine Park, Eve Blau, Shelley Tenenbaum, Jehan Kuhn, and John Rhodes for reading and commenting on various drafts of this essay. A Faculty Research Award from Wellesley College and a fellowship from the Bunting Institute, Radcliffe College, afforded me the opportunity to travel in England and to take part in a reading group on Gender and Representation at the Bunting in 1990–91.

1 See Mark Girouard, *Life in the English Country House: A Social and Architectural History* (New Haven: Yale University Press, 1978), and idem, *Robert Smythson and the Architecture of the Elizabethan Country House* (New Haven: Yale University Press, 1983); Sir John Summerson, *Architecture in Britain 1530–1830* (Harmondsworth: Penguin, 1969), and idem, ed., *The Book of Architecture of John Thorpe*, vol. 40 of *Walpole Society* (Glasgow: Walpole Society, 1966). My own *House and Household in Elizabethan England: Wollaton Hall and the Willoughby Family* (Chicago: University of Chicago Press, 1989), while primarily concerned with Wollaton, raises some of the questions with which this paper is concerned.

2 This paradigmatic approach forms the basis for my book-in-progress on houses built for women heads of households. These range from Ledoux's *hôtels* for Mlle Guimard and Mme Thélusson in the late eighteenth century to Frank Lloyd Wright's Barnsdall House (1916–21) and Mies van der Rohe's Farnsworth House (1946–51). Like Hardwick, these cases break with conventional typology and, in some instances, represent stylistic turning points. They differ significantly from cases in which women acted as their husbands' surrogates or were otherwise seen as representatives of conventional social culture. These latter are treated by Trevor Lummis and Jan Marsh in *The Woman's Domain: Women and the English Country House* (New York and London: Viking, 1990).

3 For Mulvey, see Constance Penley, ed., *Feminism and Film Theory* (New York: Routledge, 1988), where the two essays are reprinted together with other key works of feminist film criticism. Penley's introductory essay, 'The Lady Doesn't Vanish: Feminism and Film Theory,' both points out the problems that this critical venture has encountered and suggests some ways of moving forward. For Kaplan, see her *Women and Film: Both Sides of the Camera* (New York: Methuen, 1983).

4 The essays of Mary Ann Doane in *The Desire to Desire: The Woman's Film of the 1940s* (Bloomington: Indiana University Press, 1987) and in *Femmes Fatales: Feminism, Film Theory and Psychoanalysis* (New York: Routledge, 1991) are the most insightful psychoanalytic studies of female spectatorship available. Doane's work, however, betrays an uneasy oscillation between historical interpretation and psychoanalytic structure, especially in her notion of the female spectator as consumer, which leaves significant questions unresolved. See also *Camera Obscura* 20–21

(May–September 1989), a double issue on 'The Spectatrix' that offers various responses to these questions.

5 See Kaja Silverman, 'Fassbinder and Lacan: A Reconsideration of Gaze, Look and Image,' *Camera Obscura* 19 (July 1991): 54–85.

6 This distinction was made earlier by Norman Bryson in *Vision and Painting: The Logic of the Gaze* (New Haven: Yale University Press, 1983), esp. chap. 5. Bryson's notion of 'the glance' as 'a furtive or sideways look whose attention is always elsewhere' (p. 94) is obviously related to Silverman's 'look,' though Silverman emphasizes the disempowering distinction between the individual and the broader culture (or the State), while Bryson only briefly alludes to this aspect of the system of signification.

7 Jill Dolan proposes a related strategy in *The Feminist Spectator as Critic* (Ann Arbor: UMI Research Press, 1988). Following Theresa De Lauretis (notably in *Technologies of Gender*), Dolan emphasizes the construction of cultural categories and the limitations imposed by available images within theater. Both spectator and spectacle participate in a deceptively 'natural' system; Dolan focuses on the mechanisms of representation and on the ways in which conventionalized images of gender and sexuality circumscribe identity by appealing to an approved spectator.

8 See Griselda Pollock, 'Modernity and the Spaces of Femininity,' in *Vision and Difference* (New York: Routledge, 1988), 50–90. See also Mary Ann Doane, 'Film and Masquerade: Theorizing the Female Spectator,' in *Femmes Fatales*, 17–32.

9 On Hardwick, see Girouard, *Robert Smythson*, chap, 4, and idem, *Hardwick Hall* (London: The National Trust, 1976).

10 Olive Cook, *The English Country House: An Art and a Way of Life* (London: Thames and Hudson, 1974), 8–26, discusses the roots of the manor house form. Girouard, *Life in the English Country House*, chap. 3, discusses the form of the medieval hall and tower. See also

11 M.W. Barley, 'Rural Housing in England,' in *Chapters from the Agrarian History of England and Wales*, vol. 4, *1500–1640*, ed. Joan Thirsk (Cambridge: Cambridge University Press, 1967).

11 The role of the housemaid is discussed in Cahn, *Industry of Devotion*, chap 4, esp. 99–100. See also Girouard, *Life in the English Country House*, 27–8, 139, 142.

12 For literary reactions to these changes, such as Ben Jonson's 'To Penshurst,' see Don E. Wayne, *Penshurst: The Semiotics of Place and the Poetics of History* (Madison: University of Wisconsin Press, 1984).

13 See Friedman, *House and Household*, chap. 4, for an extended discussion of the type. Smythson's notebooks were published by Mark Girouard as 'The Smythson Collection of the Royal Institute of British Architects,' *Architectural History* 5 (1962).

14 See the appendix to Lucy Gent, *Picture and Poetry, 1560–1620: Relations between Literature and Visual Arts in the English Renaissance* (Leamington Spa: James Hall, 1981).

15 See Maurice Howard, *The Early Tudor Country House: Architecture and Politics, 1490–1550* (London: G. Philip, 1987).

16 *Manuscripts of Lord Middleton*, 153.

17 This was noted by David N. Durant in *Bess of Hardwick: Portrait of an Elizabethan Dynast* (London: Weidenfeld and Nicolson, 1977), 180–1.

18 Smythson and his son John worked with Charles and William Cavendish, sons of Bess of Hardwick and her second husband, on the rebuilding of Bolsover Castle (1608–40) as a medievalizing dream castle, which supports a gendered reading of these representations. On Bolsover, see P.A. Faulkner, *Bolsover Castle, Derbyshire* (London: HMSO, 1972).

19 On the use of rooms at Hardwick, see Lindsay Boynton, *The Hardwick Hall Inventories of 1601* (London: Furniture History Society, 1971).

20 Girouard, *Hardwick Hall*, 66.

Bibliography

Ackerman, J., *The Villa: Form and ideology of country houses*, London: Thames and Hudson, 1990.

Adam, R. and Adam, J., *The Works in Architecture*, London, 1773–4.

Adorno, T. 'Functionalism Today', trans. Jane Newman and John Smith, *Oppositions*, 17, Summer 1979, pp. 30–41.

Airs, M., *The Tudor and Jacobean Country House: A building history* (1975), Stroud: Sutton, 1995.

Appadurai, A. (ed.) *The Social Life of Things: Commodities in cultural perspective*, Cambridge: Cambridge University Press, 1986.

Arnold, D., *The Georgian Country House: Architecture, landscape and society*, Stroud: Sutton Publishing, 1998.

Arnold, D. (ed.), *Belov'd by Evr'y Muse: Richard Boyle Third Earl of Burlington and Fourth Earl of Cork (1694–1753)*, London: Georgian Group, 1994.

Arnold, D. (ed.), *The Georgian Villa*, Stroud and New York: Sutton, 1996.

Arnold, D., 'Palladianism and the History of Style', *The Architects' Journal*, 17 August 1995, pp. 44–45.

Arnold, D., *Re-presenting the Metropolis: Architecture, urban experience and social life in London 1800–1840*, Aldershot: Ashgate, 2000.

Arnold, D., 'Taking Stock of Pevsner's City', *Architects' Journal*, 11 January, 1996, pp. 24–25.

Arnold, D., 'Wittgenstein and the Country House', *Society of Architectural Historians of Great Britain Newsletter*, 58, Spring/Summer, 1996.

Bachelard, G., *Poetics of Space*, trans. Maria Jolas, Boston: Beacon, 1969.

Bann, S., *The Clothing of Clio: A study of the representation of history in nineteenth-century Britain and France*, Cambridge: Cambridge University Press, 1984.

Barthes, R., 'The Death of the Author', in *Image–Music–Text*, trans. Stephen Heath, 1977.

Barthes, R., 'Le discours de l'histoire', trans. as 'Historical Discourse' in M. Lane (ed.) *Structuralism: A Reader*, London: Jonathan Cape, 1970, pp. 149–154.

Barthes, R., *Mythologies* (1957), trans. Annette Lavers, London: Jonathan Cape, 1972.

Baxandall, M., *Giotto and the Orators*, Oxford: Clarendon Press, 1971.

Bennett, J.A., 'Architecture and Mathematical Practice in England, 1550–1650', in J. Bold and E. Chaney (eds.), *English Architecture Public and Private*, London: Hambleton, 1993.

Bennett, J.M., 'Feminism and History', *Gender and History*, 1, 1989, pp. 251–272.

Betjeman, Sir John, *Shell Guides*, London: Faber, 1964.

Bloch, E., 'Formative Education, Engineering Form, Ornament', trans. Jane Newman and John Smith, *Oppositions*, 17, Summer 1979, pp. 45–51.

Blomfield, R., *A History of Renaissance Architecture in England 1500–1800*, London: George Bell and Sons, 1897.

Bloomer, J., 'Big Jugs' in A. Kroker and M. Kroker (eds), *The Hysterical Male: New Feminist Theory*, 1991.

Bonfield, L., 'Marriage Settlements and the "Rise of Great Estates", the Demographic Aspect', *Economic History Review*, 2nd Series, vol. XXII, 1979, pp. 483–493.

Bourdieu, P., *Distinction: A social critique of the judgement of taste*, trans. Richard Nice, London: Routledge and Kegan Paul, 1984.

Bourdieu, P., *The Field of Cultural Production: Essays on art and literature*, ed. Randal Johnson, Cambridge: Polity, 1993.

Brettingham, M., jnr., *The Plans and Elevations of the late Earl of Leicester's House at Holkham*, 2nd edition, London, 1773.

Brod, H. (ed.), *The Making of Masculinities: The new men's studies*, Boston, MA and London: Allen and Unwin, 1987.

Brown, L., *Alexander Pope*, Oxford and New York: Blackwell, 1985.

Butler, J., *Gender Trouble: Feminism and the subversion of identity*, New York and London: Routledge, 1990.

Campbell, C., *Vitruvius Britannicus*, London, 1715, 1717 and 1725.

Cannadine, D., *Aspects of Aristocracy: Grandeur and decline in modern Britain*, New Haven, CT and London: Yale University Press, 1994.

Cannadine, D., *The Decline and Fall of the British Aristocracy*, New Haven, CT and London: Yale University Press, 1990.

Canning, K., 'Feminist History after the Linguistic Turn: Historicising discourse and experience', *Signs*, 19, 1994, pp. 368–404.

Carr, E.H., *What is History?*, London: Macmillan, 1961.

Certeau, M., de, 'History: Science and fiction', in *Heterologies: Discourse on the Other*, trans. Brian Massimi, Minneapolis: University of Minnesota Press, 1986.

Certeau, M., de, *The Practice of Everyday Life*, trans. Stephen F. Rendall, Berkeley London: University of California Press, 1984.

Chalkin, C.W. and Wordie, J.R. (eds.), *Town and Countryside: The English landowner and the national economy, 1660–1860*, London: Unwin Hyman, 1989.

Chicago, J., *The Dinner Party*, Harmondsworth: Penguin, 1996.

Clay, C., 'Marriage, Inheritance and the Rise of large Estates in England 1660–1815', *Economic History Review*, 2nd Series, vol. XXI, 1968, pp. 503–517.

Cobbett, W., *Rural Rides* (1830), Harmondsworth: Penguin, 1967.

Colley, L., *Britons: Forging the nation 1707–1837*, New Haven, CT and London: Yale University Press, 1992.

Colomina, B. (ed.), *Sexuality and Space*, Princeton, NJ: Princeton University Press, 1992.

Colvin, H., *A Biographical Dictionary of British Architects 1600–1840* (1954), New Haven and London: Yale University Press, 1995.

Colvin, H. and Newman, J. (eds.), *Of Building, Roger North's Writings on Architecture*, Oxford: Clarendon Press, 1981.

Crinson, M. and Lubbock, J., *Architecture: Art or profession: three hundred years of architectural education in Britain*, Manchester: Manchester University Press, 1994.

Crook, J.M., *The Dilemma of Style: Architectural ideas from picturesque to post-modern*, London: J. Murray, 1987.

Crook, J.M., *The Greek Revival, Neo-classical Attitudes in British Architecture 1760–1870*, London: J. Murray, 1972.

Darley, G., *Sir John Soane: An accidental romantic*, New Haven and London: Yale University Press, 1999.

Debord, G., *The Society of the Spectacle*, trans. Donald Nicholson-Smith, Zone Books, 1994.

Deetz, J.F., 'Cultural Dimensions of Ethnicity in the Archaeological Record', Keynote Address, 28th Annual meeting of the Society for Historical Archaeology, Washington, DC, 1995.

Defoe, D., *A Tour through the Whole Island of Great Britain*, (1724–26), London: Dent, 1974.

Etlin, R., *In Defense of Humanism*, Cambridge: Cambridge University Press, 1996.

Fernie, E. (ed.), *Art History and its Methods: A critical anthology* (1995), London: Phaidon, 1999.

Fiennes, C., *The Journeys of Celia Fiennes*, ed. Christopher Morris, London: Cresset Press, 1947.

Finch, M., *Style in Art History: An introduction to theories of style and sequence*, Metuchen: Scarecrow Press, 1974.

Forty, A., *Words and Buildings*, London: Thames and Hudson, 2000.

Foucault, M., *The Archaeology of Knowledge*, trans. A. M. Sheridan Smith, London: Tavistock, 1972.

Foucault, M., 'Nietzsche, Genealogy, History', in *Language, Counter-Memory, Practice: Selected essays and interviews*, trans. and ed. Donald F. Bouchard and Sherry Simon, Ithaca, NY: Cornell University Press, 1977.

Foucault, M., 'Of other spaces', trans. J. Miskowice, *Diacritics*, Spring 1986, pp. 22–27.

Foucault, M., 'What is an Author?', in Josue V. Harari (ed.) *Textual Strategies: Perspectives in Post-Structuralist Criticism*, New York: Cornell University Press, 1979.

Franklin, J., *The Gentleman's Country House and its Plan 1835–1914*, London: Routledge and Kegan Paul, 1980.

Friedman, A., 'Architecture, Authority and the Female Gaze: Planning and representation in the early modern country house', *Assemblage*, 18, August 1992, pp. 40–61.

Friedman, A., *House and Household in Elizabethan England*, Chicago and London: University of Chicago Press, 1989.

Gadamer, H-G., 'The Ontological Foundation of the Occasional and the Decorative', in *Truth and Method*, trans. William Glen Doepel, ed. John Cumming and Garrett Barden, London: Sheed and Ward, 1979.

Gallop, J., *Feminism and Psychoanalysis: The daughter's seduction*, London: Macmillan, 1982.

Gell, A., *Art and Agency: An anthropological theory*, Oxford: Clarendon, 1998.

Gideion, S., *Space, Time and Architecture*, Cambridge, MA: Harvard University, 1962.

Gifford, J., *William Adam 1689–1748: A life and times of Scotland's universal architect*, Edinburgh: Mainstream, 1989.

Girouard, M., *Life in the English Country House*, New Haven, CT and London: Yale University Press, 1978.

Girouard, M., *Robert Smythson and the Elizabethan Country House* (1966), New Haven, CT and London: Yale University Press, 1983.

Girouard, M., *The Victorian Country House*, Oxford: Clarendon Press, 1971.

Gombrich, E.H., 'The Logic of Vanity Fair. Alternatives to historicism in the study of fashions of style and taste', in Paul Arthur Schlipp (ed.), *The Philosophy of Karl Popper*, La Salle, IL: Open Court, 1974, pp. 925–957.

Gombrich, E.H., *In Search of Cultural History*, Oxford: Clarendon Press, 1969.

Hadjinicolaou, N., *Art History and Class Struggle*, trans. Louise Asmal, London: Pluto, 1978.

Hall, C., 'Gender Divisions and Class Formations in the Birmingham Middle Class, 1780–1850', in R. Samuel (ed.), *People's History and Socialist Theory*, London: Routledge, 1981, pp. 167–175.

Hall, C., *White, Male and Middle Class: Explorations in feminism and history*, Cambridge: Polity, 1992.

Hardy, J. and Tomlin, M., *Osterley Park House*, London: Victoria and Albert Museum, 1985.

Hardyment, C., *Home Comfort: A history of domestic arrangement*, London: Viking in association with the National Trust, 1992.

Harris, E. and Savage, N., *British Architectural Books and Writers 1556–1785*, Cambridge: Cambridge University Press, 1990.

Harris, J., *The Artist and the Country House*, London: Sothcby's, 1984.

Harris, J., *Lord Burlington: his Villa and Garden at Chiswick*, New Haven and London, Yale University Press, 1994.

Harris, J., 'Lord Burlington the Modern Vitruvius' in D. Arnold (ed.), *The Georgian Villa*, Stroud and New York: Sutton, 1996, pp. 41–47.

Harris, J. and Lever, J., *Illustrated Dictionary of Architecture* (1966), London: Faber, 1993.

Harris, L., *Robert Adam and Kedleston: The making of a neo-classical masterpiece*, London: National Trust, 1987.

Harvey, J., *The Medieval Architect*, London: Wayland, 1972.

Hauser, A., *The Philosophy of Art History* (1959), Evanston, IL: Northwestern University Press, 1985.

Hewison, R., *The Heritage Industry: Britain in a climate of decline*, London: Methuen, 1987.

Hill, C., *The Century of Revolution 1603–1714*, London: Oxford University Press, 1966.

Hiskey, C., 'The Building of Holkham Hall: Newly Discovered Letters', *Architectural History*, 40: 1997, pp. 144–158.

Hobsbawn, E.J., 'Karl Marx's Contribution to Historiography', in R. Blackburn (ed.) *Ideology in Social Science: Readings in critical social theory*, London: Fontana, 1972, pp. 265–283.

hooks, bell, *Feminist Theory from Margin to Center*, Boston: South End Press, 1984.

Howard, M., *The Early Tudor Country House: Architecture and politics 1490–1550*, London: George Philip, 1987.

Jenkins, F., *Architect and Patron: A survey of professional relations and practice in England from the sixteenth century to the present day*, London: Oxford University Press, 1961.

Jordan, G. and Weedon, C., *Cultural Politics: Class, gender, race and the postmodern world*, Oxford: Blackwell, 1995.

Kant, I., *The Works of Immanuel Kant*, trans. Paul Gruyer and Allen W. Wood, Cambridge, Cambridge University Press, 1998.

Kaufman, E., *Architecture in the Age of Reason*, Cambridge, MA: Harvard University Press, 1955.

Kelly, Joan, *Women, History and Theory: The essays of Joan Kelly*, Chicago: University of Chicago Press, 1984.

Kimball, F., *The Creation of the Rococo Decorative Style*, Philadelphia: Philadelphia Museum of Art, 1943.

Kostoff, S. (ed.), *The Architect: Chapters in the history of the profession*, Oxford and New York: Oxford University Press, 1977.

Kroker, A, and Kroker, M., *The Hysterical Male: New feminist theory*, New York: St. Martin's Press, 1991.

Laugier, M.A., *An Essay on Architecture* (1755), trans. W. and A. Hermann, Los Angeles: Hennesy and Ingalls, 1977

Leach, P., *James Paine*, London: Zwemmer, 1988.

Leach, P., 'James Paine's Design for the South Front at Kedleston Hall', *Architectural History*, 40, 1997, pp. 159–170.

Lees-Milne, J., *Earls of Creation*, London: Hamish Hamilton, 1962.

Lefebvre, H., *The Production of Space*, trans. David Nicholson-Smith, London: Blackwell, 1991.

Lummis, T., and Marsh, J., *The Woman's Domain*, London: Viking, 1990.

MacConnell, D., *The Tourist: A new theory of the leisure class*, New York: Schocken, 1976.

McMordie, M., 'Picturesque Pattern Books and Pre-Victorian Designers', *Architectural History*, 18, 1975, pp. 44–60.

Mandler, P., *The Fall and Rise of the Stately Home*, New Haven and London: Yale University Press, 1997.

Martins, S.W., *A Great Estate at Work: The Holkham Estate and its Inhabitants in the Nineteenth Century*, Cambridge: Cambridge University Press, 1980.

Massey, D., *Space, Place and Gender*, Cambridge: Polity, 1994.

Mingay, G.E., *English Landed Society in the Eighteenth Century*, London: Routledge and Kegan Paul, 1963.

Moir, E., *The Discovery of Britain: The English tourists 1540–1840*, London: Routledge, 1964.

Moore, H.L., *A Passion for Difference: Essays in Anthropology and Gender*, Cambridge: Polity, 1994.

Mulvey, L., 'Changes: Thoughts on myth, narrative and historical experience', *History Workshop Journal*, 23, Spring 1987, pp. 3–19.

Nussbaum, M., 'The Professor of Parody', *New Republic*, March 1999.

Osborne, P. and Segal, L., 'Gender as Performance: An interview with Judith Butler', conducted in London 1993, *Radical Philosophy*, 67, Summer 1994.

Palladio, A., *The Four Books of Architecture* (*I Quattro Libri Dell'Architettura*, 1570), New York: Dover, 1965.

Pevsner, N., *Academies of Art Past and Present*, New York: Da Capo Press, 1973.

Pevsner, N., *Buildings of England*, London: Penguin, 1953 onwards.

Pevsner, N., *A History of Building Types*, Princeton: Princeton, NJ: University Press, 1976.

Pevsner, N., *An Outline of European Architecture*, Harmondsworth: Penguin, 1960.

Pevsner, N. and Lloyd, D., *The Buildings of England: Hampshire and the Isle of Wight*, Harmondsworth: Penguin, 1967.

Pollock, Griselda, *Vision and Difference: Femininity, feminism and the histories of art*, London: Routledge, 1982.

Pollock, G. and Parker, R., *Old Mistresses: Women, art and ideology*, London: Routledge and Kegan Paul, 1981.

Port, M., *Imperial London: Civil government building in London 1850–1915*, New Haven and London: Yale University Press, 1995.

Rand, A., *The Fountainhead*, Indianapolis, IN: Bobbs-Merrill, 1943.

Roper, M. and Tosh, J. (eds.), *Manful Assertions: Masculinities in Britain since 1800*, London: Routledge, 1991.

Rowe, C., *The Mathematics of the Ideal Villa and other Essays*, Cambridge MA.: MIT Press, 1976.

Rykwert, J., *The Dancing Column: On Order in Architecture*, Cambridge MA: MIT Press, 1996.

Rykwert, J., *The First Moderns: The architects of the eighteenth century*, Cambridge MA.: MIT Press, 1980.

Saint, A., *The Image of the Architect*, New Haven, CT and London: Yale University Press, 1983.

Samaurez Smith, C., *The Building of Castle Howard*, London: Faber, 1990.

Samaurez Smith, C., 'Supply and Demand in English Country House Building', *Oxford Art Journal*, 1988.

Schmidt, L., 'Holkham Hall', *Country Life*, 24 and 31 January 1980, pp. 214–217 and pp. 298–301.

Scott, J., 'Women's History' in P. Burke (ed.), *New Perspectives on Historical Writing*, Cambridge: Cambridge University Press, 1992.

Scott Brown, D., 'Room at the Top? Sexism and the Star System in Architecture' in Ellen Perry Berkeley (ed.), *Architecture: A place for women*, Washington, DC: Smithsonian Institution Press, 1989, pp. 237–246.

Sherman, D. and Rogoff, I. (eds.), *Museum Culture: Histories, discourses, spectacles*, Minneapolis: University of Minnesota Press, 1994.

Shute, J., *First and Chief Groundes of Architecture* (1563), intro. L.Weaver, London: *Country Life*, 1912.

Sicca, C., 'The Architecture of the Wall: Astylism in the architecture of Lord Burlington', *Architectural History*, 33, 1990, pp. 83–101.

Smiles, S., *Ancient Britons*, Aldershot: Ashgate, 2001.

Solkin, D., *Richard Wilson and the Landscape of Reaction*, London: Tate Gallery, 1986.

Speck, W., *Stability and Strife in England 1714–1760*, Cambridge Mass: Harvard University Press, 1977.

Stone, L., 'On the Grand Scale': Review of *Life in the English Country House* by Mark Girouard, *Times Literary Supplement*, 10 November 1978, p. 298.

Stone, L., *The Past and Present Revisited*, London: Routledge and Kegan Paul, 1987.

Stone, L., Fawtier, J. C. and Stone J., *An Open Élite? England 1540–1880*, Oxford: Clarendon Press, 1984.

Strong, R., *The Destruction of the Country House 1875–1975*, London: Thames & Hudson, 1974.

Summerson, J., *Architecture in Britain 1530–1830* (1953), New Haven, CT and London: Yale University Press, 1993.

Summerson, J., *The Classical Language of Architecture* (1963), London: Thames and Hudson, 1980.

Summerson, J., *Georgian London* (1945), Harmondsworth, Penguin, 1978

Thompson, E.P., 'Patrician Society, Plebian Culture', *Journal of Social History*, Vol. 7, 4, Summer 1974, pp. 382–405.

Thompson, E.P., *The Poverty of Theory and Other Essays*, London: Merlin, 1978.

Thompson, F.M.L., *English Landed Society in the Nineteenth Century*, London: Routledge and Kegan Paul, 1963.

Tinniswood, A., *A History of Country House Visiting: Five centuries of tourism and taste*, Oxford and London: Blackwell and the National Trust, 1989.

Tinniswood, A., *His Invention so Fertile: A life of Christopher Wren*, London: Jonathan Cape, 2001.

Toynbee, P. (ed.), 'Horace Walpole's Journals of Visits to Country Seats', *The Walpole Society*, 16, 1927–1928, pp. 9–80.

Tristram, P., *Living Space in Fact and Fiction*, London and New York: Routledge, 1989.

Urry, J., *The Tourist Gaze: Leisure and Travel in Contemporary Societies*, London: Sage Publications, 1990.

Vasari, G., *The Lives of the Artists* (1550 and 1568), trans. George Bull, Harmonsworth: Penguin, 1965.

Vickery, A., *The Gentleman's Daughter*, New Haven, CT and London: Yale University Press, 1999.

Vitruvius, *The Ten Books of Architecture* (1914), trans. Morris H. Morgan, New York: Dover, 1960.

Walker, L., *Drawing on Diversity: Women, architecture and practice*, Heinz Gallery, 1997.

Walpole, H., *Journals of Visits to Country Seats &ct.*, in P. Toynbee (ed.), *Walpole Society*, XVI, 1928.

Walsh, W.H., *An Introduction to the Philosophy of History*, London: Hutchinson University Library, 1958.

Ware, V., *Beyond the Pale: White women, racism and history*, London: Verso, 1992.

Waterson, M., *The Servants Hall: A domestic history of Erddig*, London: Routledge and Kegan Paul, 1980.

Watkin, D., *The Rise of Architectural History*, London: Architectural Press, 1980.

Watts, W., *The Seats of the Nobility and Gentry in a Collection of the Most Interesting and Picturesque Views*, London, 1779–1786.

Webster, C., 'Architectural Illustration as Revenge: James Paine's designs for Kedleston' in M. Howard (ed.), *The Image of the Building: Papers from the Annual Symposium of the Society of Architectural Historians of Great Britain 1995*, London, 1995.

White, H., 'The Fictions of Factual Representations', in Angus Fletcher (ed.) *The Literature of Fact*, New York: Columbia University Press, 1976, pp. 21–44.

White, H., *Metahistory: The historical imagination in nineteenth-century Europe*, Baltimore, MD: John Hopkins University Press, 1973.

Whittington, G.D., Rev., *An Historical Survey of the Ecclesiastical Antiquities of France with a View to Illustrate the Rise and Progress of Gothic Architecture in Europe*, London: 1809.

Williams, R., *The Country and the City*, London: Chatto and Windus, 1973.

Williams, R., *Marxism and Literature*, Oxford, Oxford University Press, 1978.

Wittkower, R., *Architectural Principles in the Age of Humanism*, (1949), London: Tiranti, 1967.

Wittkower, R. (ed.), *England and the Mediterranean Tradition: studies in art, history and literature*, London and New York: Warburg Institute and Oxford University Press, 1945.

Wittkower, R., *Palladio and English Palladianism*, (1945) London: Thames and Hudson, 1974.

Wolff, J., *The Social Production of Art*, London: Macmillian, 1981.

Woods, M.N., *From Craft to Profession: The practice of architecture in nineteenth-century America*, California and London: University of California Press, 1999.

Index

Index fields and page numbers cited in roman refer to the main text
Index fields and/or page numbers cited in *italics* refer to extracts